The Western Marxists

The Western Marxists

by NEIL McINNES

Distributed by
OPEN COURT
Publishing Co.
La Salle, Ill. 61301

800-435-6850   or   815-223-2521

1972

First published in 1972 by
Library Press, New York

Printed in Great Britain
by Watmoughs Limited
Bradford and London

Contents

page

1 The Remystification of Marx 7

2 Georges Sorel: Alienation becomes Violence 68

3 Gramsci: Marx and/or Mussolini 88

4 Lukacs: the Restoration of Idealism 105

5 In the Shadow of Hegel: from Marx to Marcuse 130

6 Ideologists of the New Left 151

7 From the Associated Producers to the Flower People 169

8 The Irrational Totality, or the Life and Death of Reason 186

NOTES 208

Acknowledgements

Just half of the material in this book appears in print for the first time but earlier versions of chapters 3, 4 and 5 were published in *Survey* (London), nos 53, 72 and 78, respectively; chapter 6 was first published in the *Current Affairs Bulletin* (Sydney), vol 46, no 2; and chapter 7 in the *Journal of Contemporary History* (London), vol 6, no 4. The author thanks the editors of those periodicals for permission to reprint.

1. The Remystification of Marx

The socialist tradition, like others of great scope and long life, contains various strands of which several would seem incompatible, or even contradictory. For example, the socialists have usually regarded themselves as the party of theory, as the movement with a philosophy of history, and as peculiarly committed to "ideals" as against the "materialism" of the business class. And yet the Left has also long nurtured a solid tradition of anti-idealism that has sometimes become open anti-intellectualism. It saw itself as the critical party, the unmasker of bourgeois claptrap about religion, metaphysics, and morals. It was the party of materialism that saw through the hypocritical "ideology" of the ruling class to the underlying reality of how working people earned their bread.

When Karl Marx's influence first began to be felt inside the socialist movement, it was decidedly in favour of the second of these strands. For reasons that will appear in what follows, Marx is often seen nowadays as a philosopher, but for the working men and socialist militants who first encountered his views he was the anti-philosopher *par excellence*. The first French Marxists of the 1880s, led by Jules Guesde and Marx's son-in-law Paul Lafargue, actually called themselves *le parti du ventre*, the "belly party." They meant that Marx had debunked sloppy utopianism and unmasked idealist pretentiousness by recalling attention to everyday economic reality. In Italy too, the first Marxists saw themselves as the no-humbug belly party, so that an observer could say of them, "For the socialists, the working-class problem is entirely an economic problem and even, more precisely, a question of alimentation."[1]

Seeking, in 1899, to account for this determined anti-theoretical materialism of the Marxists, Georges Sorel said:

7

> The disciples of Marx, because they had to fight opponents who invoked natural law, have often thought it fair tactics to make fun of all ethical considerations and to insist on the material aspect of the struggle. It has even happened that they came to regard juridical institutions as Machiavellian tricks used by the ruling classes to maintain the existing order for their own profit. The moral foundations of the mission [of the proletariat] were left in the shadow and one spoke of a victory of the proletariat without bothering about the ethical characteristics of the conflict. This doctrine which merits the name "materialist" in the worst sense of the word, has found its most complete expression in the work of Loria. [Loria was a Darwinian popularizer of Marx in Italy.] He considers law and morality to be institutions intended to ensure the domination of the strongest. Far from protesting against these paradoxes, the Marxists have accused Loria of plagiarizing Marx![2]

The Marxists soon came to be ashamed of their philosophical nakedness. Aggressive and cynical materialism enjoyed a brief heyday in Soviet Russia in the 1920s but in the West it was left to heretics like the Wobblies (Industrial Workers of the World) to keep alive the skepticism of the belly party. Wobblies would interrupt political discussions that strayed on to generalities by chanting "What about the pork chop!" After one of their own had "gone bad" by becoming a philosopher, they turned up to jeer at his lecture on the categories, and when he asked rhetorically, "What is time?" they exclaimed, "You should know, Bert, you've *done* it!" That is, anything that diverted attention from the everyday realities of earning food and fighting bourgeois power was metaphysical humbug.

Now, this was not as far from Marx's own opinions as later "philosophical" Marxists have pretended. Marx did offer a demystifying and debunking weapon to be used on the "abstractions" of ideology. To be sure, he did not think that underneath the cant and hypocrisy of idealism there were only bellies and pork chops, but he did think that there lay there material, objective activities that could be described without philosophical abstractions. Moreover, far from dismissing metaphysics out of hand as meaningless obscurantism, Marx advanced the theory that it did symbolically convey certain information and thus could be translated back into ordinary language.

The socialists, however, ignored this aspect of Marx's work and hastened to repair the coarseness of the first Marxists by drawing a philosophy from elsewhere. The incentive for this, it is instructive to note, came not so much from the attacks of the defenders of moral order as from within the socialist movement itself, for many working men were repelled by Marxist materialism. In France, for example, Benoit Malon's *Revue Socialiste* combated the Marxists because "they have no philosophy," a charge that was taken seriously enough for the Marxist Parti Ouvrier to commission Gabriel Deville to write an exculpation.[3] As the European socialist movement was won over to Marxism, at the same time as it gained in strength, it felt the need of a philosophy and, since Marx did not provide one, it became the fashion to draw one from elsewhere. By the early years of this century, there existed combinations of Marxism with neo-Kantianism, pragmatism, Spencerian positivism, social Darwinism, Spinozism, the mechanist materialism of the eighteenth-century *philosophes*, and even Thomism. It was, in each case, admitted that a philosophical "dimension" was being supplied because Marxism lacked one and was philosophically neutral. This was the ideological compromise of the Second International, the association of reformist socialist parties.

The Third, or Communist, International founded after the Bolshevik Revolution similarly supplied Marxism with a philosophy—indeed, with a veritable established state religion—drawn from authors other than Karl Marx, and known as dialectical materialism. Being based on the new Russian state, the Communist International had even less taste than the socialists for the demystifying, debunking force of Marxism; but it did have great need, its leaders felt, of a new religion or world-view that could serve much the same function as Christianity fulfilled in rival imperialisms. So, along with coal and the railways, metaphysics was nationalized. What was then put out from Russia as Marxist philosophy was essentially a revival of the early nineteenth-century philosophy of nature as developed by Hegel and Schelling and as transmitted by the latter's pupil, Engels. Later this dogma became an obstacle to Soviet development and it had gradually but firmly to be put out of the way. It was enshrined in chapels well off the

9

path of Soviet science and industrialism, just as Christianity
had been rendered innocuous in Western countries. But no
other philosophy was allowed to grow up in its place.

In contrast to those two ways of remedying Marxism's
philosophical deficiency, the writers discussed in this book
claimed to discover that there was no need for Marxists to
borrow elsewhere because their own doctrine was already, or
potentially, an independent philosophy. This doctrine, or
nexus of doctrines, that they derived directly from Marx's
writings came to be known as *le marxisme occidental,* Western
Marxism, in contrast to the lucubrations of the orthodox
dialectical materialists. It had, and indeed still has, a certain
political importance. It enabled Western intellectuals who
would have been repelled by the simple materialism of the
first Marxists and the jejune dogmatism of orthodox dialectical
materialism to be converted to communism by interpreting it
as a variety of idealism or pragmatism such as were taught in
the academies. That interpretation had to be kept to themselves,
since it was unofficial, but that only gave it the attractions of a
secret doctrine. Communism, like some other social and
religious movements, came to have a double doctrine: one for
the ignorant and another for the educated. Beyond that,
Western Marxism proved solid enough to survive the regression
of communism in the West. It has found in recent years a new
lease of life as the doctrine of the New Left. So a study of it
could explain how, in years gone by, people who were obviously
not Marxists nevertheless became communists, and why,
today, certain non-communists call themselves Marxists.

Whereas the Second and Third Internationals ignored certain
essential assertions of Marxism, the Western Marxists re-
mystified them. Their work was a *re*mystification because
Marxism began as an attempt to demystify metaphysics. That
is, like a number of his contemporaries confronted with the
imposing systems of Hegel and Schelling, Marx wanted to
explain why people should say and believe metaphysical things.
He sought to translate those things into the language of everyday life in order to show what metaphysicians "meant," even

if they meant it "unconsciously." Marx stood out among his contemporaries in being more tenacious and more adventurous in his efforts to lead thought out of metaphysics. He wanted to show what life would be like if, as he put it, men learned to do without philosophy, meaning by that to look at society without hypocritical pretence, consoling fantasy or high-flown metaphysical mystifications. To what extent he was successful in this will emerge incidentally in the course of what follows, where the main point, however, will be to show that Western Marxism has taken the opposite course of reinstating the very metaphysics Marx sought to debunk. It has invented the contradiction in terms "Marxist philosophy" to designate a body of doctrines of the same sort as those that Marx diagnosed as symptoms of social malaise.

It might seem odd that some idealist metaphysicians should pursue this roundabout course of claiming to derive their philosophies from a sworn enemy of metaphysics. Why did they not put them forward as simply their own work or as a continuation of familiar religious and philosophical traditions? Why try to foist them on Marx? There could be, on one calculation, much to be gained from decking out old ideas as the last word in Left thought. If popular support were wanted, if a mass backing were sought, if the thrill of modernity were relished, it would be better to present irrational anti-scientism as Marxist anti-capitalism. Opposition to industry, to democracy, to rising standards of living and to wider education would be better received if done up in Marxist wrapping, though of course it would have to be a "philosophical," esoteric, and superior Marxism. A similar calculation is responsible for the appearance among the Marxist philosophers of the "Marxist theologians," to use another contradiction in terms. When men in both the Catholic and Evangelical churches came to the conclusion that the real enemy of religious faith was not that "godless communism" that their superiors inveighed against but the increasing prosperity, security, welfare and conformity of neo-capitalist existence, the alliance of metaphysics and anti-capitalism was bound to suggest itself. It was soon to take shape as yet another variety of Marxist philosophy.

The Hegelian Dream

For there are several varieties of the philosophical remystification of Marx. The main ones will be described in this book but first it is necessary to show the nature of the original demystification which Marx claimed to carry out on German metaphysics and notably on Hegelianism. He was not, as has been noticed, quite alone in this. Indeed, demystification of metaphysics was the *coqueluche* of the German universities in the twenty years after Hegel's death in 1831. It was practised not only on Hegel and Schelling but on philosophy generally. Marx took a doctorate by doing it to Epicurus, showing that the ancient materialist was "talking behind a mask," speaking in allegories and symbols that Marx could decipher. For example, when Epicurus (or Democritus) spoke of the trajectories of atoms, Marx said he was really talking about the relations between individuals in society. Still, it was the spectacular course of German thought from Kant to Schelling that most attracted the demystifiers, especially when that line of metaphysicians reached a paroxysm of incomprehensibility or ambiguity (some said dishonesty) in Hegel. An incentive to this effort to debunk metaphysics and religion was the use made of them by the reactionary and repressive Prussian state to limit freedoms and protect privileges. Hegel became the favorite target not only because he was the most metaphysical of philosophers but because he almost gave the game away. In reading him one commonly feels (as, alas, one never does in reading Schelling) that one *almost* sees what it is all about. Certain of Marx's contemporaries put this by saying that Hegel *really* knew what the everyday meaning of his high-flown metaphysics was, but he dared not declare it because it was subversive; so he preferred to disguise it in such manner that one only caught glimpses of it. Marx brushed this aside and said Hegel was sincerely unconscious of the real meaning of his system but that he was great just because he had produced an exact allegory, that is, a mystification that only needed to be interpreted point by point to yield a description of the most important features of social life.

To understand the vexed question of Marx's relation with Hegel one might imagine a psychiatrist who has been having difficulty understanding a particular neurosis until one day he comes upon a patient whose symptoms are so crystal-clear in their symbolic meaning that one only has to interpret them one by one to have the etiology of the malady laid bare. Such a patient would go down in the literature (one is thinking of some of Freud's early cases) as a classic whose unconscious had written a perfect account of a typical mental illness in symbolic or mystified form. What was the Hegelian dream in which the world appeared upside-down, needing only to be stood back on its feet, that is, interpreted?

Hegel offered to perform in his philosophy a eucharistic miracle. He would transubstantiate the humble bread and wine of this world into spirit. Needless to say, Hegel's work, like the priest's feat at communion, would leave the bread, the wine, and all the universe physically unchanged but they would have received a consecration. Our attitude to them thereafter would be radically different. Things would have been spiritualized and humanized so that men could live among them without ever again feeling puny or miserable. Objects would remain what they were and yet they would have lost that cold, indifferent—even threatening—objectivity that assumed hallucinatory proportions for Sartre's character Roquentin but which is felt by all idealists. Objects would thereafter appear to be parts of ourselves, created by us and still within our spiritual power, indeed as striving to come back to us or more exactly to that "Spirit" in which we participated. In all this, Hegel was a characteristic idealist, for idealism consists in the refusal to accept minds as occurrences among other non-mental occurrences and insists that mind dominates all else, in some sense produces everything else. He was, more particularly, typical of modern German idealism in saying that this state of affairs was not given from the beginning but was the program of a historical activity. It was something that was coming to pass, getting truer day by day. Therefore it was an activity in which folk could take part, if only by *thinking* in certain ways. In this way Hegeliansim could lead to a popular "idealist" ethics, to the exhortation to humanize the world by affirming the supremacy of spirit and the immense power (even if only in *imagination*) of the divine spark in man.

Hegel performed his eucharist by inviting belief in an elaborate mythology, the adventures of Spirit. He said that Spirit, Logos, or the pure Idea, created matter and history out of itself. It assumed the form of material objects and historical institutions, which were simply other ways of its existing, its spatial extension and temporal development: alienated Spirit. It did this in order to know itself, for in the beginning Spirit was not self-conscious. It could become so only by self-externalization, by laying itself out in objects which it then could contemplate. These objects did not know they were spirit in unconscious form but they included one creature, man, who could come to see that fact. In him, Spirit could reach the self-consciousness that it had created the world to attain. Yet it could achieve this goal only if man cancelled out the world in his thought, annulled its objectivity, and saw it as Spirit alienated. In that cognitive act, Spirit was reclaiming its own alienated self from the objects it created, ending its division from itself and returning from self-estrangement. This was no easy matter because the objective world presented itself to man as hostile, strange and absurd; it was self-contradictory, for example. So it called for heroic spiritual effort on man's part to overcome finite, brute fact, to pierce its illusory substance and bring it back to Spirit. Yet it was worthwhile because once externality was subdued, it was recognized as simply Spirit's own activity, all its own doing, and hence incapable of dominating or misusing us.

This mythological cycle of self-externalization, lapse into alienation and then cancellation of that alienation by an act of knowing, is what Hegel calls dialectic. It is a process capable of repetition, as when Spirit generates successive new civilizations; but in each cycle there is progress in the self-knowledge of Spirit. In that way history moves onward and ever upward in a sinuous dialectic of self-divisions, self-contradictions, and self-reconciliations of Spirit. The process will have a stop only when Spirit has run through all its possibilities of self-externalization and overcome them all in turn, whereupon absolute knowledge will have been reached—Spirit knowing itself as spirit. There is dispute as to whether Hegel thought this ultimate goal had been reached in his philosophy. That is of less relevance to Marxism than another disagreement that still divides the Hegelians; the locus of self-contradiction. The majority opinion, which Marx seems to have shared, is that the only self-contradiction that Hegel called dialectical, meaning a necessary and wholesome stage in progress, was Spirit's negation or contradiction of itself in the creation of material objects, which in turn were negated when men saw them as Spirit's doing. Thinkers under Schelling's influence, such as Engels, have argued, in contrast, that material objects themselves contain self-contradiction permanently and by their very nature. A whole metaphysics has been built on this foundation, dispensing with the law of contradiction (that X cannot both be and not be Y) and called dialectical materialism. It has nothing to do with Marx, who wrote nothing to indicate that he did not accept the usual view that, for Hegel, the self-contradictoriness of things was only apparent and transient, part of the horror and absurdity of the world that vanished as soon as it was understood as Spirit.

Mystified Economics

It was common ground for those who tried to demystify this bizarre construction that, for all its universal or ontological pretensions, it was really about society, not about "Being" in general. The things that were to receive spiritual consecration without being actually changed were the Christian family, the Prussian monarchy, and all the institutions of Protestant German "civil society," notably the competitive economy for which Hegel had a solid respect. On that basis various attempts were made to decipher Hegelianism by Feuerbach and the Young Hegelians; but it was Marx who found the most far-fetched and unexpected solution which was yet the one that offered the greatest number of point-to-point correlations between the allegory and its interpretation. Briefly, he declared that the meaning of metaphysics was economics.

What Hegel had given was not an account of the structure of Being but a description, in "obscure, unclear-to-itself and mystifying form," of the social process of production. This process went on in a dialectical series of conflicts and divisions but its real hero was the labor of men, not Spirit. Using terms that Marx introduced only some years later, one can say that he saw Hegel's dialectic as the mystified version of the tension between productive forces and productive relations. Productive forces, which appear in Hegel's allegory as Spirit, are the creative powers men apply to supporting themselves and their fellows. Productive relations, which figure in Hegel's story as objectification or alienation, are the various arrangements they enter into in the course of their work and the legal and political systems that codify those arrangements.[4] It was perfectly natural and inevitable, despite the horrified language Hegel used in talking of the melancholy state of alienation, that man's productive powers should objectify themselves in such shapes. It was natural, too, and this was where Hegel's dialectic was a correct account of the social process, that any given set of productive relations should be eventually swept away, "negated," to make way for others better suited to the development of productive powers. This sweeping away, however, could not be accomplished by a mere act of knowing, for these were perfectly objective, solid social arrangements that had to be liquidated. But they would not be superseded until men saw, as Hegel wanted them to see, that all these objectifications were their own doing, products of their own activity, and thus remained susceptible to their evolving needs.

What was not natural, said Marx, and what deserved the pejorative name of alienation, was for any one set of productive relations to harden, to become a fetish, and to be allowed to block the smooth, sinuous evolution of society by damming back productive forces under the pretence that it was natural and not a man-made dispensation. Hegel, unknown to himself, had given an allegorical description of just such an event. This was no accident, for there would be no need of metaphysical systems unless something had gone wrong in society. The mysterious mumbo-jumbo of the philosophers was a symptom of social malaise, a neurosis as we would say, set up by the damming back of productive forces by unsuitable productive relations. Hegel's metaphysics was a mental by-product of the primitive accumulation of capital in Germany. That process involved, as Marx was to go on to argue in detail, the corruption of men's goods (the normal objective upshot of their work) into commodities and capital (the abnormal, alienated but equally objective relations between goods). The proper resolution of the problems that Hegel's philosophy posed was not some other and cleverer metaphysical system but the abolition of the underlying social crisis that had given rise to it. That abolition would take the customary dialectical course of history. It would start with men's recognition that commodities and capital were nothing but their own labor laid out in alienated shape, and then it would progress to men's reclaiming of their own—not just in thought but in actuality, by replacing that set of productive relations with another. Hegel had not only given an accurate though upside-down description of a social situation; he had shown how to get beyond it and, incidentally, how to get rid of metaphysics by abolishing the circumstances that gave rise to it. As Engels said years later in his pamphlet on the end of classical German philosophy:

> It is with Hegel that philosophy in general ends, on the one hand because in his system he resumes its whole development in grandiose fashion and on the other hand because he shows us, though unconsciously, the way that leads out of that labyrinth of systems toward the genuine, positive knowledge of the world.

Hegel was so good at metaphysics that he gave the game away and made metaphysics thereafter unnecessary for anyone who could read off the true meaning of what he said.

Marx said that Hegel found "only the abstract, logical, speculative expression of the movement of history." The same might be said of anyone, poet or metaphysician, who told a dialectical story in which some creative, productive force continually generated and then cancelled successive institutions. But Marx went further and said that Hegel got it all upside-down and had the dialectic walking on its head.[5]

By that he meant that Hegel made the productive, creative force something mental, the Idea or Spirit, whereas in reality the metaphysician's notion of Spirit was just the sign of a breakdown in the dialectic. It was the distortion produced in men's minds by the failure of the dialectic of productive forces and productive relations to work smoothly. What was a by-product of a breakdown was presented in Hegel's metaphysics as the root cause and demiurge of the whole process. That could fairly be called an inversion. Yet Marx's figure of speech —which was not his own but was borrowed precisely from Hegel who had applied it to the Convention during the French Revolution and to Anaxagoras, because both made society rest on reason, i.e., stand on its head—later led to an extraordinary misunderstanding. If Hegel's upside-down dialectic concerned ideas, then by standing it back on its feet, Marx must get a dialectic that works in matter. Matter, too, would then be held capable of contradicting itself and thereafter progressing to higher forms by overcoming that contradiction. This was the blunder of the founders of dialectical materialism and it is still solemnly taught as one variety of Marxist metaphysics. In truth, Marx's dialectic, being the historical interpretation of Hegel's, worked in history, not matter. It was standing on its feet because it took Spirit, metaphysical notions, not as the subject of history but as the distorted reflection of an historical crisis.

The Two Deaths of Philosophy

Marx did not decide all at once that when Hegel wrote "Spirit" he meant "social labor" and that when he wrote "object" he meant "commodity." At first, from 1841 to 1845, he was confused because he was running together two other demystifications of Hegel: Feuerbach's, according to which Spirit alienating itself in objects meant mankind alienating itself in an imaginary god, and Moses Hess's, according to which the same Hegelian formula meant man alienating himself in money. It was at this period that Marx produced such odd phrases as "logic is money" and "money is god."[6] Gradually, he got his own theory clear in his mind. It was that the Hegelian dialectic represented—tellingly misrepresented, rather—a principle of general sociology about the creation of social forms, their hardening into obstacles to free activity and their eventual re-appropriation by men, in revolution. At the particular period Hegel wrote, one such cycle had reached a critical phase: social labor was being alienated in commodities, that is to say, men's activity was being perverted in the institution of the capitalist market. Had he wished, Marx could perhaps—like those later Marxists who saw what he was getting at—have worked out in detail the interpretation of the Hegelian metaphysics as mystified economics.[7] But he was not concerned to do so because he now had in hand a scientific hypothesis about society which could be shown to be true or false by empirical research. It had been suggested to him by Hegel but it was not, for that, metaphysical; on the contrary, it could be tested against facts. So Marx threw himself into the relevant social research and it occupied him intermittently for almost forty years. He had drawn his hypothesis from a philosopher, as scientists in other fields have done (e.g., atomism) but he had an explanation for using such a source: philosophy was confused economics and it arose out of socio-economic tensions. Therefore it could happen that a metaphysician like Hegel could suggest a hypothesis about society, whereas it was less likely that he would suggest a useful one about zoology or physiology (subjects on which Hegel also had metaphysical opinions).

One is now in a position to judge the long debate about when, if ever, Marx dropped his youthful philosophical preoccupations and when, or whether, he became a social scientist. The evident analogies between his latest economic theories and his earliest philosophical notions (e.g., between commodity fetishism and alienation) have seemed to make a decision difficult. The analogy is explained by the fact that the scientific hypothesis was drawn from a metaphysical theory while at the same time offering to show how a metaphysical theory could come to suggest the truth about society. It has been possible for people who saw only Marx's points of departure and arrival but not the intervening development (which Marx did his best to hide by not publishing the relevant documents while referring to them in mysterious asides) to maintain either that there is no connection between them or that, on the contrary, Marx stayed a philosopher to the end. The matter is further complicated by the circumstance that, like Newton or Pasteur or the rest of us, Marx did carry to the end of his life philosophical impedimenta of whose weight he scarcely seemed aware—but they were not of Hegelian origin. Such prejudices as that of the whole, "rich," all-rounder personality (which lies behind the denunciation of abstract labor in *Capital*) came from an older ethical tradition that runs back to Schiller, Kant, and Rousseau. Other prejudices and passions played a role in Marx's social theorizing too, but there is nothing of philosophical interest or importance in that, however damaging it may have been for his scientific work. Philosophy for him was the source of a hypothesis and one whose implication was that philosophy of the Hegelian sort was an illusion that could be cured by social action.

At first Marx took the Young Hegelian stand that the way to be rid of philosophy was to "realize" it. This view became familiar 130 years later when the idealist Marxists revived it.[8] Obviously, to believe that metaphysics can be realized, can be made to come true, one must first believe that it is saying something relevant, even if in arcane language. One must believe that its doctrines contain a promise or a prefiguration of, say, freedom, or happiness, or a better life. On that view, what needs to be done is to translate them into material reality by means of political action. The philosophers' concepts of Reason and Liberty would become realities, whereupon there would be nothing left for philosophers to do. In that sense philosophy would be "abolished," but it would be vindicated too, by providing the "intellectual weapons" for a revolutionary movement. It was in this mood that Marx wrote in his 1841 dissertation, "There follows the consequence that making the world philosophical is at the same time making philosophy worldly, that its realization is at the same time its downfall . . ." Three years later, after his political failure as a bourgeois liberal, he took the working class as the vehicle for the realization of philosophy:

> The *emancipation of Germany* will be an *emancipation of man. Philosophy* is the *head* of this emancipation and the *proletariat* is its *heart.* Philosophy can only be realized by the abolition of the proletariat, and the proletariat can only be abolished by the realization of philosophy.[9]

Marx soon progressed to a more radical point of view: philosophy could not be realized but only destroyed because what it contained was not hidden promise but distorted economics. The analyst who thinks his patient's fantastic dreams could be made to come true has caught his patient's neurosis. The real cure is to rearrange life so that fantasy vanishes without trace. The point, Marx now was saying, was to "put philosophy aside," to "become an ordinary man again" and to study that real world that "is to philosophy what sexual love is to masturbation." As Engels said later, philosophy on this view is "as superfluous as it is impossible." It was in this mood that Marx wrote in *The German Ideology,* speaking of German philosophy:

> The phantoms formed in the human brain, too, are necessary sublimations of man's material life-process, which is empirically verifiable and connected with material premises. Morality, religion, metaphysics and the rest of ideology and their corresponding forms of consciousness no longer seem to be independent. . . . Where speculation ends, namely in actual life, there real, positive science begins as the representation of the practical activity and practical process of men's development. Phrases about consciousness cease and real knowledge takes their place. With the description of reality, independent philosophy loses its medium of existence.[10]

The aim now is the liberation from metaphysics by means of social theory, a theory that will illuminate and powerfully assist social action.

It is important to have clear the distinction between these two attitudes because one can then see how much of Western Marxism is retrogression to Young Hegelian notions that Marx abandoned in his twenties. Neither of the eventualities he spoke of in turn—the disappearance of philosophy thanks to its social realization, nor the destruction of philosophy by analytical criticism of its causes—would seem to lend much encouragement to metaphysical speculation. Yet by blurring the distinction between them, so as to continue the first while claiming to be a Marxist (a member of a mass movement), philosophers have been able to keep alive the program of all idealism: the promotion of the idealist ethic, the exhortation to humanize the world by realizing philosophy, i.e., by affirming the supremacy of noble thoughts. Among the neo-Marxists, Merleau-Ponty was franker in recognizing the blank contradiction between Marx's successive attitudes to philosophy but he was also typical in deploring it. The youthful Marx, he complains in effect, while still so young and having written nothing worth remembering, had already betrayed "occidental Marxism" to "naturalism."[11] True enough, he had deserted Hegelian metaphysics and Young Hegelian moralizing for a hypothesis that could be set against facts.

Even granting (what would take a separate enquiry to prove) that metaphysics belongs to the pathology of thought and that, therefore, it calls for diagnosis and demystification, it is clear today that Marx did not find the whole explanation for the malady. Since he wrote, not only has historical materialism, which is implicit in his diagnosis, been subject to damaging criticism, but equally plausible suggestions as to the etiology of metaphysics have come from elsewhere. The psychoanalytical suggestion that metaphysics is literally neurotic (e.g., that the yearning for the Whole runs back to infantile narcissism) or the linguists' suggestion that it results from the bewitching of thought by language are, on the face of it, less "wild" than the assertion that it is dream economics, that the Absolute is capital and its self-identity is profit. Moreover, if Marx had convincingly demystified metaphysics, new metaphysical doctrines could hardly have arisen in his name. Yet that is precisely what happened.

The Resurrection of Philosophy

It has been argued that this happened because the march of events showed that Marx's scientific hypothesis was wrong and that then his theory could only be preserved as philosophy, as a theory immune from historical disproof. Yet those who first saw that Marx's specific predictions had been mistaken did *not* seek to remystify him. Sorel, for example, said that by 1908 everyone saw that Marx's theories were wrong and they were being kept alive as myths, as belief's proof against facts. That did not lead him to a remystification of Marx but, rather, to a pioneering study of social myths. Similarly with others who saw that Marx had gone wrong in parts of his social science: they tried, starting from Marxism, to work to more scientific theories of the evolution of capitalism, of imperialism, and of revolutionary movements. Still others took parts of Marx's theory and tried to work them up into scientific subjects such as the sociology of knowledge, the sociology of work (based on Chapter 13 of *Capital*), or the formal theory of social classes. Whatever success those efforts had (and it was naturally very unequal), they did not amount to a restoration of metaphysics.

One of the few who between Marx's death in 1883 and 1910 called for an original and distinctive Marxist philosophy was the Roman professor, Antonio Labriola; but he gained no hearing.[12] For the rest, those men of the Left who wanted a philosophy drew it from elsewhere and the very variety of sources shows that the prevailing view was that Marxism was philosophically neutral, like other scientific theories. The most successful combination seemed to be of Marxism with pragmatism, as effected by Arturo (not Antonio) Labriola and Georges Sorel. The least happily inspired was Plekhanov's combination of Marx with Spinoza. The combination no one thought of was of Marx with Hegel—in part because Hegel was out of fashion (a "dead dog," Marx had said in 1873)[13] until the revival of interest in him began in the academies in the first decade of this century, and in part because Marx's earliest analyses of Hegelian philosophy were then unpublished or neglected.

In short, there occurred between Engel's death in 1895 and 1910 the break-up of an ambitious system into scientific studies and philosophical eclecticism, a process already seen in the systems of Saint-Simon and Comte. The reproach that could be made to most of those who tried to carry on what was scientific in Marxism is that they neglected the general sociological theory that Marx had read into the dialectic: the view that social arrangements are transient creations based on domination and ever liable to challenge from a new social movement. To treat them, instead, as natural science regularities to which social movements must bow would be, as Marx said after writing *Capital*, both empirically false and socially conservative.[14] It would be both because it would issue in a sociology of the supposed permanent, unchangeable features of social life that overlooked their origins in domination and their susceptibility to disruption by innovating movements and moralities. Not all the social scientists who set out from Marxism made that error. Though they did not call their style of thought dialectical (a term henceforth discredited by Engels's sallies into the philosophy of nature), they took over from Marx the notion that sociology was about institution-creating activities and they sought to purge it of its monist assumptions in order to arrive at a theory of social movements. It was left to a later generation, starting from 1923 and reaching its triumph after 1945, to remystify exactly this sociological theory into Hegelianism. That is Marxist philosophy.

One way to arrive at a Marxist philosophy is to ignore what Marx said about philosophy and to argue that since his starting point was Hegel, he remained a Hegelian to the end. For example, one recent historian says, ". . . Karl Marx takes his place in the history of Hegelianism in spite of his exclusively scientific pretensions and *Capital* is an authentic product of German philosophy."[15] This overlooks so much in that work that plainly is not philosophy that others feel obliged to save those appearances by arguing that Marx was indeed a philosopher but a poor one. The progression from metaphysics to social science, then, is due to Marx's philosophical incompetence; one might as well go direct to Hegel for authentic metaphysics.[16] However, that solution would deprive contemporary idealists of their Left patent, since Hegel's progeny were not all on the Left; far from it. Some were of a political color nowadays decidedly out of favor. So Marx's philosophical originality and competence are vigorously defended[17] in order that theologians might still concern themselves with him directly.[18] Still, there is so much in Marxism that is unphilosophical, to say the least, that an ancillary hypothesis is needed.

It is one that appeals to theologians because it has often been applied to Christianity. Marxism begins as pure philosophy but it has a tendency to "degenerate" into social naturalism because of the encroachments of "materialism," which must be combated by means of successive infusions of idealism. A series of such infusions, or revivals of pristine purity, is studied below;[19] the method still has adepts.[20] Even such *revivalism*, however, can only get us back to the economico-philosophical manuscripts—that is, to documents where something else besides philosophy is also in question. The foreign matter can be dealt with by being ignored; one can "lay the stress" on the philosophical parts and hand over the rest to the secular arm, to professional economists.[21] This practice is made to seem more reasonable by the publication of various extracts from Marx's works which collect the passages apparently dealing with philosophy and omit (as too technical, or as since proven wrong) those dealing with economics. To take the philosophy and leave the economics must seem an arbitrary way to deal with a theory that says the meaning of philosophy is economics, but it is the quickest way to the metaphysics of alienation (to which we shall return).

Obviously, it was necessary for more scrupulous Marxists than the theologians to face squarely the fact that Marx not only said he wanted to end speculative philosophy but actually did drop that subject by turning for busy decades to social research aimed at proving a hypothesis suggested unconsciously by Hegel.[22] One of the first to do this was a German communist politician and editor of a Communist Party theoretical magazine, Karl Korsch. In 1923 he wrote in *Marxismus und Philosophie*:

> ... the dialectical materialism of Marx and Engels ... absolutely must be considered according to its theoretical nature as a philosophy. . . . As Marx says, "You cannot surpass philosophy without realizing it." It is thus established that for the revolutionaries Marx and Engels, *at the very moment* they abandoned Hegel's idealist dialectic for dialectical materialism, the surpassing of philosophy meant something very different from its simply being put aside.[23]

To grasp the sense of this it is useful to know that it was promptly denounced as heretical by the Communist International and that three years later Korsch, then a deputy in the Reichstag, was expelled from the party. For what Korsch was protesting against was the coarse, tough-minded Bolshevik dogma that philosophy, by which was meant primarily ethics and political morality, was dead bourgeois ideology to be replaced now by a "scientific" Leninist amoralism. Korsch replied that this was poor social theory and it would lead to political defeat in the West, where cultural and ethical issues were vital, whatever might be true in Russia. Korsch, who was a professor of law and had been Minister for Justice in Thuringia, was keenly aware of the resistance that would greet a party that claimed that law and morality were outdated metaphysics. So he sought to put some "philosophy" back into communism by reviving Marx's Young Hegelian pronouncement that the "realization" of philosophy was the real aim of the proletariat. In thinking that idealism could repair a bad social theory, Korsch stands out as one of the fathers of Western Marxism.

Karl Korsch's views were to find no support in the communist movement, which was duly Bolshevized before being Stalinized; but they were taken up a decade later by German university socialists seeking to create the intellectual climate for the Popular Front, in the years after 1934. For them, collaboration between communists and liberals against fascism presupposed that the Marxists gave up their anti-idealist stance. If Marxism could be reclaimed for the idealist philosophies then regnant in the universities, it would be possible for the intellectuals to take the lead in the campaign for the Popular Front. Marcuse saw in 1932 that the readiest way to do this was to revive, as Korsch had suggested, Marx's Young Hegelian plans for the realization of philosophy. Then the proletariat and "its" party would appear to be on the same side as the university idealists. He wrote:

> In [even] the most rabid of Marx's attacks on declining German philosophy there expresses itself a philosophical *élan* that one would misunderstand completely if one confounded it with a will to destruction.[24]

The consequences of this view were the same in the 1930s as Marx had seen them to be in the 1840s. The combination of missionary idealism and social theory leads to the annihilation of the second: society is asked to find its new and more rational shape by passing through mind, by copying a mental pattern. All the talk of realization of philosophy comes down to intellectuals dictating to social facts, as Marcuse's subsequent career showed. Besides, it runs into fatal logical difficulties. Realization or culmination of a theory can only refer to the application-syllogism: a philosophical proposition appears as major premise in an argument where the minor contains a reference to needs and the conclusion concerns an action. In that syllogism the theory has been applied or, if one wishes, has been realized, has been made actual—but it has not culminated or disappeared for all that. Philosophical propositions are still available after figuring in application-syllogisms to figure in other syllogisms, including perfectly philosophical ones. The plan to abolish philosophy by realizing it turns out to be empty; it is an "eschatological fiction."[25]

That difficulty was met by another communist leader, Antonio Gramsci, who had helped found the Italian Communist Party and later died of maltreatment in Mussolini's jails. Gramsci saw that he was in jail in part because Korsch's presentiments had been correct. The Western working class had refused to rally to an amoral party that dismissed ethics and culture as bourgeois ideology. A party of Leninist "technicians of revolution" had, in their brusque changes of policy and their unscrupulous use of temporary political allies, overlooked empirical ethical facts, namely, the moralities formulated by social movements and incarnated in their institutions. To retrieve its defeat, Gramsci felt, Marxism needed a philosophy—not in the sense of a metaphysics but of an ethics. The Young Hegelian formula about the culmination of philosophy would serve but it received, in Gramsci's hands, a new meaning, one derived from the brand of idealism Gramsci was trained in: Crocian idealist historicism. Philosophy meant morality and it was not to be destroyed or put to one side, as Russian materialists had argued, but rather to be

27

"realized" or to "culminate," in the sense of winning a mass backing and becoming a popular faith. Marx had not wanted to reject or supplant philosophy (this was aimed, like Korsch's protest, at the Bolsheviks) but its realization did not mean its appearance in some application-syllogism that would leave philosophy untouched. It meant its transformation into a popular culture, a mass religion, a myth.[26] Such transformation was a normal fate because, on the absolute-historicist view Gramsci adopted, the only "proof" of a philosophy lay in its becoming historically effective. As a populist, he saw historical efficacity in mass ideologies.

> Ideologies, thus, are "true" philosophy because they are those philosophical "vulgarizations" that carry masses to concrete action, to the transformation of reality. That is, ideologies are the mass aspect of each philosophical conception which, in the "philosopher," looks abstractly universal, beyond space and time . . .[27]

In other words, philosophy is not, as the optimist Marx had hoped, a curable neurosis but a condition whose proper end is to become an epidemic: by winning minds after turning into political propaganda and popular religion. Gramsci clung, as Korsch had too, to the hope that one far-off day all philosophy might indeed disappear in a rational society.[28] But meanwhile, in the hard world of Hitler, Mussolini and Stalin, the struggle was one set of lies against another, one political propaganda against another, one popular faith against another. (Gramsci even allowed that Marxism had become a superstition.)[29] In the struggle between our lies and theirs, the only "proof" would be who won the masses. The reason for preferring the victory of our religion is that we have on Marx's authority what they deny: that one day all metaphysical mystification will end, in a transparent society. This is the interpretation of Marxism of a Western communist politician caught between Stalinism and fascism.

The Metaphysics of Alienation

By the time it became known, with the publication of Gramsci's notebooks from 1947, this interpretation was of little use because in the interim fascism had discredited the doctrine that philosophy was politics and truth was historical by showing that it reduced everything to propaganda. Another way to remystify Marx was then available, however, because Marx's youthful work had become better known. It was being read by Western Marxists in a way that derives not from Korsch's book but from another communist heresy published in the same year, Lukacs's *History and Class Consciousness*.

Marx had, as he thought, demystified Hegel's story about Spirit alienating itself in objects and civilizations by saying that this symbolized social work creating goods and institutions. There was no need for Hegel to speak of it as a painful and mysterious process.

> It is entirely to be expected that a living, natural being endowed with objective (i.e., material) capacities should have real natural objects corresponding to its nature and also that its self-externalization should establish an actual objective world. . . . There is nothing incomprehensible or mysterious about this. The contrary, rather, would be mysterious.[30]

Where there *was* room for indignation was when this normal process of externalization broke down, when social labor began to be throttled in one outdated set of productive relations, maintained in place by domination. That was indeed a painful and (for its victims) a mysterious process, called alienation or reification, because it converted productive relations from activities into something given, imposed and cruel. This was not, as Hegel had suggested, a universal, ontological state of affairs but always a concrete historical happening, affecting such and such a class of producers, here, now and for these reasons. Marx eventually dropped the term alienation as too philosophical,[31] preferring the related notions of "commodity" and "abstract labor," whose exact economic meaning he sought to define, and the similarly related concept of a tension between productive powers and productive relations.

The remystification of Marx on this point consists in transferring his juvenile pathos about alienation (and his life-long opposition to commodity-production, abstract labor, and outdated productive relations) to the general conditions of social life. What thereby seems imposed and cruel is not anything particular in history but the human situation generally. Alienation once again becomes Hegel's objectification, that painful act whereby Spirit tears the world out of its ghostly bowels, and it is suffered by no social class in particular (not the proletariat, for instance) but by *anyone* sensitive enough to dislike work, laws, and the various conditions of cooperation.[32]

This misunderstanding was prepared by Lukacs who later admitted he had mistakenly re-Hegelized Marx. By then, the error was well launched on a long career as a principal tenet of Western Marxism because it provided the opportunity for rhapsodies on the sufferings of man's essence (the humanist version of Hegel's Spirit) in modern society. It enabled an attack on contemporary industrialism to be mounted by idealists and theologians under "Marxist" auspices. It helped self-styled Leftists reject as alienation cooperative work in the founding of institutions, in favor of a non-alienated life of sex, ecstasy, contemplation, or privacy. It made it possible for "Marxists" avowing no allegiance to a cause to repudiate as alienating any particular set of objective conditions while they held out for the illogical fantasy of a life without conditions.[33]

Communist critics complain that it has also allowed existentialist Marxists to deplore objectification without incriminating capitalist alienation, i.e., to pass off as the "human tragedy" something that could be corrected by revolution. There is no question that to deplore everything social as alienating can, in certain cases, lead to indifference not only to revolution but to participation in any innovating, institution-creating activities. Heidegger's Marxism was such a case. At the same time, it is no less clear that indignation about supposedly pervasive alienation and the chiliastic vision of a completely de-alienated society have led to anarchistic, destructive attacks on all institutions—to blind revolutionism.[34]

The vague notion of human alienation suffered by no particular social subject was welcome to those who wished to retain an oppositional stance when the proletarian victims of alienation deserted them. By giving the term a general, anthropological sense, what had been developed by Marx as the analysis of a concrete social situation (admittedly at first in the humanist language of Feuerbach) could be converted into the description of a timeless, constant structure, whether of society or of Being itself.[35] Thereupon, the proletariat's desertion of its revolutionary mission was no cause for idealists to abandon their action stations. They had found new tasks in an eternal battle where no allies could ever betray them: the war on the conditions of social existence.

It is important to notice that this theory arose among German Jewish Leftists in the 1930s and it reflects their despair at the defeat of the German working class by Hitlerism. It expresses their conviction that, even if opposition to fascism no longer had a powerful mass base, it nevertheless deserved to be kept alive as theory by small groups of intellectuals.[36] This attitude resembles that of East European intellectuals thirty and forty years later, in countries where there is no mass movement of protest and where it is safer to deplore ontological unhappiness and anthropological alienation than to specify historical cases of it. Hence the progress of anthropological Marxism in Yugoslavia and Czechoslovakia; it has even made its appearance in Russia.[37]

In contrast, in the West since 1950 this attitude could only be maintained if one avoided asking why the once alienated proletariat had deserted the philosophers, why the once oppressed social subject had left the idealists high and dry with a concept of alienation that no longer had historical content and had to be used metaphysically. An answer would be that the proletariat had been de-alienated to the extent that collective action had won for it a measure of control over the conditions of its existence and had made productive relations better accord with present productive powers. That very de-alienation was, perversely enough, deplored as "integration" by some opponents of alienation. If the workers' *victories* could be made to look like workers' *defeats*, the hopeless situation of Germany in the 1930s would be recreated in imagination and theories then coined would gain new currency. Among the survivors of the 1930s, Horkheimer admits that this confusion will not serve; but Marcuse insists that totalitarianism prevails under neo-capitalist democracy as much as under Hitler and so the theories of despair are still seasonable. Needless to say, theories that empty Marxism of historical content and look for an anthropological or ontological fundament common to vastly different ages go back not only beyond Marx but beyond Hegel, too, to Kant.

Totality versus Facts

To separate Marxism from history was a feat but it was matched by other Marxist philosophers who converted that would-be scientific doctrine into the most resolutely anti-scientific of all philosophies, absolute idealism. This latter is the faith that, to use the words and the capitals favoured by its devotees, the Truth is the Whole, that there is a Totality of Reality compared to which all constituent parts are incomplete and for that reason false. This denial of the independent existence of things is viciously anti-scientific because whereas science consists in the positive treatment of subjects, absolute idealism entails the rejection of all subjects. For it, there could be only one subject, the Whole or the Absolute, and nothing scientific can be said about *it*. Concerning any matter short of it, we can only say things that are incomplete, relative, interim or in some other way marred by falsehood. Surely enough, the transmutation of Marxism into absolute idealism has led to the denial of all the social sciences in favor of disquisitions upon a whole called Praxis or History.

In that way it has led back to doctrines whose abstractness and sham generality Marx mocked. Yet there is no denying that Marx gave the absolute idealists a handle in that some of his remarks about social affairs were colored by monism, by the assumption that society was a unity. When he had to analyse a particular society, say France under Napoleon III, Marx dropped that monism, but it reappeared whenever he sought to give an account of his methods. In particular, it showed up in summaries of two of his theories, economic equilibrium and historical materialism. Instead of following Marx's own practice, as later social scientists have done by abandoning monist assumptions in treating the social connections that those two theories point to, the Marxist philosophers have preferred to exacerbate gratuitously the monist or solidarist language Marx sometimes used, until they got a Whole, a Totality, in which they could find rest from facts.

The innovator here too was Lukacs and the prime disciple Marcuse; the Italian and East European exponents of Praxis have followed, by elaborating a dogma of totality whose connections with Marx's work are quite tenuous. They have arrived at a curious perversion of the dialectic. For Marx the dialectic symbolized a social fact, but for them it is a new version of traditional absolute idealism. Marx said Hegel's dialectic symbolized the social fact that productive labor generates objective institutions that can get in the way of continued free activity and need to be revolutionized. The Marxist philosophers, on the other hand, say that social labor is the Whole and that the institutions that successively objectify it, obstruct it, and then are swept aside by it, are the parts. These latter are those untrue finites which Hegel said it was idealism's job to destroy. They are instances of that incompleteness and dependence, that inferior or relative mode of being that idealism finds in all particulars. Naturally, there can be no science of them; all the social sciences from demography to economics are false. The only science is the One Science, the Human Science, which consists in reflections on the Whole, on Praxis. Praxis is the lone reality in social affairs; all the rest is its temporary appearances or manifestations. Alienation or reification, therefore, do not consist in the historical situation where productive forces are throttled back by outdated institutions but in the general ontological circumstance that the Whole has parts. Any part of history, any institution, is a temporary alienation or reification of the whole of history; its meaning and its destiny are re-integration into the fluid totality of Praxis.

Lukacs's interpretation of Marxism begins this line of thought:

It is not the predominance of economic themes in the explanation of history that decisively marks off Marxism from bourgeois science. It is the point of view of totality. The category of totality, the universal and determining domination of the whole over the parts, constitutes the essence of the method Marx borrowed from Hegel. . . . So for Marxism there is not, in the last analysis, any autonomous science of law, of political economy, of history, etc.; there is only one science, historical and dialectical, unique and unitary, of the development of society as a whole.[38]

c

This "Whole" looks like Hegel's Spirit in yet another of its disguises, and indeed Lukacs revealed that it was the subject-object long sought by German idealism. It was the continuing activity of which all social realities were the transient creations[39] and which enjoyed a superior degree of reality compared with the mere facts of experience.[40] That onward-rolling totality consisted of men's activity or Praxis. It embraced everything they did in society. Its tragedy has been that till now it has been unconscious, in the special sense of not being aware of itself as men's activities. That tragedy is shortly to end and it will end—like Hegel's sufferings of Spirit—in an act of cognition. The acquiring of class consciousness by the proletariat will be the coming to consciousness of history, the arrival on earth of the subject-object.

This is not a demystification of Hegelianism. It is a parody of it. As will be seen below, it is a parody that has enjoyed a long career, down to the New Left. In 1936 Marcuse took over the theory that the dialectic was identical with absolute idealism. The object of the "materialist dialectic," he said,

> ... is the totality of the process of social evolution [which] appears as an inherently multidimensional, organized structure. ... In relation to this process, every individual factor, considered as an isolated unit, is "inessential," in so far as its "essence," i.e., the concept of the real content of an appearance, can be grasped only in the light of its relation to the totality of the process.[41]

This is the familiar absolutist assertion that in order to know anything at all one needs to know something about everything. It returned thirty years later in Marcuse's essay, "Repressive Tolerance." There he claims to place his New Left call for "total revolt" under Marxist auspices by arguing that:

> According to a dialectical proposition it is the whole which determines the truth—not in the sense that the whole is prior or superior to its parts, but in the sense that its structure and function determine every particular condition and relation.[42]

Meantime, the same conception of society as a perfect unity and a concrete totality, under the name of Praxis, has been adopted by the philosophical opposition in East European communist states.[43]

The starting points for the absolute-idealist mystification of Marxism were, as I have noted, Marx's theories of economic equilibrium and historical materialism. Whenever the absolute idealists seek to derive their philosophy from Marx, they quote one or other of a small number of citations referring to these subjects. These are passages in which Marx says either that an economy is an unstable equilibrium in which a change in one part (say, production) entails a change in another part (say, consumption), or else that the productive relations of any one epoch hang together to form a characteristic culture.

As to the first of these ideas, it came to Marx from Ricardo and Quesnay; none of them managed to give it precise expression. It was to be formulated mathematically later by the School of Lausanne, that is, by Walras and Pareto, as the theory of economic equilibrium. (And as soon as it was, it was borrowed by a theorist a few miles down the lake, the Geneva linguist, Ferdinand de Saussure, and applied to yield the first theory of linguistic "structuralism.") This line of thought owes nothing to absolute idealism, except perhaps that people in Marx's day were made receptive to the notion of organism and of organic interaction by the raptures of Hegel and the Romantics on the subject. But they had taken the idea in the first place from the budding science of physiology, and they had done nothing to carry it any further. The reason they made a metaphysics out of it was to protest against the French Revolution's contempt for irrational, organic societies. Some applications of the idea to social affairs, such as the Historical Law School around Savigny in Marburg, were all too obviously inspired by the Restoration's ideology of social unity and gradual change; and Marx despised the Historical Law School. In taking over from the economists the notion of an economy as an interacting unity, he was not accepting metaphysical organicism but adopting a hypothesis of economic analysis. He made it clear that interdependence was so far from flowing from the structure of reality that, in economics, it was only gradually coming to be true, thanks to bourgeois force. In other words, the extensive interdependence of economic facts was attained only in the advanced capitalist societies.[44] Yet it is on references by Marx to economic interactions that Lukacs bases his importation of the category of totality into Marxism.[45] In reality, the hypothesis of organism can be applied to an animal, an economy, or a language without the least concession to the idealist notion of two levels of being, the superior Whole and the barely half-real parts. There is nothing idealist in an input-output table, which is what Marx (who well knew Quesnay's *tableau économique*) was getting at in his references to economic equilibrium.

There is a second pretext. In the theory for which he has always been best known, Marx argued that the culture—law, politics, ideologies—of an era formed a unity which he dubbed "productive relations" in order to suggest their dependence on productive forces, on the way men gained their subsistence at that time. The doctrine of historical materialism has never, in Marx's hands or later, received satisfactory expression. Either it is made precise and can easily be disproven, or else it is put so generally that it is safe but of little use. The quest for convincing formulations continues.[46] What concerns us here is not its general validity but the difficulties Marx got into by trying to state it monistically, as true of *societies*. Sorel and Max Weber were later to show that everything valuable in the theory could be saved by applying it to social movements, to ways of living. One has less trouble showing that moralities, ideas, and institutions arise in the day's work and evolve in intimate association with practical affairs, and especially with the most important of practical affairs—the securing of supplies of whatever material it is the movement requires (capital, means of production, laboratories, churches, artistic materials or whatever, depending on what sort of movement it is). On the contrary, by trying to say this of *all* society at a given epoch, the historical materialists were committed to arguing that a society is a single movement in need of only one set of materials (food, shelter, clothing) and that all its ideas depend on that. Worse, they fell into the sort of culture-morphology later associated with Oswald Spengler: each culture became an organic whole and there were no laws applying to successive structures or blocks of productive relations.[47]

Now this was grist to the mill of the absolute idealists. If Marx had said that the economy was One and if he also said that each culture was One and if he finally had said that culture depended on the economy, then they felt entitled to jump to the concrete totality of history, the Whole of which everything specific is an aspect. There is not to my knowledge any place in Marx's work where he connects the notion of the *tableau économique* (of economic equilibrium) with his assertion that each set of productive relations is a system (that cultures have a certain unity). Yet the idealists have run them both together to get the dialectic of totality. Rather, they already had the totality, it being the stock in trade of absolute idealism; what they jumped at was the pretext to connect it with the most vigorous social movement of the day, with Marxism. There were various reasons for doing this; that is, absolute idealism could serve several social functions. As combined with Marxism (whereas it has mostly served Rightist social forces), it could fill either a post-revolutionary conservative function, or else a mock-revolutionary anti-reformist one. It does the former in the hands of Lenin and Mao; the latter with Herbert Marcuse, Frantz Fanon, and (as Marx saw long ago) the Young Hegelians.

The Uses of Totality

When Lukacs, whether defending Lenin in 1922 or Stalin in the 1930s, insisted that history was a whole whose course could be known to a few, he was disqualifying as partial, and therefore false, oppositional criticism, which necessarily was based on less-than-total experience and interests. When Mao Tse-tung in his little red book recalled Lenin's saying that you need to know *all* a thing's aspects, relations, and mediations in order to deal with it, he was using absolute-idealist logic for the same purpose. When a Yugoslav philosopher rules that the administration can adopt "the standpoint of the Whole" and find "the one true general interest," absolute idealism is again put to its traditional conservative use.[48] One would imagine that such shifts would be too gross for Marxists, since Marx was so scathing when the Right of his own day used them. But the application of absolute idealism to social affairs produces a characteristic habit of thought in its addicts, whether of Left or Right. The clue to it lies in that philosophy's devaluation of everything that falls short of the supreme reality, the Whole. In the religious sphere, this attitude leads to a masochistic self-effacement of the individual (the particular) before the ineffable Whole. In politics, the particular that is to be effaced cannot be the individual man; if politics is to have any subject, men must retain their material, corporeal existence. What is to be devalued is everything in between the individual and the social Whole. It is to that in-between range that is applied the absolute-idealist critique of the finite as false. It is possible to put this in Hegelian language as the abolition of "mediations," or sub-totalities, between particulars and the Whole.[49] It is plainer to say that it means the dissolution of all independent, intermediate institutions, political factions, unions, churches and the like. All such groups and all the purposes they serve are incomplete, partial and false over against the true society and the authentic historical purpose of the totality. The parts, the factors, the particulars and the "inessential" isolated units denounced by absolute idealists and awarded by them an incomplete measure of reality are simply, when politics is in question, all associations other than the central committee of the ruling party, which represents the Whole. The Whole is the Revolution and the parts are counter-revolutionary.

The mock-revolutionary use of the doctrine may be seen in the totalist, New Left sociology of Frantz Fanon.[50] Whatever social fact he took up—whether the relationship of Arab girls with their fathers or how families listen to the radio—he at once passed to the social whole, in which such details had their meaning and which alone could be changed. Fanon was remarkable among the neo-Marxists in developing the absolute-idealist logic in a way familiar in other fields, namely to the point of denying that one can make distinctions within the Whole. One can see only a blur, a whole culture, and the only conceivable political action would be to leap from one cultural structure to another. The banality that we perceive things in a context is twisted into the very denial of the distinction between things and contexts: we can only see the whole lot and cannot hope to distinguish, much less reform, any part.[51] Marcuse draws the same conclusions from his allegation that society is a perfect unity. If it is a repressive society, one cannot make distinctions within it, *everything* there will be repressive— including the exercise of civil liberties. The only solution is to revolutionize the totality. Any attempt to draw distinctions is counter-revolutionary.[52]

Such pronouncements sound extremely radical. Yet, as Hegel well knew, total revolutions can exist only in imagination. The only way to change things totally is to change our minds about them, to see them in a new light. For that, it is not necessary that they be *really* changed. Indeed, any partial change—a reform or even a very considerable revolution—would fall so far short of total change as to cut a pale figure alongside the eucharistic miracle of transubstantiation. In this way, mock-revolutionary absolute idealism can lead to conservatism. Marx said of his Berlin student friends that their plan to liberate men's minds

> . . . reduced itself to the demand that the existing be differently interpreted, i.e., that it be accepted thanks to another interpretation. Despite their use of "world-shattering" phrases, the Young Hegelian ideologists are the greatest conservatives.[53]

The same attitude has come back, under absolute-idealist auspices, with the New Left. What many New Left revolution-aries are dissatisfied with is not so much what we do as our reasons for doing it, the spirit in which we do it. Since improve-ment of the lot of the poor mass of humanity presumably counts among their aims (as among almost everybody else's), a high level of economic activity would have to be maintained after their revolution, but it would be on a new, non-economic basis. Their revolution would give a new *meaning* to life. We should still be going about our wonted tasks but "a radically new ethos of work" would appear.[54] On this view such details as the re-allocation of resources are the concern (by definition) of the Establishment and aspirants to it and all other partial concerns are mere sectional interests, reformism, or vile traffic. What matters is not such futile finites but the Whole, the need for the totally other. One of Sartre's fictional characters is a *grand bourgeois* who considers himself more radical than the reddest revolutionary, because the first step in *his* revolution would be to turn the whole of society upside down. Admittedly, the second step would be to put everything back in its accustomed place, but then everything would appear in a new light. Thereupon, the poor radicals would be left far behind," *là, loin derrière moi, agitant leurs mouchoirs.*" This has long been a familiar type of Right thinking. What is new is that it now also flourishes on the Left.

The Reflection of Locke in Lenin

One way of covering over Marx's hostility to philosophy has been to argue that what he was actually doing was making a contribution to the theory of knowledge. Indeed, if Marx were an *epistemologist*, he would be welcome in the academies. If his contribution to the "knowledge problem" were the theory that thoughts are reflections of the material world, he would fit nicely into the Leninist academies and he would incidentally serve as starting point for a materialist metaphysics. If, on the other hand, he were a pragmatist (with only occasional backslidings to Locke's reflection theory of knowledge), he would be acceptable in the American universities. Either way, as one who had wrestled with the supposed problem of how we gain knowledge of the "external world," he would be *salonfähig* among the very philosophers he sought to put out of work. Unfortunately for that hope, Marx was not an epistemologist nor did he seek to be one. He did not put up a Leninist theory of perception and he was not a pragmatist.

On the first point, it is generally accepted—gladly by the Leninists, sadly by the Western Marxists—that Marx adopted the theory of knowledge later made orthodox for communists by Lenin. This is to the effect that the ideas in our heads are pictures, or representations, of material things outside in the "external world." The evidence for this is such passages as this one from *Capital*:

> For Hegel, the thought process (which he actually transforms into an independent subject, giving it the name of "idea") is the demiurge of the real. In my view, on the other hand, the ideal is nothing other than the material when it has been transposed and translated inside the human head.[55]

Yet this remark is drawn from a passage referred to above in quite another connection, in the matter of how Marx's dialectic differed from Hegel's. For Hegel, the demiurge of the historical process was Spirit. Marx replied that Spirit was a metaphysical notion and one that arose as a distortion, as a symptom, of a situation in the economy. History was not "the outward manifestation of Spirit"; on the contrary, Spirit was a meta-physician's metaphor for social labor, and that material process was only "transposed and translated inside the human head" *because* it was being alienated in a social system that meta-physics was trying to sanctify. So Marx here is not talking about knowing but about *not* knowing, about the origin of meta-physical illusions. This is clear also in various similar passages in his work where he stipulates that the transpositions and translations inside the human head which he is contrasting with social reality are "apparitions, specters, fancies . . . idealist humbug"[56] and that the "representations" he is attacking are "ideological reflexes and echoes of this life process. The phantoms of the human brain . . . morality, religion, metaphysics and other ideologies."[57]

This is (to prefer one anachronism to another) not the world of Locke but of Freud. It is not about how we gain knowledge but about how we fail to do so and, instead, suffer delusions, in particular the metaphysical delusion that Spirit rules the world. A reader of Hegel, after all, could scarcely fall back on Locke's "images," for Hegel was caustic about the theory that ideas are images of "things outside." Thus when Lukacs re-Hegelized Marx he was quite consistent in throwing out the reflection theory of knowledge professed by Lenin.[58] Granted that Marx was writing—like Pareto with his cumbersome "residues" and "derivations"—before more convenient terms were introduced by psychoanalysis, he was entitled to call delusions "representations," because he was insisting that they were not arbitrary or meaningless but did represent something. They represented it "upside-down, as in a camera obscura."[59] Like a neurotic symptom, they tellingly misrepresented something. Metaphysics, religion, and other ideology were illusion but a natural and sociologically explainable one, in that they resulted from certain forms of social organization. They expressed the truth erroneously and in that sense reflected the social process.

This diagnosis of metaphysics has nothing to do with the metaphysical theory that ideas represent matter (or substance), a view of Locke's so decisively dealt with by Bishop Berkeley that it has enjoyed little currency since then (that is, outside Russia and the communist parties).[60] Lenin accepted, in *Materialism and Empirio-criticism,* what seemed to him the simple, robust, common-sense belief of mankind that *"outside of us* and independently of us there exist objects, things and bodies [and] that our perceptions are images of the outer world." Lenin was combatting as "nothing but sheer idealistic foolishness" the theorem that bodies are complexes of sensations. In so far as Lenin meant that things can exist in independence of a mind, he was taking up the naturalist position common to Marx and other men of scientific temper. But Lenin has no justification for calling those mind-independent things "matter" (nor hence for calling his theory "materialism") because they include other minds—which are also occurrences that exist independently of being known. Apart from that "materialist" importation, Lenin's image theory runs into the difficulties of any representationist theory. How do we know the image is an accurate copy unless we compare it with the original? And then if we can see the original, for the purpose of this necessary comparison, why could we not see it directly in the first place without having to go via a copy? Lenin's attempted answer, drawn from Engels, is that "action proves the conformity of our perceptions with the objective nature of the things perceived." Now, it is indeed true that action (and the same is true of argument and contemplation, of course) can show that beliefs we used to hold are wrong (or right) but it cannot show that "being right" meant "having a correct image."[61] In finding out during action that our notions about something had been wrong (or right), we would still need to compare idea and thing—whereupon the idea is shown to have been all along an otiose entity, since direct knowledge can be had without it.

The upshot of Lenin's dogmatic argument is that orthodox Marxists have felt obliged to imagine all the minds in the world being submerged together in a submarine called Mentality and peering anxiously through the periscope at images of the rest of the universe, called Matter. The captain of the submarine has orders not to surface, so the only way to check the accuracy of the periscope's images is to cruise around without hitting anything—which is *Praxis*. This is, clearly, a very inadequate account of knowing; but the important point for the development of communist metaphysics is the assumption that all the minds are in the one submarine and all the matter outside. Hence the dogma of materialism, which confounds the naturalist assertion of the mind-independence of things with the arbitrary claim that what is independent of a mind is non-mind, matter. The realization that minds, too, are independent occurrences among material ones allows everyone to clamber out of the submarine, and the materialist voyage is over.

It should never have begun. Marx, at least, was not one of the organizers. In saying that religion, metaphysics, and "idealist humbug" had social causes and could not be got rid of by cleverer philosophies but only by social change, he was not putting up a theory of perception nor asserting the primacy of "matter" over "mind." In saying that a metaphysical illusion could be explained by a particular way of organizing productive life, he was not saying that ideas were copies of external reality. He was saying that some ideas were useless, mystifying distortions of it. Yet in the name of Marxist philosophy, Leninists are still defending Lockean "ideas," hoping to cover over the weaknesses of the copy theory with sophistry about "structurally isomorphic images." Having also taken over from Engels the illogical notion that matter is self-contradictory (this is called the dialectic of nature), they then can make no sense of a mentality that is an exact copy of matter, for it would have to be self-contradictory, too. This farrago is the compounding of two metaphysical theories (representationism and the dialectic of nature), neither of which comes from Marx.[62]

How they made a Good Pragmatist out of K. Marx

Engels and Lenin, we have seen, said that practice was a crucial element in the obtaining and verification of knowledge. This was in part an attempt to deal with an evident difficulty in the copy theory of knowledge; but it was also in sympathy with the gathering vogue of pragmatism in the last years of the previous century and the first decade of this one. By 1909 Marxists like Arturo Labriola claimed to have found that Marx had actually anticipated pragmatism. Since pragmatism at that date was laying emphasis on experiment and industry, as against immaculate clean-handed ways of acquiring knowledge, this discovery was congenial to a proletarian socialist movement concerned to "liberate" science and industry from clean-handed entrepreneurs. The further development of pragmatism revealed that it contained a relativist notion of truth. What was true was ultimately, on this view, decided by the relevant social authorities, the folk whose expert practice dealt with that particular field, and they decided it by ruling what was expeditious rather than what was absolutely the case. These relativist notions of truth, and the implicit devaluation of pure science as against getting things done, were soon taken up in Europe by anti-socialist forces. Pragmatism was for a time one of the official philosophies of Italian fascism; and, in a romantic, "biologized" version, it provided the original ideology of Nazism. The claim that Marx was a pragmatist before the word was, therefore, allowed to drop, and the arguments of the pragmatist Marxists of the first decade of this century (e.g., that science *is* industry) came to be strongly opposed in Soviet Russia.[63]

Marx the pragmatist was rediscovered in American universities in the 1930s by intellectuals sympathetic to the new liberal Left, who drew their pragmatism from John Dewey. The texts in which they thought to make this *trouvaille*—mainly the Theses on Feuerbach—were interpreted by the neo-Hegelians in a very different sense and are interpreted today by the New Left as neither pragmatist nor Hegelian but as a justification of revolution.

Briefly, the pragmatists imagined that in the Theses on Feuerbach Marx was asking "How do we know?" and was answering, "By activity." In fact, Marx was asking, "What is it *that* we know?" and was answering, "Social activities." Marx was not talking about knowledge in general but about society, just as he held metaphysicians were, whether they knew it or not, also talking about society. He was arguing that society is not made up of objective things *given* to man (as the materialists said) but of things men were *doing*. This is what the idealists like Hegel had meant, Marx added, by making the world (i.e., society) man-dependent. But they mystified their discovery by making "man-dependent" into "mind-dependent," as if the activities going on in society were mental, as though social labor were Spirit, and as though society could be changed by taking thought. On the contrary, social institutions were objective, real and "out there" (as the materialists said), but they were just men's activities, as Hegel has hinted in his bizarre story about the world being alienated Spirit. It was necessary, Marx argued, to give up the fatalism of the materialists *and* the mentalism of the idealists in order to see that society was the product of concrete work. Once men saw that, they would understand that society was plastic and subject to their joint intentions. They would cease submitting to social circumstances as though these were determined by natural (or maybe supernatural) powers, and they would realize that they could do better than put up mythological interpretations of society: they could change it.

Arturo Labriola claimed that "no one will ever understand anything in *Capital* unless they start from the notes of Feuerbach." Whereupon he proceeded to misunderstand those notes as a sketch of pragmatist relativism: "Matter, far from being the *primum datum* of reality, is a construction of our spiritual experience."[64] Of wider influence was the similar misreading by Sidney Hook a generation later. Hook thought that in the first Thesis on Feuerbach[65] Marx was asking "to what extent man is active in knowing" and that Marx was finding in all previous philosophies "one fundamental defect, an inability to explain the facts of perception and knowledge—in short, the facts of meaningful consciousness and action."[66] Marx wanted, according to Hook, to take over from idealism "the illumination it sheds upon the relation between acts of consciousness and the *contents* of consciousness," which would entail seeing that

The Western Marxists

"knowledge presupposes some active subject who approaches it with *this* category rather than *that*."[67] The whole affair for Hook is about "things and consciousness" and "man and nature," and he reads into Marx the characteristic social relativism of the pragmatists:

> Praxis could not be contrasted with science for science has a praxis, too. The scientific objects which the scientist studies are essentially related to the practices of scientists. These in turn are related to the basic practices of the culture which supports science. . . . For Marx knowledge gives power by virtue of the activities it sets up in transforming things on behalf of social needs.[68]

Continuing this imputation of Dewey's philosophy to Marx, Hook found that Thesis Five[69] meant: "For Marx sensations were not merely experienced effects of things acting upon the body; they were effects of an interaction between an *active* body and things surrounding it."[70] Hook added, "In the light of his genial [sic] insight, he [Marx] would urge scientists to examine their conclusions in terms of the operations and practices necessary to achieve them and to set forth the meaning of their theories as prescriptive guides to specific action."[71] In short, Marx was a solid American pragmatist do-gooder, almost fit for a job with the New Deal: ". . . the fact that action is thoughtful makes it possible to achieve beliefs which are *truer;* the fact that thought leads to action makes it possible to achieve a world which is *more just.* This, I believe, is the sense of Marx's final '*Thesis on Feuerbach.*' "[72]

Now, Marx was so far from the pragmatist opinion that an "act of consciousness" was involved in knowing anything that he considered all talk of "acts of consciousness" or the "activity of Spirit" to be a mystification drawing attention away from concrete work. "Consciousness" contributed nothing to our world, which was the product of men's real activities. At first, in a slave-owning or feudal society, the *made-ness* of our world (the fact that society is made up of human activities and their product) would not be stressed. The workers were mere objects, owned body and soul by their lords, and the instruments of production were natural forces like wind, water, and soil. Such a society would espouse materialist, contemplative views of social affairs, according to which institutions were out-there, given once for all, and unchangeable.

In contrast, modern societies exhibit their *made-ness*, the fact that they are composed solely of human activities and their products. The workers in them are no longer objects but free men, and the instruments of production are capital goods which (as the classical economists had shown) are accumulated labor. But these societies, Marx complains, are capitalist: they separate the free workers from all control of the capital goods. The *making* that constitutes such a society has to be mystified, disguised, by being presented not as the real labor of working men but as the mental effort of capitalists. It is the ingenuity of the investor, the cunning of the speculator and the craft of the merchant that get the rewards; so those activities must be privileged over and above the devalued, discredited, and dehumanized work of the proletariat. Such a society will espouse idealism, with its cant about "acts of consciousness" and the "active subject" and "spiritual labor." At least the British and French bourgeois were content to stop at that hypocrisy, enshrined in their science of economics; but the Germans, who (according to Marx) substitute fantasy for real social enterprise, had to mystify it by converting "spiritual labor" into the "labor of Spirit." Hence the Hegelian rigmarole about Spirit, which was the mystification of a hypocrisy, i.e., the metaphysical form of economics. Hegel was the metaphysical thinker of capitalism because he dressed up its apology of spiritual activity (i.e., making money by your wits) into a mythology about the travail of Spirit.

The old-materialist, pre-capitalist world had had a passive, hopeless, and detached view of itself. It did not see itself as produced, as product, yet it did correctly see institutions as real, solid, and objective. The new, idealist, capitalist world sees all society as activity, as Praxis, as a producing; but it pretends that the producing is mental work, i.e., what the capitalist does, not what the workers do. In the first Thesis on Feuerbach, Marx suggests combining these two views of society: fusing the unproduced object with spiritual production to get objective production, to get the notion of society as concrete work.[73] The old materialist, contemplative attitude persists into the modern polity as the attitude of single individuals in the market: for each one of us, by himself, society (especially its economic "laws") looks to be overwhelming, natural, and unchangeable.[74] But with the new materialist standpoint, arrived at by the combination Marx is suggesting, it will be possible for men once they rise above the individualism of the market place to envisage joint social action.[75] Then they will see society as concrete work, as the product of producing, as the institutions thrown up by social labor. Whereupon they will realize that it is subject to change by joint activity, and subject to real revolutionary change, not just spiritual sanctification as in the Hegelian philosophy. Since it is composed of *their* activities—all their own doing—different activities will make a different world. At that point the cause of metaphysical interpretations of the world will be seen to lie in social difficulties. Men will turn away from religion, from abstraction, from mysteries and mysticism, to the practical task of new activities, to the creation of new institutions.

The pragmatists with their "active subject" would have seemed to Marx to remain in the mainstream of idealism. For him, idealism's theory of mental activity—of the dependence of the "world" on mind—was a disguised apology for entrepreneurial profits and an open denigration of real work, of wage labor. Far from anticipating pragmatism and Hook's active subject, Marx rejected them and pointed to the active object. The only object in question was social, since Marx held that metaphysicians were always talking unconsciously about society. As for non-social objects (for the perception of which Marx adopted a realist, Greek view), they were rarer than philosophers' thought.[76]

In saying, then, that objects are activity, Marx meant that society is a lot of doings—so we can change it by doing something else. This point was always clear to the Marxist neo-idealists but they gave it a characteristic twist. Lukacs saw that Marx was inviting us to approach society as activities, but he added that the trouble to date was that these activities were unconscious and that the revolution would consist in them becoming conscious. That act of cognition would be the work of the proletariat; in fact, since the proletariat seemed incapable of it, it would be the work of a party acting in its name, the Leninist party.[77] Lukacs translated this back into the language of German idealism by saying that the objects (social activities) would become subject in the proletariat, whereupon history would have a single subject-object. There is no doubt that for Marx an act of cognition came into it. Men would have to become aware that society was all their own doing (e.g., that economic values were their labor objectified) before they would set out to mold it to their desires. But by stopping at the act of cognition, Lukacs virtually restored Hegelianism, according to which de-alienation, the abolition of the dead, objective obstacles to Spirit, was something that happened in mentality. It was the attainment of omniscience, the perfect transparency of the world to itself. Whereas Marx had said that social objects were activities, concrete work, and thus liable to change by different forms of concrete work, Lukacs made it all a matter of unconscious activities becoming conscious. He thus restored idealism.

In the face of the plain fact that the proletariat did *not* become the "subject-object" or the "subject of the thought of society," Lukacs had to pass on that task to the party of Leninist revolutionaries. That party had not awaited Lukacs's invitation to substitute itself for the Western working class, but Lukacs's theory made its pretensions more acceptable to some Western intellectuals. Even so, the restoration of idealism was to bear its full fruit only after the defeat of the communist movement in Western Europe. An isolated minority then took up as "Marxism" the doctrine that history could come to consciousness in a small group, and that society could be changed by an act of cognition.

The everyday meaning of that claim in the 1930s was that the economic laws described by bourgeois economists as natural and unchangeable (though they appeared to have led to the depression and to Nazism) could in fact be overruled by a national plan in which the planners would undertake to refashion all Western society. As though to confirm Marx's jibe that Germans are doomed to mystify British and French

D

economics, this claim was put forward by Max Horkheimer in 1937 in language that came from Lukacs's idealist reading of the Theses on Feuerbach. Thus: things seem to us as individuals to be natural and given, but in fact they are historical products; to date they are the product of unconscious activities (uncoordinated entrepreneurial ventures), but they can become conscious (planned), so that all society is the object of "planned decision-making and rational goal-setting."[78] This was put forward by Horkheimer as a metaphysics, including a new logic, under the name "critical theory." It was perhaps a fair version of Marx's views of 1845, though it is worth recalling that Marx did not publish those views and left them "to the mice" as too juvenile. He preferred to devote years of work to determining the conditions under which such things might come true. On the contrary, Horkheimer within a few months (in response to favorable comment by Marcuse) expanded his critical theory into the "struggle for a state of affairs in which what men want is also necessary, in which the necessity of things becomes a reasonable, mastered evolution"[79]—i.e., into the demand that the wish coincide with the reality. This was the fantasy revived by Marcuse thirty years later, and taken up by the New Left as neo-Marxism.

Abstract Labor

The last way of remystifying Marx that we shall examine is to work back from the criticism of abstract labor in *Capital* to the "radical humanism" that Marx sketched in some youthful notes he left unpublished.

Here we are not dealing with Hegelian opinions that Marx rejected or interpreted, nor with juvenile views he later expressly repudiated, but with philosophical prejudices that Marx retained to the end, while seeking to rationalize them, to give them scientific form. Like any philosophical prejudice imported into empirical enquiry and treated as a datum instead of as a hypothesis, this one had deleterious effects. In fact, it vitiated Marx's economics. Those who find that opinion too strong would have to agree that the scientific procedure has been to criticize the ethical assumptions concealed in the concept of abstract labor, to get them out into the open and to continue, if possible, the task Marx attempted of bringing it down to something empirical. Remystification of Marx has consisted in taking just the opposite course of complacently resuscitating the radical humanism from which Marx set out. To see where it was he started from, one needs to go back a few years.

The industrial revolution introduced a new and unfamiliar division of labor in society. It was not of course the first division of labor; society, once it developed past the most primitive levels, has always known complementary tasks and specialization; but the term seems to have been introduced first at this time—by Mandeville in the *Fable of the Bees*, the final version of which dates from 1729. As the system of manufactures progressed, the thinkers of the Enlightenment reacted with increasing distaste to its parcelling out of tasks, the humblest of which were limited, repetitive, and degrading. Adam Ferguson, the philosopher of Augustan Edinburgh and one of Adam Smith's teachers, was typical in denouncing the division of labor in manufactures for repressing reason and feeling in workers, who were reduced to operating as parts of "an engine." In saying that, he passed close to a discovery made by a later generation of industrial managers, namely that the system he was criticizing was nefarious not because it divided labor but because it required human beings to do the very thing they are worst at, imitate parts of an engine, which is also the very thing they least need to do, since a machine can do it and do it better. Ferguson however missed that point (which is not surprising since, as Peter Drucker has shown, Henry Ford missed it too), and declared that "we are creating a nation of helots and we shall have no more free citizens." The immediate resort to a classical metaphor is characteristic of the Enlightenment with its classicist airs. Instead of comparing the lot of European workers in the first manufactures with their lot in rural Europe just prior to that time, it set the fashion of contrasting the conditions of *ancient* and *modern* labor, on the assumption that the ancients had been perfect all-rounders with a well-balanced personality. This fashion was powerfully aided by the work of the eighteenth-century German art historian Johann Winckelmann, who founded classical archaeology and originated the idea of Grecian man as the perfect specimen of humanity, the most beautiful and the most balanced, endowed with a spiritual wholeness that was reflected in the unity of the *polis*, that perfect political form. It was with this paragon of all the virtues (as well as with a handful of universal geniuses of Renaissance times) that the workers in the manufactures were compared, to the discredit, naturally, of that system. Their inferiority was ascribed to the new division of labor. Yet it was one of Adam Ferguson's pupils, Adam Smith, who, while accepting Ferguson's strictures on the system, also demonstrated in the *Wealth of Nations* how it was creating new wealth and advancing humanity's condition. The advantages of economic progress by way of the system of manufactures became increasingly obvious as the eighteenth century wore on. So one sees in writers at the close of the century an ambivalence: a nostalgia for the unity of the personality, allegedly lost because of the division of labor, and a respect for the new study of political economy and its justification of the industrial system.

Schiller is an example, and one that was to have its influence on Hegel and Marx. In the sixth of his *Letters on the Aesthetic Education of Man* (1794–5), Schiller brought up the standard comparison—or rather the "astonishing contrast between contemporary forms of humanity and earlier ones, especially the Greek." The Greeks were credited with "natural humanity" (Winckelmann had said that to imitate the Greeks was the same as imitating nature) and with a simplicity and completeness that "puts us to shame." For they did not suffer the division of labor.

> How different with us moderns! . . . we see not merely individuals, but whole classes of men, developing but one part of their potentialities, while of the rest, as in stunted growths, only vestigial traces remain.

Schiller asked, "What individual Modern could sally forth and engage, man against man, with an individual Athenian for the prize of humanity?" The reason was that the modern community, i.e., the economy of the industrial revolution, "insists on special skills being developed with a degree of intensity which is only commensurate with [i.e., matched by] its readiness to absolve the individual citizen from developing himself in extensity. . . . Thus little by little the concrete life of the individual is destroyed in order that the abstract idea of the Whole may drag out its sorry existence," i.e., so that national wealth should increase. Yet Schiller was aware of the benefits and advantages of the new division of labor and he recalled them in language that echoed both Mandeville and the political economists.

> I readily concede that, little as individuals might benefit from this fragmentation of their being, there was no other way in which the species as a whole could have progressed. . . . If the manifold potentialities in man were ever to be developed, there was no other way but to pit them one against the other. . . . One-sidedness in the exercise of his powers must, it is true, inevitably lead the individual into error; but the species as a whole to truth.

Schiller did not explain how there could be benefits for the whole of society which no individual members enjoyed. Even if the improvement in the lot of the workers who performed the most-divided, meanest tasks were not apparent to him, the accumulation of capital in other hands should have been. In any event, Schiller was not convinced by the argument of the political economists, for he concluded, "however much the world as a whole may benefit from this fragmentary specialization of human powers, it cannot be denied that the individuals affected by it suffer under the curse of this cosmic purpose [*unter dem Fluch dieses Weltzweckes*]." Can the purpose of economic growth by way of the industrial arts justify the loss of Greek wholeness of personality?

> But can Man really be destined to miss himself for the sake of any purpose whatsoever? Should nature, for the sake of her own purposes, be able to rob us of a completeness which Reason, for the sake of hers, enjoins upon us? It must therefore be wrong if the cultivation of individual powers involves the sacrifice of wholeness . . . it must be open to us to restore by means of a higher Art the totality of our nature which the arts themselves have destroyed.[80]

Now, the Enlightenment saw only the system of manufactures. It did not see the introduction of machinery and the beginning of large-scale industry.[81] These brought with them a new division of labor which seemed to make workers not parts of an engine, of which the other parts were men like themselves, but mindless adjuncts to wooden and iron machinery—parts of an engine on a footing with its metal parts. The neo-classicist ambivalence of Schiller now seemed to the Romantics callous and heartless, for they saw in the new mechanized factory an intolerable degradation of man. They reacted with a shrill intellectual Luddism. A more reasonable view (one is here wise long after the event) would have been that there was progress rather than degradation in the replacement of at least some of the human motions in a factory by mechanical motions. Men were not being lowered to the level of wood and iron but being extricated from the "engine" and relieved, in part, by wood and iron. Years later, after long research and after much progress in the factory system itself, Marx admitted that that was what had happened. He came to see that modern industry, just because it was a permanent technological revolution, had no use for the narrowly specialized workers of the first manufactures, those part-men who so horrified the Enlightenment. Perpetually advancing industry required, rather, "a many-sided mobility of the worker" and "the utmost possible versatility of the workers." Its functioning called for, not "the detail worker, who has nothing more to perform than a partial social function [but] an individual with an all-round development, one for whom various social functions are alternative modes of activity."[82] This tendency to repair, for the economy's own sake, the initial specialization of mechanical functions has gone much further since Marx admitted it, and it is continuing with the introduction of computers and process-control. It began with those very technological innovations that the Romantics (and young Marx) denounced as a further assault on man's "whole nature." They took over and carried to absurd lengths one half of Schiller's case, the lament for lost totality, and they often flatly denied the general benefits of the industrial system. Hegel, who corrected most Romantic exaggerations when he absorbed the main doctrines of Romanticism into his philosophy, took over unamended the view that the Greeks had embodied perfect wholeness in politics and in art and that this had been destroyed by the division of labor. Thus he was capable of such remarks[83] as, "When we speak of educated men, we mean, primarily, those who can do everything that others do." It is against this background that one must set Marx's youthful rejection of the division of labor in favor of a visionary "radical humanism."

The terms he used were the Romantic commonplaces. The division of labor had "changed man into an abstract being, a machine tool" and had "reduced him to a physical and intellectual monster."[84] A little later he wrote (and, to his credit, never published) one of the silliest passages of this whole Romantic outcry against the division of labor:

> For as soon as the division of labor begins, each man has a particular, exclusive sphere of activity, which is forced upon him and from which he cannot escape. He is a hunter, a fisherman, a shepherd or a critical critic and must remain so if he does not want to lose his means of livelihood; whereas in communist society, where nobody has one exclusive sphere of activity but each can become accomplished in any branch he wishes, production as a whole is regulated by society, thus making it possible for me to do one thing today and another tomorrow, to hunt in the morning, fish in the afternoon, rear cattle in the evening, criticize after dinner, in accordance with my inclination, without ever becoming hunter, fisherman, shepherd or critic.[85]

These puerilities would be of no interest were it not that from the start Marx went beyond declamations about "whole man" to attack the new science of political economy which was justifying, or at least rationalizing, the industrial economy and its division of labor. It did so by showing how the various divided tasks and special occupations fitted together via the market, by being measured on a common scale, by being quantified in money terms. Marx called this, right from 1844, the "reduction of the greater part of humanity to mere abstract labor."[86] "Abstract" is used here in its logical sense, as referring to something abstracted from, or considered apart from, its proper context. The market economy works, Marx said, by abstracting from each man's different labor a quantifiable aspect, expressed in money terms, and by neglecting all the other aspects of his work, notably the personal satisfaction it procures him as a means of self-expression. From that point on, it would appear, the argument has been transferred from the ethical and aesthetic level where Schiller and the Romantics carried on their denunciation of the industrial division of labor, to the specifically economic level. Marx has set out on the course that will lead to *Capital*, where the identical term "abstract labor" is a key concept. He need never again attack the division of labor as such but only the production of commodities, which are goods to be exchanged on the market according to how much abstract labor they contain. So it is possible for a critic to say, "After *The German Ideology* Marx never mentioned the possibility of abolishing the division of labor and the deliverance of the individual from its constraints. ... No trace of it can be found in Marx's mature works."[87]

At all events, it had disappeared underground, absorbed as a hidden emotional charge attaching to the purportedly exact economic terms, "commodity" and "abstract labor." What *had* disappeared without trace (to surface again 130 years later in the remystification of Marx) was the Romantic vision of a society of Grecian whole men, knowing no division of labor nor even any unequal development of talents, living harmoniously together without the need of any special coordinating agencies (like market or state) because, fundamentally, they were all identical and omnicompetent. That vision was Marx's forgotten footnote to the millennian history of philosophical communism. He said at the time that his utopia was superior to traditional or "raw" communism in that instead of laying the emphasis on who owned property, on whether it was private or socialized—a matter of concern only to owners and consumers—he laid the stress on the association of propertyless *producers*. So it is not difficult to understand why, when Marx discovered in socialism a real-life force supposedly dedicated to just that cause (to the liberation of industrial production from restraints imposed by property-owners, without a care for age-old fantasies about equal and just consumption), he discarded the whole-man vision of the Romantics and tried to work out the conditions under which socialism could succeed. His economic analysis of the commodity market was a contribution to that study.

The question that arises, however, is whether some of the Romantic complaints about the industrial system and its division of labor did not live on, in disguised form, in Marx's economic theory. So many readers of *Capital* thought that Marx *was* attacking the division of labor that Engels later had to write in a passage, in the text of the first chapter, explaining that this was *not* so. Commodities, goods incorporating a quantity of abstract labor, are not just goods made by one man and consumed by another, explained Engels. There was nothing wrong with that, i.e., with the division of labor, as long as the tasks were allocated by a family, a church, or on some conscious plan. Goods become commodities only when they are exchanged via the market, because then labor is being divided and tasks allocated by an external, "natural" force.[88] The market can do this only if all tasks are put on a common scale and measured in terms of something abstracted from them, abstract labor. So the objection is to exchange via the market, not to the division of labor combined with exchange on some other basis.

Capital contains many criticisms of the free market which, even when mistaken, are empirical or analytical material of the sort one finds in any economic discussion. The basic criticism, however, which is concentrated in the notion of commodity, is of a quite different sort. It is the objection that the only way the market can compare things is by ignoring the humanly important differences between them. The only way to get an equivalence between coats and linen is to ignore—nay, to deny—the differences between tailoring and weaving and to highlight something humanly unimportant they have in common. This involves outraging the personal wholeness of the tailor and the weaver by reducing each to one aspect of himself. This is the aspect that happens to facilitate the natural division of labor but which overlooks everything that might make tailoring and weaving pleasant and satisfying expressions of the whole man. This anonymous aspect is generic, general, undifferentiated, abstract, impersonal, non-individual work. To highlight that aspect—which Marx does not deny exists, i.e., he allows that you can rationally quantify tasks—is a scandalous proceeding because it negates each worker's personality and the peculiarities of each calling. It levels their diversity and inequality to a flat common denominator.

> When the use-values of commodities are left out of the reckoning, there remains but one property common to them all, that of being products of labor. But even the product of labor has already undergone a change in our hands. If, by a process of abstraction, we ignore its use-value, we ignore also the material constituents and forms which render it a use-value. It is no longer, to us, a table, a house, or yarn, or any other useful thing. . . . It has ceased to be the product of the work of a joiner, a builder, a spinner; the outcome of some specific kind of productive labor. When the useful character of the labor products vanishes, the useful character of the labor embodied in them vanishes as well. The result is that the various concrete forms of that labor disappear too; they can no longer be distinguished from one another; they are one and all reduced to an identical kind of human labor, abstract human labor. . . . Nothing is left of them but the before-mentioned unsubstantial entity, a mere jelly of undifferentiated human labor. . . . Such an equalization of utterly different kinds of labor can only be achieved by ignoring their actual unlikeness, by reducing them to terms of that which they all share as expenditures of human labor power—abstract human labor.[89]

The pathos here is precisely that of Marx's earliest protests against the market economy and the division of labor. Men's personalities, he said in *Capital* as he had said years before, are mutilated once their labor is quantified, reduced to a common denominator. "Commodity exchange begins where community life ends."[90] What makes men personalities is their different producings. What fits them together in a divided economy is their identical product, lumps of anonymous labour-stuff. Abstract labor is an insult to human individuality.

Marx claimed to be making a scientific discovery in this account of how markets operate. The British physicist Joule, who was born in the same year as Marx, made a similar discovery about this time. He found that there was a common sort of stuff in different physical phenomena: heat and conduction of an electric current; and he quantified it by providing the law for the relation of one to the other. Yet Joule did not report it as a scandal that Joule's law had crippled and mutilated heat and electricity by robbing them of their distinctive characters and denying their differences. He did not conclude that heat and electricity could never again appear as subjects in sentences but were condemned to function only as predicates to a subject that was the thing they had in common and of which they were the mere vehicles. This is the conclusion Marx drew from his supposed discovery of abstract labor as the common stuff in all marketable commodities. That he should do so shows that he was operating with a firm prejudice about the uniqueness and wholeness of each human personality: properties that were damaged if men were regarded in a unilateral way, from the point of view of their place in a quantified division of labor.

The comparison with Joule's law is unfair in that Marx said *his* abstraction was not just a mental act (though it depended ultimately on a frame of mind) but was a real social force of growing power, the market. It was the market that treated men as producers of commodities and as bearers of quanta of abstract labor stuff. This social fact mutilated their personalities by separating their products from them as abstracted and divorced pieces of themselves. Neglecting for the moment the questions whether the market actually does this, and whether there is anything else in modern society *besides* the market, the point to note is that Marx reveals his assumptions by immediately comparing the market with religion.[91] It, too, abstracts parts of the human personality and fetishizes them—as gods. Thus we are back to the Feuerbachian humanism in the midst of the discussion of the foundations of Marx's economic system. Feuerbach, too, had assumed, like a whole generation of opponents of the industrial economy, that there existed a unitary, whole personality from which no faculty should be divorced and treated as a separate power. The concept of abstract labor depends as much on that assumption as did Feuerbach's criticism of religion, and as much as did Marx's attack on such Hegelian abstractions as Logos. In each case, the critic's claim is that an attribute of the whole individual personality has been split off, given a spurious autonomy and set up to rule over the individual as, respectively, the market, god or reason. Marx's line of thought here is exactly parallel with his critique of Hegel's philosophy decades before. He charged then that Hegel took the human activity of thinking and set it up as thought, as something external to and superior to men, and made *it* do all the thinking, merely using men as its predicates, or vehicles. That, said Marx then, was an improper abstraction, a mutilation of the true subject, the undivided human personality.

In so far as the market did something similar (here the separation is of abstract labor instead of thought), it too was to be condemned in the name of the whole man. It took the craftsman who had a "natural bent to make something independently" and who was "competent to carry on a complete craft, [to] practise it anywhere and finds means of subsistence,"[92] and by separating the anonymous, quantifiable part of his work (for the purpose of fitting him into a division of labor organized by the market), reduced him to a vehicle of abstract labor power. Thereby it made him no longer the subject of his own talents but an "accessory," an "appurtenance of the capitalist's workshop." It was because Hegel's philosophy, with its abstraction of *thought*, symbolized this perfectly real abstraction of *labor*, that it was the allegory of capitalism and needed interpretation. Marx's prejudice in favor of the whole man of the neo-classicist and Romantic opponents of industrialism is so evident here that it is no wonder that the most patient of critics (and not only the hasty readers whom Engels corrected) have asked whether Marx to the end was not as much opposed to the division of labor as to exchange via the market.[93]

Scientific discussion of Marxism has, on this point, entailed separating his economic criticism of the market from his philosophical attack on it in the name of humanism. It has involved the logical demonstration that to compare things is not to say they are identical; to say that things have a certain aspect is not to reduce them to that one aspect; to give things a price is not to deny that they have other, "priceless" characters.[94] More technically, it has involved the long debate over *what* it is that the market is quantifying and measuring. The neo-marginalist economists very soon proved that it was not measuring the abstract labor in goods, that is to say, that Marx's labor theory of value was defective. Later economists have found fault with the neo-marginalist argument, but no one has gone back to the opinion that the market is measuring labor alone, or even mainly. Once it is seen not to be so, Marx's humanist attack on it fails. If it is measuring *other* things in goods, things that are not related to the producers' personalities, then quantification is no improper affront to them.[95]

Finally, supposing that it is established that opposition to the market can be maintained without any hangover of humanist prejudice against the division of labor, there remains the question of how labor *is* to be divided. If the various complementary tasks are not to be allocated by the market, how is it then to be done? This is the equally long debate about economic planning. Marx has been of little help here, for although he was explicitly in favor of the "rational . . . common control . . . of the associated producers," i.e., of an economic plan, he gave no hint of what it would be like, nor of how it would be preferable to the allocation of tasks by the market.[96] In the void he left, others have improvised. There is nothing to show that Stalin was not, in intention, quite faithful to Marx's thinking in so far as Marx assumed that *any* way of allocating tasks would be better than the free market. Stalinism was even compatible with lip service to the most impractical of Marx's youthful effusions against the market.[97]

Whereas, then, rational discussion of Marxism has, in this regard, centered on the theory of economic value and on planning versus the market, the remystification of Marx revives, full strength, the radical humanism that merely taints Marx's mature work. In doing so, it revives notions that can be had, as well or better, in other places, namely, in the European literary and philosophical opposition to early industrialism. All that was specific in the young Marx's acceptance of that line of thought was that he at once gave it an economic foundation and thereafter stayed in the field of economics. To neglect this original and characteristic twist and to go back to his Romantic sources and call *them* Marxist betrays either an ignorance of Marx's place in history or else a persistent will to confuse matters. Such confusion would be advantageous if old-fashioned opposition to industrialism were being resuscitated in the usurped name of an industrial movement, socialism.

A first step in that direction would be to ignore the fact that Marx's thought was rigorously economic even when it was overly optimistic. He saw that if nothing else were scarce, *time* would be. So there would always be the need to fix priorities, to quantify alternatives, and to measure human activities. If this were not to be done by means of the market in abstract labor, then it would have to be done in terms of time[98] or of the economy of effort.[99] Whatever the measuring stick, society would thus remain an *economy*. To invoke Marx in support of a vision of total de-alienation beyond economics—where there is no more getting and spending, neither business nor a national plan, no materialist engrossments but just living one's hobbies— is mystification.

It requires no violence to the texts, on the other hand, to get from young Marx a condemnation of the division of labor, though there is no reason for drawing this commonplace from him unless one is out to suggest that it is essentially Left. What I have called the persistence of that prejudice into Marxist economics might more sympathetically be called the effort to prove or support the Romantic ethic; but then its value would lie in the rational refinement of the prejudice and not in its coarse literary form. To revive the latter is either to repudiate society (which is always a division of labor on some principle) or else to resurrect the "butterfly" fantasies of Fourier, according to whom we could make job-diversification a ritual. Nor is the absurdity of rejecting the division of labor disguised by the claim that it only means that we should "as readily engage in" one activity as in another or that there can be "reciprocal participation" between folk engaged in different activities.[100]

The statement that some forms of the remystification of Marx involve repudiation of society may seem a critical exaggeration. Yet it is important to note that this is indeed the implication of several of the views now paraded as neo-Marxism. In this, they join that long tradition of idealist philosophy that repudiates society by denigrating the natural, spontaneous and unthinking cooperation of men and pleads for voluntary, planned, and conscious collaboration. (This was Collingwood's idea of politics, for example, as it was Plato's.) This second sort of cooperation has surely existed in important institutions, notably since the rise of capitalism; but it has never characterized a whole society, a multiplicity of institutions. A society cannot be one factory, one project nor even one movement (like democracy or communism). In the face of the fact that men simply do cooperate naturally and without taking thought, idealists have argued that this inferior or insect-like sort of coexistence should be replaced by a conscious plan. This is the meaning of Marx's lifelong objection to the market as a natural and unconscious ("behind-men's-backs") way of coordinating activities and his preference for a voluntary, planned association. As applied to a nation, this could only mean a preference for economic planning. Needless to say, given the remoteness from individual choice that is entailed by the inevitable delegation of sovereignty to a planning board, the plan is as natural— and as alienating—for the majority as any market; the elaborate domestic propaganda machine of the Soviet Union cannot make it seem otherwise. Yet to reject both the market, which is "natural" cooperation, *and* the plan, which is the only practical form of "voluntary" cooperation, in favor of truly *agreed* society where there is universal participation in everything, is to set conditions that no society can satisfy. It is to reject society for a small community, or a parasitical group, in which some such conditions could be met—for a time. In Pop Marxism and Zen Marxism, Marx's demand for voluntary as against natural cooperation is invoked in this sense: to support transient, parasitical associations. It is no accident that this should be accompanied by that other way of rejecting society, the call for the realization of a total self and the satisfaction of "real" human needs.[101]

That call has its echo in the earliest of Marx's unpublished work, though no more there than in a host of other humanist writings and not at all in his mature and important work. Marx for a time accepted the notion of a human essence (the *Gattungswesen*) and though he soon renounced that illusion (e.g., in the *Communist Manifesto*), he continued to operate with a prejudice about what the properly human personality was like and what were correct human needs. The authoritarian consequences of notions about "proper" humanity are considered in a later place,[102] but what is at issue now is the anti-social and anti-political implications of putting individual human nature and needs at the forefront of thinking about society. This was the practice of the young Marx, but it necessarily disappeared when Marx went on to make positive contributions to social and political studies.

First of all, to demand the realization of one proper human type is to ask for the suppression of society and its replacement by one man multiplied many times. If everyone is much the same, as they must be if they are all to be perfect incarnations of one acceptable sort of personality, the distinguishing features of society—conflict and complementarity—vanish. Sorel later remarked that Engels's raptures about final communism implied a society where everybody was called Frederich Engels, and indeed some such assumption is needed for the hope that all conflict—both between individuals and between the institutions that represent them—shall cease.[103] Secondly, this attitude involves going behind and below what plainly makes up society—the plurality of causes in which individuals take part but whose conditions of existence are not the same as those of individual existence—in an attempt to reach a supposed individual human nature. It is a turning away from "a world I never made" to *me*, and thus it is individualism. For Marx in 1844–5 the "true" individual was all work and gregariousness.[104] That point of view is rejected by those contemporary neo-Marxists for whom work is a curse and *l'enfer, c'est les autres*.[105] To put sex and ecstasy, or contemplation and privacy, in place of work and gregariousness (or any other "governing objectives" such as the idealist theory of mind requires) changes nothing as to the main point: which is that individualism is replacing an interest in social and political affairs, i.e., in the things that are open to individual adhesion but that are different from, and longer-lived than, individuals.[106] No continuing enterprise can be defined in terms of individual, subjective needs.[107] So "anthropological philosophy," or humanism, or more simply individualism, is always anti-political and anti-ethical. Abuse of these strains in young Marx has led, in the worst cases, to a relapse to the philosophical communism that Marx scorned even in his youth. Thus with Marcuse, neo-Marxism shows the features of what could be called the chiliasm of anti-economic communism. Man can get beyond economics[108]—and even beyond laws[109]—because abundance is henceforth possible,[110] leaving distribution as the sole economic problem,[111] if only he will undergo the moral regeneration[112] that will reconcile him to frugality and reasonable needs.[113]

After Marx

What I have here called remystification is by no means a fate peculiar to Marxism but can affect other doctrines too; it has affected Freudianism in certain of its heresies. There are good reasons why men should confuse a new idea with old conceptions it was meant to contradict and expose. That such retrogressions occur disposes of Hegel's contention that thought progresses to a higher stage in each epoch, but it does *not* show that progress does not occur. For example, ways *forward* from Marx have been found. They just do not, in point of fact, lead into the blind alleys of Marxist philosophy. They begin from the criticism of Marx's monism, his unitary view of society. On this score, the first Revisionists have done work not since surpassed. They showed that the dialectic was not about history or society in that there were no self-liquidating societies, e.g., no capitalism inevitably doomed to total revolution. It was, rather, about certain activities that went on in society, namely institution-building movements. The case the Revisionists were concerned with was the socialist movement, which they thought might replace bourgeois economic institutions; but Sorel soon broadened their argument to take in all sorts of innovating social movements. Thereby Marxism, which began as the critique of political economy, was continued as criticism of the categories of all the social sciences. Its critique claimed to show that a social science could be objective and could provide a rational description of a particular set of institutions, the way classical economics was a description of capitalist institutions. (That was the "materialism" spoken of in the First Thesis on Feuerbach.) Yet it would be an incomplete science as long as it did not reveal the origins of those institutions in the practice of a particular social movement, their continued dependence on force and other forms of domination, and their vulnerability to revolutionary moralities that create original and opposing institutions. (That was the "idealism" of that same Thesis.)

To continue Marxism in that way, as the sociology of the institutions of morality-movements, entailed getting rid of its monism. It meant describing various, independent, conflicting or successive movements, rather than the Hegelian figment of a "universal movement" that could create a whole society in which everything would be "made by us" and nothing would be "natural." Inspired by Hegel, the Marxists were right to reject supernatural, zoological, and fatalist views of society and to recall that any part of it, from the birth rate to technical invention, could be (and at one time or another had been) *made* and thus was not subject to unchanging laws but to collective intentions. Any part of it, that is, could be revolutionized, made over again, by a new morality arising (as historical materialism meant to show) in practical life and in institutionalized practice. But the Marxists took too much from Hegel when they accepted the notion that there could be *one movement* that could change *everything*. Society as such could never be a cause to which men could adhere and, more important for the revolutionaries, the rest of society outside the scope of their cause is indeed a natural obstacle and an indifferent context.

Finally, to correct Marx's monism ruled out in advance that staple of Marxist philosophy: the movement that is unaware of its historical mission. The defect of this communist theory does not lie in the notion of "mission." Missions, duties, moralities are the very stuff of social theory and a tough-minded "value-free" social scientism that dispenses with them deprives itself of a subject. The defect of the theory was the claim that a group's mission flowed not from its own character but from its place and its relations in a whole that was to be revolutionized. Now that is a role of which a group would necessarily be unaware. So Marxist philosophers would have to enlighten it, make it conscious, or else stand in for it—in either case changing the world by an act of knowing, by making the unconscious conscious. On the contrary, however ignorant of its total relations to a supposed whole, a movement is not ignorant of its mission. Indeed, its mission, in the sense of its characteristic morality and the duties of its station, are just what a movement is most conscious of, for it constitutes its points of difference from other ways of life. If men do not see "what is to be done," it is because in social life seeing what is to be done is not a knowing but a doing, a way of living. It is a morality come to life in real institutions. Men might not, at a given moment or ever, adopt a certain way of life, a particular mission; but it cannot happen that they do so and then not know it.[114] Purveyors of a consciousness of the requirements of the total system—which is what philosophers have mostly been, and not only Marxist philosophers—have no place in social theory and only a mystificatory role in political life.

The metaphysical reason for preferring labor to capital is that continuing creative activity is held to be prior, both logically and chronologically, to its products. Capital is accumulated labor, said the classical economists; so Marx could argue that there was something absurd and immoral about it dictating to labor, worse, battening on it and claiming to be the employer of its own creator.[1]

The inert products of past activity thus came to be a dead hand laid heavily on present activity. While granting the solid reality of capitalism (it was no illusion to be wished away, as utopians imagined) and while granting too its immense utility in the recent past, Marx hoped to see the "normal" state of affairs restored, that is, the priority of labor over capital, of present creative work over the products of past work. When stated thus in very general terms, this hope can be fairly called *the* revolutionary attitude. Something like it will, in all ages, attract the instinctive sympathy of those who prize innovation, creation, experiment, and invention above the inherited, the traditional, the accepted, and established (even when they admit that these latter are the products of activity that was, in its day, no less enterprising than their own). Not that Marx did rest content with stating it in such general terms. In the course of detailed enquiries into economics, of which the results may be judged independently of such general statements of faith, he seldom reverted to the vague, metaphysical formulation he started with. When he did, it was to recall that it came from Hegel and was called the dialectic; for dialectic is the metaphysical priority granted to the fluid, ongoing and creative forces over all their temporary, reified products.

68

The trouble with metaphysics is that it produces sham generalizations. It restates problems from many different subjects so that they *sound* the same, and then it proposes one bogus answer to them all, offering a key to fit every door. The Hegelian dialectic was a perfect case. It claimed to have universal application, but Marx argued that it really fitted only one door, economics, which he proceeded to unlock. The vice is common to various philosophies. If you restate puzzles in sufficiently general, vague terms, you can make them all sound rather similar and thus encourage the hope that something of substance (i.e., not just something logical) can be said about them all. Charles Fourier entertained this illusion in an almost lunatic form, but more subtle varieties of the malady can be found in metaphysical systems that reduce many subjects to one subject so as to find an answer to everything, an answer that can be uttered in one breath. We shall see another case of it now, a case that closely concerns the history of Marxism in the twentieth century and with it the birth of fascism and contemporary irrationalism. A man who stood at just the intellectual crossroads we are headed for was Georges Sorel.

Within a few years of Marx's effort to bring the sham generality of Hegel's dialectic down to the specific, empirical problem of labor's relation to capital, Marxists with a philosophical itch began to confound that question with a variety of others that could be made to sound very much like it. The first such question was that of the status of science. This issue was precipitated by the failure of several mechanist hypotheses in physics around the turn of the century.[2] There followed a variety of attacks on mechanism, attacks led by positivists, pragmatists, neo-Kantians and outright anti-scientific irrationalists. One of the theories propounded during this debate, and which achieved its most literary expression in Henri Bergson, was that reality, in all the subjects studied by science, was a fluid, ongoing confusion that science unsuccessfully attempted to grasp with a set of frozen concepts. Rigid scientific notions were useful for practical purposes but they did not yield genuine knowledge. They were profitable on week-days but come Sunday, when you really wanted to understand the world, you had to use other ways of knowing, such as participation, empathy, and "fluid concepts."

It is clear (or if it is not clear, it becomes so after sufficient reiteration) that this can be made to sound rather like Marx's translation of the dialectic. There is something fluid, ever-lasting and inexhaustible (labor—or reality) that enjoys priority over any temporary, profitable, utilitarian effort to fix it in one mold (capital—or science). So it is not surprising to find leading Marxists annexing this theory of knowledge to their own doctrine. Engels had already worked back from Marx's historical dialectic to the claim that dialectic meant *another* way, additional to scientific ways, of studying nature, a way that laid emphasis on its fluidity. Before long Lenin would exclaim that dialectics meant "universal elasticity of notions." Sorel belongs here too, for he thought to find in Bergsonism a revivifying philosophy for the Marxist movement, and he suggested that "we must beware of too much strictness in our language because it would be at odds with the fluid character of reality . . ."[3]

At the level of intellectual doctrine, this attitude concorded with the concurrent rise of modernism in Catholic theology. Dogmas, for modernist theologians, were like capital or science; they were improper and outdated attempts to *fix* something eternally progressive and creative—which in religion was non-dogmatic faith, i.e., vague religiosity. Much more widely felt was a concordance between these intellectual attitudes and the social malaise created in many parts of European society by the growth of the great modern business corporation and by the progress of parliamentary democracy.

The first decade of this century saw the rise of giant business enterprises. They achieved their large size not only by the application of new industrial mechanisms (i.e., bigger factories) but also by new managerial techniques (i.e., bigger companies running more factories). Often they applied these latter techniques in a series of ruthless mergers and amalgamations. It was obvious, in the U.S.A. (thanks to General Electric, Rockefeller's Standard Oil, Westinghouse, and Bell Telephone) as well as in Europe (thanks to Siemens, Shell, Marconi, and the chemical concerns later merged into I. G. Farben), that something new had arrived on the economic scene. It was something that directly threatened both the small business-man's place in the traditional economy *and* the status of skilled workers inside the factory. Among the rational reactions to this novelty were the Anti-Trust laws in the U.S.A.[4] and the theories of "finance capitalism" or of some such new "stage" of industrialism propounded by European Marxists (Hilfer-ding, among others).[5] Among the less rational reactions to it were revolutionary syndicalism, and the first stirrings of radical attitudes later identified as fascist. Common to both of these was the feeling that science and capital, united in the new phenomenon of big business, were corroding all that was natural, vital, and organic in the traditional economy. The sentiment that a cold intellectual approach to work (exempli-fied by assembly-line Taylorism) was promoted by big business was most keenly felt by those working men in small businesses (notably in France and Italy where capital was very little concentrated) who had retained inside the plant the status of artisans. They had long since lost control of their means of production, it is true, and they smarted under employer and overseer. But they retained the pride, technical expertness, and self-respect of their independent forefathers. For a generation they had been anarchists and Proudhonian federalists. Now, faced with the threat of social and professional demotion on the assembly lines of the newer, bigger, more automated and more rational factory, they embraced the "direct action doctrines" of, first, revolutionary syndicalism and, later, fascism. Many quit the factory rather than accept the new system and went into petty commerce. When that in turn was crushed by the emergence of gigantism in distribution, they went over to fascism.[6]

It required some glossing over of very significant differences to equate the artisans' resentment of big business with Marx's theory of labor's relation to capital, for Marx had not expli-citly defended old-fashioned workers against rational, large-scale manufacture. Still, the parallel was plausible enough for Sorel to argue that the revolutionary syndicalists had salvaged

71

"true" Marxism from the bureaucratic betrayal it was receiving in German Social Democracy.[7] The parallel between the artisans' attitude to big business and Bergson's praise of the intuitive over against the intellectual needed no argument at all, for it was obvious in Bergson's work. Bergson repeatedly took the large automatic factory as the expression of the intellectual attitude he was out to devalue. For that matter, all the critics of mechanism in physics had complained that the scientists were describing the universe as though it were "a factory,"[8] and their attack on that type of theory had distinctly anti-industrial overtones. Sorel suggested that all Bergsonism had a "technological model," as though Bergson's two ways of knowing were symbols for two ways of producing, two types of economy. As plausibly as it can be argued that Hegel's philosophy reflected the primitive accumulation of capital in Germany, it can be maintained that Bergson's philosophy was a reaction to the emergence of finance capitalism, Taylorism, and automation.[9]

An apparently unrelated social phenomenon going forward at that time introduced another complexity; or, rather, it contributed another problem that could be stated generally enough to be conflated with those mentioned so far to give an additional element to the new metaphysics. That phenomenon was the progress of parliamentary democracy against the resistance of older social authorities in countries like France, Germany, and Italy. In France this process was symbolized by the Dreyfus case, which ended with the discredit of the Church, the Army, and the Courts, and with the triumph of new mass parties backed by a sensationalist popular press.[10] The progress of the new system naturally had the support of most citizens but it also encountered significant opposition. Indeed, it awakened both loathing and anxiety, not least among Marxists who remembered their master's warnings against "merely political" movements that lacked a social soul. A republic of journalists and professors who were hand in glove with finance-capitalists (of the sort implicated in the Panama scandal)—who tortured their consciences about the innocence of a bourgeois army captain and took that as a pretext to seize Church property and expel the orders while their police shot down striking workers—such a regime was bound to be detested not only by the traditional Right but by Marxists, syndicalists, nationalists, monarchists, proto-fascists and social Catholics. For all of them such a regime represented another victory for that cold rationalism, ignorant of vital organic reality, that had already celebrated its triumph in capitalism, in science, and in big business.[11]

Given a temperamental inclination to confuse separate problems in order to arrive at a metaphysical generalization, one could easily run together all the four topics mentioned so far and argue that there was an organic vital reality that was being violently *atomized* by the leading forces of the young twentieth century; by capitalism, by science, by big business, and by democracy. Just as the free creativity of labor was oppressed by its own dead product, capital; just as the fluid reality of life was misrepresented for base utilitarian purposes in science; so, too, the natural and informal production methods of artisanry and small business were being crushed by the rational big business corporations; and so, too, the natural authorities of an organic community were being discredited and expropriated by intellectualist parliamentary bureaucrats. Metaphysics, which Marx thought he had debunked by reducing its sham generality to one particular problem, was thus restored, by confounding that problem with a number of others that could be made to sound like it. Since Hegel's metaphysics was about the recurrent cancellation of reifications by the dialectical progress of the demiurge, it enjoyed a revival at just this time, in the first decade of the century. It was, thereafter, ready at hand to assist the thinkers of fascism and of irrationalist Marxism.

As will appear in a later chapter, the confusion of the first pair of notions, i.e., the passage from anti-capitalism to anti-science, became explicit in Georg Lukacs and this founded an important lineage of Western Marxism. Yet the general feeling for this metaphysical conflation of problems dates from the earliest years of the century. It accounts for those surprising migrations between Marxism and fascism, from Benito

Mussolini down to Jacques Doriot. It was Sorel that best represented this connection of various problems, and yet he did so in an unexpected way. What the new metaphysicians denounced, he approved. While he agreed that there was a common metaphysical fundament involved, his feeling about it was the contrary of that of his contemporaries. What the Marxists deplored as the alienation of labor in capital, Sorel approved as bourgeois violence. What the Bergsonians denounced as the intellectualist falsification of nature, he approved as experimental scientific violence. True, he attacked big business and democracy as immoral *force,* but he pointed out that they could be replaced only by other social systems that would do just as much violence to men's natures. His systematic insistence on the role of violence derived from his basic pessimism. When his optimistic contemporaries complained that capital, science, big business and democracy were doing violence to an underlying reality that needed to be liberated and grasped in its true character, Sorel replied that the underlying reality of man, nature and society was decadent, obscure, lawless and wasteful and so it well deserved to have violence done to it. Only *conscious violence*, applied according to an ethic, could reduce the fatuity and vanity of human spontaneity to a truly progressive economy; only *it* could reduce the chance wastefulness of nature to scientific law and to an economy of forces; only *it* could establish social forms morally superior to big business and democracy.

Of these various issues, the one that most occupied Sorel was the philosophy of science.[12] He accepted the view that arose in his day that scientists were not *discovering* the hidden mechanisms of nature, as the ontological mechanists imagined, but were *inventing* or manufacturing models. Scientific laws were accounts of the working of experimental machinery into which a part of nature, after being purified or simplified so as to make it homogeneous with the man-made laboratory mechanism, had been incorporated. There was no reason to suppose that such machines were models of natural mechanisms. Indeed, Sorel said, there was no sign that determinism of any sort operated in nature when left to herself (with the exception of astronomy). Indeterminism, however, was no grounds for skepticism, as the theorists of the "bankruptcy of science" were proclaiming at the time. Exact science was *still* possible, but its sole domain was man-made mechanisms, such as laboratory equipment and industrial plant. Determinism existed only where men created it, in machines that did violence to nature by shutting out chance interference. So science was about "artificial nature," the manufactured phenomena of experiment and industry. It had nothing to say about "natural nature," where hazard, waste, and entropy were uncontrolled, where our knowledge was limited to statistical probability and where our intervention was restricted to rule of thumb. Sorel accepted the pessimistic conclusions being drawn in his day from the second law of thermodynamics, to the effect that there was absolute chance in nature and that the universe was "running down" to a heat-death.[13]

Against that malevolent nature of chance and waste—typified in the phenomena described in the law of Clausius, phenomena that threatened the accuracy of science and the efficiency of industry—humanity struggled in a hopeless effort of "dis-entropy," seeking to establish and maintain regions of determinism (in science) and of economy of forces (industry). Science, industry, and engineering were part of a vast human enterprise of control by violence, the rebellion of a part of nature against its senseless confusion and "running down." Himself an engineer, who had been a youthful mathematical prodigy, Sorel set out this theory in much technical detail, carrying it through to its most startling implications. For example, he maintained that geometry was about architecture, not nature, because its figures and proportions existed only where men had created them.[14]

The pragmatists of the day were emphasizing the practical element in the acquisition and verification of knowledge, while the Marxists were arguing the connection between intellectual activity and mechanical, economic labor.[15] Sorel's theory may be seen as the extremist version of both doctrines. He felt that he stood at the meeting place of the lines of thought originated by Charles Peirce, William James, and Henri Bergson, on the one hand, and Karl Marx on the other. Yet what gave him his significant place in modern social thought was that he worked out a theory of culture exactly parallel to that philosophy of science. Culture and institutions were, he held, forever threatened by relapse into that disorder and barbarism that came naturally to men. Against a chaotic background of decadence, men occasionally fought heroically to set up limited areas of law, order, and historical significance. To make any sense of a tract of history, they had to lay a hard discipline upon themselves and do violence to their own nature. They had also to reject the claims of so-called "social science" that it could lay bare history's laws, that it could make sense of history without our intervention. Sociology or social science, in so far as it alleged natural regularities common to human affairs in various ages and countries, became Sorel's *bête noire*. He pursued it with ferocity and sarcasm because he thought it was the cover for some immoral force that was seeking to pass off arrangements profitable to itself as if they were "natural."

His general case lies in the assertion, "Nature is not a teacher." He argued that nature does not teach men science, which is rather something that men do to nature. He showed, too, that nature did not dictate modern industrial technology, which creates, rather, unnatural phenomena (e.g., light that comes not from burning but from a non-burning, as in an incandescent lamp). This view he carried over into social theory by arguing that nature (or history taken as *la nature sociale*) did not prescribe men's policies. In this, he attacked the notion of "scientific policy" or what he called *intellectualism*: the belief that culture is imitation of nature and that it progresses by men discovering what nature or history requires of them, and then accepting its models and bowing to its necessities. On the contrary, Sorel protested, all parts of culture were like science in this: that they were artificial, creative human activities going forward in a man-made context, an artificial milieu, under the leadership of specialized liberal authorities and *in spite of* nature and natural obstacles. Culture is not the description nor the imitation nor the acceptance of nature (if it

if culture rebellion
than capital must constrain

were, it would depend on those best at that, viz. the intellectuals). Culture is rebellion, defiance, mastery.

It was in this spirit that Sorel accepted, and later criticized, Marxism. He accepted it because it destroyed the pretension of economics to be a natural science, by showing that economics described only the social dispensation brought about by bourgeois force. Marx had contested economic science's universal relevance without impugning its objectivity, by providing an historical criticism of its categories. He admitted that its laws pointed to regular, repeatable connections and thus its claim to be a science was not absurd. However, by raising the question of the origin and duration of those objective regularities, Marx had shown that they were imposed by capitalist violence. Sorel drew the inference that they were therefore liable to decay if not constantly supported by a vigorous capitalist movement, whereupon capitalism would "run down" into a disorderly, unpredictable economy. Sorel gave a description of such an economy, under the name of "capitalist degeneration," that reads like a forecast of the contemporary welfare state.[16] Sorel drew the further inference that the capitalist mechanism could be annulled by another violent movement, provided this latter were willing and able to dedicate itself to production, innovation, and discipline, as had the capitalist class. For as long as he considered the proletarian movement was such a historic challenger, Sorel counted himself a socialist.

He attacked Marxism in turn when, instead of rationalizing the faith of a movement more vigorous than capitalism, it took itself for a scientific policy based on a precise reading of a social determinism. This pseudo-scientific part of Marxism, he said, had to be separated out by a process of "decomposition" from what was valuable in that doctrine, namely the anatomy of the capitalist and socialist movements. The socialist movement, Sorel argued, contained the promise of a new social order of which, one day, another "social science" like bourgeois economics might be written. Meanwhile, its progress provided a thread of historical sequence and rational meaning running through the chaos into which European society was heading as the capitalist mechanism broke down because of the bourgeois "failure of nerve."

The trouble with Engels and Kautsky (and hence with the majority of Marxists before Lenin) was, Sorel argued, that they were not content to see the socialist movement as the promise of a future and hypothetical social science, that is, as the force that might one day generalize its own discipline; they wanted it recognized as from now as a work of science, *based on* sound historical science. Whereas (as Sorel saw it) it was an aspiration toward a new *artificial* order, an order foreshadowed in the law and institutions of the movement itself, the orthodox Marxists saw it as the inevitable outcome of a *natural* order written into the laws of history. What he took for the heroic and promising attempt to install something artificial and hence insecure, they took for the operation of an immanent necessity. That sort of Marxism, Sorel warned, was an intellectualist pseudo-sociology that was storing up bitter disappointment for workers gullible enough to listen and to believe.

The critique of this Marxist pseudo-sociology centred on what Sorel called the "revolution schema," the mechanism that Marx claimed to have discovered in history, that carried over each social form into the next. Marx had described it in general terms in this way:

> At a certain stage of their development, the material productive forces of a society find themselves opposed by existing relations of production, or, if one takes the juridical point of view, by the property relations within which they had progressed till then. Instead of being forms of development of productive forces, those relations become chains on them. Then begins an era of revolution. With the change in the economic base, all the gigantic superstructure is, more or less rapidly, overturned.

That was Marx's account of that crucial moment in the dialectic when the objective institutions that till then have expressed social labor begin to throttle it and are cancelled out. The *Communist Manifesto* gave an account of the previous historical instance:

> The means of production and exchange on which the bourgeoisie based its formation were engendered in feudal society. At a certain stage of development of these means of production and exchange, the relations

within which feudal society produced and traded, the feudal organization of agriculture and manufactures, in a word feudal property relations, no longer corresponded to the productive forces that were already developed. They were limiting production instead of promoting it. They had become chains. They had to be broken. They were broken.

This formula, which is at once a translation into ordinary language of the Hegelian dialectic *and* a suggested sociological law, will find its application, Marx implies, in the transition from one to the other of the "pre-historical" economic forms: the asiatic, the antique classical, the feudal, and the bourgeois. So it will apply also to the next transition, from capitalism to socialism.

Sorel could show[17] that in fact Marx had only one case that answered his description, and that was the French Revolution, which Marx described, moreover, in a singularly tendentious way so as to suggest an analogy between it and his own day, and thus enhance the plausibility of another similarly profound revolution. Marx was saying that bourgeois property relations, like feudal, had unleashed productive forces that they could not contain and which they were restraining. This period of contradiction could not long endure but would end in the passage to new property relations, to a new form of society.

So the revolution schema, Sorel said, eventually came down to an analogy between 1789 and 1847. That analogy was false from start to finish. The ancien régime with its chaotic tax system, feudal vestiges and meddlesome regulations did often restrain productive forces, but that situation bore very little resemblance to a system in which production was brutally cut back by depressions occurring perhaps once a decade and due (on Marx's theory of the business cycle) to prior over-production. Depressions created poverty, unemployment, and bankruptcies—but not in the way, or even in the sense, that the ancien régime did. Permanent restraints on enterprise were not comparable with cycles of boom and slump. Sorel supposed, for his part, that the alternation of prosperity and depression was due to the vagaries of consumption in a market where consumers were free; at all events, it was not due uniquely to the private property relations of the bourgeoisie in the way feudal property relations could be held to have trammeled European men of business enterprise.

Secondly, the French Revolution, on Marx's peculiarly limited account of it, consisted in getting rid of useless, obstructive idlers who stood in the way of independent and experienced entrepreneurs. A proletarian revolution in Marx's day would have consisted, on the contrary, in getting rid of experienced industrialists in favor of a class so far innocent of any acquaintance with the direction of economic affairs. That was not striking analogy but blank contrast.

Finally, Marx had reduced the French Revolution for the sake of his argument to the expropriation of feudal privileges in restraint of enterprise. The disproportion between the feudal vestiges of 1789 and the immense structure of contemporary capitalism was so enormous as to make it adventurous to speak of "suppressing" the one as readily as the other. The minor economic transaction of the night of 4 August 1789 was no precedent for the assignment of destroying capitalism. Besides, noted Sorel, if the French Revolution really consisted in that act of liberation from feudalism, then the French bourgeoisie would seem to have chosen an extremely costly way of freeing itself. In other countries the bourgeois could easily afford to buy feudalism out, so great were their gains from free enterprise. Should one, then, draw the analogy with a socialism that buys out private capitalism, as has often been urged for the past century?

With the revolution schema reduced to a single dubious analogy, the succession of social forms had lost the specific mechanism or the hidden spring that could have distinguished Marx's historical theory from Hegel's gallery of national portraits or from historical evolutionism. The dialectic, the successive cancellation of social reifications by social labor, had lost all necessity. Unless Marx could show how, by a recurring automatism, each type of society developed all its potentialities (occupied every position on its orbit) until, for that reason, it had prepared the successor-type of society (touched off the next automatic cycle)—unless he could show that, he was simply relying on a disguised *Weltgeist*, hidden under the language of that evolutionism for which the older Marx came to have a taste.

Despite this rejection of Marxism as the science of historical determinism, Sorel remained a student of Marx. He felt that although a doctrine was not science it could still be instructive, in that it might contain a rationalized, striking, and influential formulation of the mentality of a social movement. Therefore, on Sorel's account of how social science arose, it might be of great interest as foreshadowing the possibility of a new social order exhibiting enough regularity to be described in a science like economics. It would then be a "myth": a dramatic account of the future of a movement. Sorel claimed that the very people who "believed" a myth did so in a curious way; they cared for it strongly and yet they did not bother to establish its plausibility. They treasured it not as demonstrably true but as an inspiring picture of what the world would look like if one day their ethic won all men's allegiance. Myths were a present morality stated in the future tense. It followed that intellectualist criticism of them was not only socially ineffectual (people would not give them up because of contradictory evidence) but presumptuous, because intellectuals did not know any more than myth-makers what the future held. Their "social science," on which they based their forecasts of the future, was bogus because there was no regularity in history except when great, violent myth-making movements put it there. It was the myth-makers who fashioned the future, because their myth epitomized the aspirations of an enthusiastic mass, and thus it could well be the shadow of things to come. On the contrary, the sociologist's scientific blueprints for the future preceded nothing but ridiculous disappointment. They heralded nothing but the rule of intellectualist planners and the spread of the consumer mentality among the dupes waiting for the promised good times.

The future, said Sorel (following Bergson), was radically unknowable. There were two possible attitudes to it: Myth and Utopia. Myth deserved respect as the product of intense social wills that might well decide the future, whereas Utopia deserved scorn as the divagations of intellectual charlatans, the

81

F

"social scientists." In continuing to think that Marxism was important though a myth, Sorel was thought by some to be advancing the paradox that it was demonstrably false but should nevertheless be believed in. In reality he meant that, after the breakdown of the capitalist order and of the economic science that described it, there was only one movement in Western society at the start of the twentieth century that held the promise of a successor-order which a new science would describe; and Marx had stated that movement's myth in the form of a supposed historical determinism.

This view of Marxism was quite unacceptable to even the most revisionist of the pre-1914 socialists. They reasoned that if Marx had incorrectly identified the natural tendencies of capitalist societies, they would be able to identify the real ones. For example, if it turned out that there was no *fatal trend* toward increasing inequality of wealth and sharper class conflict, it could be that there *was* a trend toward increasing equality of incomes and class collaboration. They would not envisage the possibility, Sorel suggested, that there might be *no trend at all* in the confusion of decadent capitalism until a vigorous movement put one there. Sorel claimed the socialists would not entertain this possibility because they knew that any such movement would have to show energy, morality, and discipline, whereas it was so much easier to drift along with decadent capitalism. That attitude, he insisted, was most marked in the very party that claimed to be Marx's heir.

> German Social Democracy, which claims to have received from Marx a very profound understanding of the economy, of politics and of history has never produced a doctrine fit to occupy an honorable place in modern philosophy. But it correctly awards itself the glory of possessing the most perfect type of contemporary democracy, because it has succeeded better than any other popular party in grouping multitudes of devoted electors around its intransigent negation of national traditions. Thanks to its tireless agitation, the German proletariat sighs for the day when the Prussian Army, the schoolmasterish bureaucracy and magistrature that issued from the old universities, as well as the authority of the churches, will all have disappeared. . . . All our contemporary democracies in Europe show phenomena similar to those we see in particularly striking form in German Social Democracy.[18]

The tragic events of 1918 in Germany seemed to Sorel to confirm this diagnosis. He already saw in them the mentality that was soon to be exploited in Hitlerism:

> In the advanced democracies one observes among the plebs a profound sentiment of the duty of passive obedience, the superstitious use of fetish words and a blind faith in egalitarian promises. . . . Envy is one of the most efficacious forces in democracy.[19]

For the most part, Sorel was simply contemptuous of that sort of democracy, the one that triumphed after the Dreyfus case, because it was "motivated solely by the instincts of destruction" and resented any social force that could not be brought to the common market of political brokerage, whether that force was one of the old social authorities or a new revolutionary movement. He was moved to a passionate denunciation of democracy when some social scientist or intellectual (typically a professor-parliamentarian) presented it as the natural or most progressive arrangement of human affairs, the one in which a knowledge of social necessity was winning out over barbaric violence. Sorel's reply was that there was no natural order; in any polity, some particular force was always gaining satisfaction. If it took the fraudulent line of disguising itself as Everyman, it must be because it had a bad conscience about its pre-eminence. It was only a "Might" that feared it had no "Right." In contrast, the older social authorities had never shrunk from receiving the respect they thought due to them because of their superior energy and morality; and no more would a new revolutionary movement be ashamed to affirm the importance of its mission and, if need be, it would break the heads of the governmental peacemakers sent to corrupt it into conformity.

Much of the argument Sorel advanced in this connection was sheer moralistic prejudice, of which the origins are plain in the society from which he came. The Jansenist fire that still smoulders within one tradition of French provincial Catholicism and the memory, still lively in one born in 1847, of the days when republicanism (i.e., the rule of a class of liberal entrepreneurs) had been a heroic enterprise to be carried to the corners of Europe—both were sentiments out of tune with an age of Modernist theology, social democracy, and welfare capitalism. Those sentiments would incline an elderly Proud honian to the thought that they found an echo in the morality of working men and artisans who refused both big business and big unions, in favor of revolutionary syndicalism; and they would predispose him to sympathy with *any* faction—royalist, anarchist, or Catholic-revivalist—that met the disguised and hypocritical force of parliaments and plutocracies with open and unashamed violence.

Such predilections would be of no general importance were it not that they obliged Sorel to worry the question of how one would define, or at least identify, a might that was also a right, a social force that not only could sweep away the dead institutions and ideologies deposited by past enterprise but would be admitted by contemporaries and historians, however grudgingly, to have a *right* to do so because it would be doing it in the name of a new creative morality. In this, Sorel was looking for the empirical reality of the social dialectic. That is to say, he was trying to identify those forces that create and annul institutions and that are the only subject of a social science. Hegel had dreamed of them as *Geist*, as Spirit; and Marx, who successfully recognized one of those forces in the shape of proletarian socialism, had lost it again in a spurious sociology. Sorel thought to find forces in morality-movements, in organizations around some practical ethic, that attain sufficient solidity to give sense and continuity to an era of history and thus to deserve comparison with the determinism that the experimenter forces on lawless nature.

He described such movements as having a particular "psychological, sentimental content": namely, that they promote "the spirit of responsibility, the value of personal dignity and the energy of initiative." They "bring into the world a new way of judging all human actions or, following Nietzsche's celebrated phrase, a new valuation of all values." They set themselves before existing society as "its irreconcilable adversary, threatening it with a *moral catastrophe* much more than with a material catastrophe." They oppose to present society a new juridical system and a new law. They "find in their conditions of life the nourishment for sentiments of solidarity and revolt."[20] They are movements that conceive liberty not formally but as "activity productive of useful things for a purpose chosen by ourselves" and that conceive revolt not anarchically but as "the collective struggle for the conquest of rights"; thus they are independent enterprising initiative going forward under its own native law. They are movements of men "persuaded that the work they are devoting themselves to is *grave, formidable and sublime,*" so that they will consent to sacrifices that procure them no honors and no profits;[21] movements that "reinforce the sentiments of heroism, sacrifice, and union."[22] Such movements do not "put themselves on the utilitarian plane" like interest groups but nevertheless they defend certain "interests," conceived as what furthers a characteristic spirit.[23] They promote in adherents the feelings of personal responsibility or individualism, of productiveness, of exactitude in fulfilling tasks and of disinterestedness or anonymity.[24] They are, finally, movements that revive the notion of the sublime and of grandeur in a context of mediocrity and decadence,[25] that arise in hazard but do not have hazard for their law, that lift men out of mediocrity under the pressure of certain constraints and thus react against the normal human tendency to ordinariness.

Sorel studied at length examples of such movements in the history of religion, art, science, and republicanism. He said it was such movements that Marx had in mind[26] when he described the return from capitalist alienation (the historic goal of the socialist movement) as being free cooperative production, "the work of men freely associated and acting consciously as masters of their own social movement." For Sorel, Marx's "associated producers" were another instance, like Gothic artists or Puritan entrepreneurs, of the morality-movement.

Now, if forces of that sort provide the true thread of history in that they alone allow a coherent treatment of social affairs, then Sorel has not so much shown that physics and social studies have a common method (the construction of artificial determinisms) as that ethics and social studies have a common subject matter: the moralities of liberty. After all, any attempt to divide history into absolute hazard and limited determinism must fail. Difficult enough to maintain in physics, in history it fails twice over. Few observers, however skeptical of the claims of sociology, see the usual course of human affairs as being as much a matter of random chance as the weather or the trajectories of molecules. On the other hand, even fewer would allow that the occasional regularity and predictability introduced into history by dominant social movements deserve comparison with the precise determinisms of physics. So the distinction between chance and determinism is blurred at both ends. Social life, it seems, is never as chancy or as determined as Sorel contended. For all that, in his description of artificial social determinisms Sorel singled out forces that can from time to time make history consecutive and regular: the plurality of enterprises undertaken in a certain progressive spirit, the successive attempts at cooperative self-government. Thereby Sorel led Marxism, which began as an interpretation of the Hegelian dream about the Spirit that alternately creates and annuls the world of men, onward to a theory of social movements.

To be sure, that theory has not progressed very far since his day, in part because of the metaphysical trimmings Sorel attached to it. These led to Sorel being persistently classified with the fascists and irrationalists who started with the same metaphysical assumptions. It is quite true that Sorel shared with them the view that in science, in capitalism, in big business and in democracy, the *natural* and the *real* were being violated. Like them, too, he saw error and hypocrisy in the Edwardian optimism that accepted science and the prevailing social order as based on natural determinisms, independently of any human force and contribution. From there on, however, Sorel took another path. He sought a new, non-natural or *voluntary* basis for rationality, law, morality, and science, whereas the fascists and irrationalists wanted to revert to a supposed primitive nature in order to escape just such artificial determinisms. Thus, the metaphysical running together of distinct and separate problems for the sake of an over-riding attitude to all of them had the customary effect of introducing inextricable confusion. In this case, it led to the association of doctrines of mindless brutality with the theory that social movements (including the activity of scientists) were rational violence applied to secure new law, new ways of living inside original institutions.

If, because of this confusion, Sorel's development of Marxism had a limited effect, at least it criticized in advance the most influential form of neo-Marxism of the second half of the twentieth century. This is the Western Marxism that goes back to the juvenilia of the master in search of an apology for the de-alienated life, for the life free of mediation via reified institutions, for the life of emancipation and anarchy. Combined with *fin de siècle* pathos about the bankruptcy of science, this irrationalist Marxism refuses capitalist institutions *and* scientific concepts (both lumped together as "the positive" by Marcuse and Adorno) as twin forms of reification. Against that, Sorel argued that there was no life of consequence without the rational imposition of alienation and violence on recalcitrant nature. In seeking to show that there was no science of "natural nature," Sorel added that human nature cannot even be systematically described apart from its appearance in some distinctive and violent culture, despite all the efforts to get behind society to "the truly human" and its "proper wants." The world of men is nothing but inconsequential confusion until grasped by the discipline of a forceful liberal tradition that harnesses and reinforces creativity by setting limits to fatuity, waste, and chance.

3. Gramsci: Marx and/or Mussolini

The contrast between the abundant publication of Antonio Gramsci's works in Italy and the scarcity of translations into other languages[1] is so striking that it has invited Machiavellian explanations. Ignazio Silone told the Parisian Weekly *L'Express* several years ago that the political party that has custody of Gramsci's manuscripts had been urged by its sister-party in Russia to be prudent in publishing them, for they contained suspect matter. Specifically, said Silone, the Italian communists were given a "licence" to print Gramsci in Italy, where his original variety of Marxism would be useful in bringing anarchists to communism, in return for an undertaking to restrict publication in other languages.

That Gramsci's manuscripts are published in obedience to political considerations is evident even in Italy itself. The books printed under his name are, for the most part, selections, made according to principles that are not revealed, from a mass of material to which independent scholars do not have access. Where comparison is possible, as with the letters and newspaper articles, expurgation and arbitrary omissions have been alleged; and Gramsci's earliest writings, which some would have found embarrassing during the Stalinist era, were held ten years and published only after the 20th Congress of the Soviet Communist Party. Scholars, already sufficiently hampered by the fact that Gramsci has become a political and ideological symbol and the object of a cult, have appealed to those who hold the keys to his work to allow a complete critical edition "without censorship or prejudice."[2]

I mention these things without polemical intent, simply as a warning of the limitations of any account of Gramsci's life and thought such as follows. For what could be the polemical intent? In Italy the usual one is to reclaim Gramsci from a political party that is exploiting his renown, by proving that he was really a less orthodox Leninist than is believed. But at a time when no one is agreed on the content of "Leninism"—certainly not Moscow and Peking, nor the Revisionists and Stalinists inside other parties—this would be a vain task. Its only conclusion would be that Leninism and Gramscism have both become, in the course of ideological controversy, amorphous, polyvalent doctrines between which it is easy to stage "battles of quotations." Yet both definitely belong to the same tradition and there can be no point to "rescuing" Gramsci from the political party that has made him its intellectual standard-bearer. Indeed, for all the difficulties of elucidating his thought—we shall return to them in studying his Prison Notebooks after outlining his life and political career—it is plain that some of the most effective things in it are his defences of Lenin from the anti-Bolshevik Marxists.

Antonio Gramsci[3] was born in Ales (Sardinia) in 1891, one of the seven children of a modest clerk. His childhood in that extremely backward island was poor but not unhappy, though he started work (ten hours a day) at the age of eleven and always suffered indifferent health. He proved himself a good student, and after secondary education in Sardinia he won a scholarship to the University of Turin in 1911. Living poorly on his bursary, supplemented by odd jobs, he distinguished himself in the faculty of letters as a brilliant student of linguistics and philology. More important, the big industrial city brought him into touch with the socialist movement; and while still an undergraduate he joined the Italian Socialist Party (P.S.I.) and wrote in the local socialist press. By 1914 his choice was made and, to the despair of his professors, he abandoned an assured academic career to become a "professional revolutionary." That meant, at first, editing a Turin socialist weekly, *Grido del Popolo,* which was to be closely associated with the factory council movement in that city. After the collapse of the five-day armed insurrection of the Turin workers in August 1917, Gramsci was elected secretary of the Turin section of the P.S.I.[4]

The party was soon to be rent by the division of the Second International, and Gramsci espoused Lenin's cause, as far as he could then have understood it. Lenin's theoretical works were not yet translated and Gramsci saw the Soviets through the veil of his experience with the Turin *consigli di fabbrica* or factory councils. From May 1919 these latter found a new organ in the daily *L'Ordine Nuovo*, which Gramsci joined as an editorialist along with his fellow-student Palmiro Togliatti. During and after the May 1920 general strike that paper represented the Third International Opposition inside the P.S.I. It printed the Turin section's "Program," which Gramsci seems to have drafted and which Lenin explicitly approved. The inevitable split came at the Leghorn conference of the P.S.I. in January 1921. The official history has it that Gramsci led the opposition out of the P.S.I. and thus founded the Italian Communist Party. But there is evidence that he was unenthusiastic about the formation of a new political party, preferring to place all his revolutionary hopes in direct action by the factory councils.[5] "The Italian state," he wrote at this time, "must be decapitated in Milan, not Rome, because the real capitalist governing apparatus is not in Rome but Milan. . . . Rome has no function in Italian social life; it represents nothing and will submit to the hard laws of the workers' state against parasites."

These opinions were regarded as "syndicalism" and "economism" by some of his companions, whom Gramsci in turn suspected of "Blanquism" because they identified the dictatorship of the proletariat with the dictatorship of a party. Such differences were, in our own time, described as mere nuances by Togliatti, and indeed they did not prevent Gramsci playing a leading role in the new party. It was, however, an oppositional role at first. Gramsci criticized the first secretary, Bordiga, who held that the Communist Party was the principal, if not the sole, force capable of standing against fascism. Gramsci called this attitude sectarian, demanded a broad alliance of anti-fascist elements, and continued to argue that workers' and peasants' committees were the real expression of the socialist movement. The Communist Party could develop only in a parallel course with such autonomous proletarian institutions. This latter notion caused some embarrassment in the Third International when it was asked to referee the dispute, as may be seen in the ambiguous Theses of the 5th Congress in Moscow in 1924. On the one hand, the development of workers' soviets is declared, in general, impossible "before the revolution," while on the other hand, in a special recommendation to the Italian party, the factory councils are warmly approved.[6] The whole affair is obscure because one must rely on party sources, to a large extent, and Bordiga's and Gramsci's positions have inevitably been re-interpreted in the light of later events.

In the meantime, Gramsci had been sent to Moscow in 1922 as the Italian delegate to the International. During a year's stay there he met all the Bolshevik leaders (and, incidentally, married). In 1923 he watched developments in Italy from Vienna, and on returning home was elected secretary of the C.P.I. and, in the April 1924 elections, a communist deputy. As chief of the party, he founded *L'Unità*, conducted the struggle against fascism, led the opposition out of parliament after the assassination of the socialist deputy Matteotti, and back in again when the attempt to found an "anti-parliament" failed. All his efforts to form an anti-fascist coalition, either in or out of parliament, came to nothing and his proposal for a general strike was rejected. Mussolini's "laws of exception" were introduced and Gramsci was arrested under them in November 1926. At his trial in May-June 1928 the prosecutor asked for a sentence that would "stop that brain working for twenty years." Gramsci was condemned to twenty years, four months, and five days' imprisonment.

In truth, that brain could not be stopped working even by the inhuman conditions of fascist jails, which told sorely on a frail constitution. Soon after his arrest Gramsci calmly planned an immense labor of research and meditation, and he went on to execute part of it in an achievement that has few equals for tenacity and sheer intellectual heroism. Between 1929 and 1935 he filled thirty-two notebooks (almost 3,000 pages of minute handwriting, the equivalent of 4,000 typed pages)

The Western Marxists

with notes and essays on politics, philosophy, and literature. All of it was subject to prison censorship and anything subversive enough to strike a fascist jailer would have led to interruption of the trickle of books and papers that kept Gramsci in touch with the outside world. Two serious breakdowns in 1931 and 1933 brought him to death's door, and by 1936 he was utterly exhausted; deliberate ill-treatment appears to have played a role. He died in April 1937 in a Roman clinic a few days after his term, commuted by various concessions, had expired. He had lived forty-six years, eleven of them in jail.

The Prison Notebooks, from which editors have extracted most of the published works by grouping passages on related subjects,[7] are certainly the most important part of his achievement, but it is useful to look first at his journalism in the *Grido del Popolo* and *L'Ordine Nuovo*.[8] It is not all political, as against the cultural interests that predominate in the Notebooks. Gramsci was an adept of Crocean idealism from 1917; he kept up his linguistic studies during his political activities; and as drama critic of *Avanti!* in 1919–20 he was already working out a theory of "national-popular literature" that he developed further in prison. Yet the main interest here is naturally Gramsci's reaction to the Bolshevik Revolution, and his participation in the Italian socialist movement's affairs until its liquidation by Mussolini.

Grido del Popolo: One of his first articles, published early in the war, supported Mussolini's doctrine of "active neutrality"; the first step toward Italy's entry into the war on the side of the Allies. This was a false start, and Gramsci was silent for a year before re-appearing as a partisan of the contrary Zimmerwald line. His youthful political options are less significant than his early concern for the "spiritual conditions" of a proletarian revolution, for this was to be an abiding interest. He wrote in January 1916:

> Every revolution has been preceded by an intense labor of criticism, of cultural penetration, of permeation of ideas through groups of men initially refractory and engrossed with solving day by day, hour by hour, their own political and economic problem.

It had been thus with the French Revolution and it would be thus again with socialism. The conception of revolution as, in the first place and above all, cultural preparation, entailed no concession to democratic reformist doctrine because, Gramsci argued, "the socialist state . . . does not continue the bourgeois state; it is not an evolution from the capitalist state . . . but continues and develops systematically the professional organizations and local bodies that the proletariat has been able to generate spontaneously during the individualist regime."

The Bolshevik Revolution, when it came, was patently no more in accord with this Sorelian schema than with orthodox social-democratic Marxism, but Gramsci hesitated no longer than Sorel did: the Russian Revolution was right and all the Marxist theorists were wrong. It was a revolution "against Karl Marx's *Capital*," or at least against the mechanical interpretation of Marxism given by such as Kautsky. As for its no less evident inconsistency with Gramsci's own theory of revolution (for a determined minority played a greater role in Russia than any cultural preparation of the masses), Gramsci admitted that it was an "exception," due to the "peculiar circumstances" in Russia. But the workers' soviets would soon re-establish the rights of proletarian spontaneity against the dictatorship of a minority.

L'Ordine Nuovo: These reservations about Leninism are attenuated in the immediate postwar years (to re-appear in the Prison Notebooks), but Gramsci's notion of socialism remains intact. It means a free, democratic, decentralized society based on the autonomy of the producers' own institutions. Because the situation in Italy, as in the rest of Europe, is ripe for revolution, Bolshevik tactics can and must be used. Yet they cannot be the whole of revolutionary action. They are to be deployed in step with the growth of specifically proletarian organizations, such as the *consigli di fabbrica*. The political party and the trade union are typical creations of the liberal-bourgeois period and cannot characterize the new proletarian society. They are "agents," and however crucial their role at revolutionary moments, the "principal" remains the proletariat's own original political creation: the system of workers' and peasants' institutions which alone are capable of replacing the democratic, parliamentary state.

> The class struggle, in the present period of capitalist industry's history, realizes itself in a new type of proletarian organization which is based on the factory and not on the craft, on the unit of production and not on the trade unions born of the division of labor. This new type of organization . . . arises on the job, it sticks closely to the process of industrial production, its functions have to do with the job, in it the economy and politics meet, in it the exercise of sovereignty is one with the act of production.[9]

It is clear that, while unreservedly accepting Leninism, Gramsci is putting it in a wider context, just as Sorel was doing at that time.[10] What that context was has already been glimpsed in his earlier articles, and the matter will be worked out in his prison notes. Meanwhile, his position seemed ambiguous, and would become more so as the C.P.I. was "bolshevized" in the period 1924–6, as the soviets disappeared as a live force in Russia, and as Stalin's conception of an omnipotent party leadership emerged. By then Gramsci was performing constant mental acrobatics on the question of the party's relations with the factory councils. His confusion made it possible for Togliatti to deny later that he and Gramsci ever believed that the councils "contained in themselves the solution to the problem of power, that is, of the conquest of power and the construction of a new state." On the contrary, Togliatti said, the theory of spontaneous workers' institutions was meant to lead up to the consolidation of a party dictatorship. It would seem that the veteran communist leader was looking back across Stalinism and re-interpreting Gramsci's (and incidentally his own) ideas in that light. However precarious Gramsci's balancing of party and *consigli* may have been, his idea was explicit enough. Sovereignty resides in the workers' native institutions formed at the place of work, and these are the embryo of the new state, whereas the party is an indispensable but dependent instrument—and one, moreover, ever threatened with bureaucratization.

The Prison Notebooks: This account of Gramsci's political ideas during his years of freedom may explain why the official presentation of his thought dwells relatively briefly on that part of his career—just long enough to emphasize that he was Italy's "first Leninist" and "the founder of the Communist Party"—and then passes to the books extracted from the prison notes. Here the outlines of Gramsci's politics are harder to grasp. Leaving aside the criteria on which the extracts may have been selected and grouped, there is the fact that Gramsci passes to a higher plane of abstraction. For one thing, he had to. He could not, without attracting his jailer's attention, refer to Marx, Engels, Marxism, or Lenin, so he denoted them by nicknames: Lenin became Ilic, Marxism "the philosophy of Praxis," Marx and Engels "the first and second founders of that philosophy," etc. The disguise is often more impenetrable than mere nicknames: political forces show up as general ideas, partly because the necessity of subterfuge became the habit of talking indirectly, but partly for more profound reasons. The first of them seems to have been that Gramsci practiced a sort of self-censorship, shrinking from identifying certain targets even under a disguise. Thus, "some people" are accused of having debased and vulgarized Marxism, and if one thinks he means Lenin one cannot always prove it. Again, Bukharin is criticized for his mechanical Marxism but there is no sure sign that Gramsci realizes that he is actually attacking Stalin's philosophical views. The second is that Gramsci had passed—and would have had to, even if he had remained at liberty—from political action to contemplation on the causes of the defeat that revolution had everywhere suffered by the 1930s. So he is naturally led to taking a more general view of political affairs, to the extent that adversity and disillusion make us "philosophical." Thirdly, enforced leisure allowed him to resume the speculative enquiries that had interested him as a student.

As if this greater abstraction were not a sufficient obstacle to a simple reading of Gramsci's work, there is the circumstance that it is fragmentary, inchoate. The jottings seldom attain the length of short essays; so, even after the re-arranging by the editors, his "books" remain a mixture of argument, suggestions, book reviews, bright ideas *da vedere* (to be looked into), and sketches of vast research projects that read like the scholar's equivalent of the delicious menus composed by concentration-camp prisoners. Lest this be taken as belittling them, I hasten to add that on almost every page we have the precious sight of a free mind armed with considerable learning and inexhaustible curiosity ranging over most of the domain of modern culture. That this demonstration of intellectual enterprise should come from a sick man in jail (and that it should be accompanied, in his personal letters,[11] by evidence of a noble and generous character) is extremely touching; but it is still inadequate to sustain the claim commonly made in Italy that Gramsci made an important contribution to modern philosophy. However, the following account of his ideas may enable readers to judge for themselves.

Since those ideas are nowhere systematically exposed, it is hard to know where to begin, but one may well take as fundamental Gramsci's project (first formed in 1917) of writing an "anti-Croce" that would be parallel to Marx's inversion of Hegelian idealism to produce the philosophy of dialectical materialism.

> It is necessary to practise on the philosophy of Croce the same reduction that [Marx and Engels] practised on the Hegelian philosophy. This is the only historically fruitful way of bringing about an adequate renovation of the philosophy of Praxis [i.e., Marxism], of elevating that philosophy, which has been "vulgarized" for the immediate needs of practical life, to the level it must attain . . . [namely] the creation of a new integral culture which will have the mass-character of the Protestant Reformation and the French Enlightenment as well as the classic character of Greek culture and the Italian Renaissance, a culture that will, in Carducci's words, synthesize Maximilian Robespierre and Immanuel Kant, politics and philosophy, in a dialectical unity. . . . For us Italians, to be the heirs of the Crocean philosophy, which represents the modern, world version [*momento*] of the classical German philosophy.

And this fresh synthesis between Marxism and idealism will belong, not just to Italians, but "to Europe and the world."[12]

Disregarding the naive cultural nationalism that casts Italian neo-idealism for this universal role, one asks why any such synthesis is necessary. Why should Marxism, which Gramsci's companions took to be a self-sufficient or even definitive philosophy, need a re-invigorating blood transfusion from idealism, Italian or any other? Obviously because Gramsci felt that it had suffered a "materialist" degeneration in his time, and that in three senses. Its official metaphysics had relapsed to a mechanical materialism (in Stalinism), rather of the sort that the Hegelian Marx had criticized a century before. Secondly, it had been given a narrowly political interpretation (in Leninism) to the neglect of the cultural, and especially ethical, factors in social change to which Sorel's theory of proletarian spontaneity had drawn attention. Thirdly, it had been simplified for the purposes of mass indoctrination, to win the support of plebs whose intellectual capacity, or incapacity, reflected merely vulgar prejudice and naive realism.

This triple debasement was perfectly understandable; and Lenin was not to be castigated for his role in it, any more than Saint Paul could be castigated for having simplified Christ's message. Paul and Lenin stand for action, organization, and the diffusion of the ethic created by their masters, for its transposition into a social reality. The duality science/action is represented in the very name "Marxism-Leninism," and we could similarly call Christianity "Christism-Paulinism."[13] Besides, Engels had been wrong in saying that Marx left the proletariat the secure "heirs of the classical German philosophy." Any such heritage is inevitably exposed to dissipation, especially in the conditions of political action. The reduction of idealism to a practical philosophy (which means, concurrently, the elevation of practice to a philosophical plane) is not a once-for-all affair, as Engels's phrase suggests, but a Vico-style cycle that needs to be repeated by each generation, at ever higher levels. The time had come, Gramsci felt, for a new fusion of political practice and speculative idealism; and it would take the form of an anti-Croce written by a Marxist.

For all the historical (or historicist) justification of Leninism as a necessary phase in Marxism's progress, it is clear that Gramsci feels about it the way a theologian does about simple-minded "popular religion": it is the opium of the

97

G

people. It is also evident that Gramsci is rejecting the doctrine drawn from the last Thesis on Feuerbach ("The philosophers have only interpreted the world in various ways; the point however is to change it"), that philosophy culminates, once and for all and without residue, in revolutionary action. This had been taken to mean that proletarian action, endowed by Marx with all the philosophy it needed, had replaced philosophy, leaving no more room for mere speculation. On the contrary, said Gramsci, philosophy never culminates in the sense of ending, and men of action are never dispensed from reckoning with speculative idealism. Politics will always have a philosophical dimension, and revolution will always include cultural creativeness. In plainer terms, the simplification of revolutionary action, by (or at least since) Lenin, to the strategy and tactics of a minority intent on seizing power is a dangerous approach to the vast work of liberation—which must begin with a revolution of ideas, progress through the adoption of a new morality by the masses, and culminate in the social hegemony of that new ethic. The Leninist mistake is not to concentrate on installing a new state (whatever anarchists might say), but to fail to see that "the foundation of a ruling class, that is, of a state, is equivalent to creating a new worldview," that is to say "a new intellectual and moral order"; so it is primarily a philosophical assignment.[14]

The "conception of [Marxism] as a popular modern Reformation," of revolution as the coming to hegemony of a new ethic, Gramsci explicitly draws from Sorel. In general, all his ethical theory and his philosophy of revolution, as far as it is reaction against, or reservations about, Leninism, comes from Sorel, who was certainly a major influence over Gramsci. His "maximalist" opponents had seen this from 1919 when they accused the *Ordine Nuovo* group of being "neo-syndicalist, spontaneist, Bergsonian,"[15] and it is patent throughout the prison writings. Yet Gramsci is no Sorelian, in that he dissociates himself from the Frenchman's anti-intellectualism, anti-Jacobinism, and his "Jansenist fury against the stupidities of parliamentarism and political parties." For those are the things (the role of intellectuals, Jacobins, political parties) that Gramsci wants to synthesize into his political philosophy, which will combine Robespierre (i.e., Lenin) with Kant (i.e., Sorel). His insistence on the necessity of disciplined political action under party leadership, even for a revolutionary movement whose content is ethical and cultural, is among the most effective things he wrote. This is why Ignazio Silone could say that, for all their anxieties about Gramsci's philosophy, the communists would find him invaluable, at least in Italy, in bringing anarchists, idealists, and romantics to see the need for party discipline.

Lenin's and Trotsky's apologies for minority leadership and party discipline had been peremptory and polemical, and often came down to the local, historical argument, "Russia is at war!"; and it quite failed to convince Marxist opponents of Bolshevism. Gramsci wanted to show the general, theoretical necessity, in all revolutionary action, of the sort of political leadership Lenin had provided. On the one hand, he argued that anti-Jacobinism is at best an honest theoretical error in such as Sorel, but more often serves as the cover for a rival group's bid to displace existing leadership. For all movements have political leadership. None is really spontaneous in the sense of being unled. Anti-Jacobinism and rejection of Bolshevik discipline are pretexts for passivity, and thus well suit the ruling class. Besides, revolutionary movements will find their opportunity only at a moment of social breakdown; and if they do not then resort to Jacobin-Bolshevik tactics, the ground will be swept from under their feet by a right-wing counter-revolution, which is precisely the characteristic product of moments of social breakdown.

On the other hand, the political leadership that a Leninist party offers the working class is not Blanquism, an external, authoritarian discipline imposed on the movement. Rather, it is a directing, educating force, a specialized function of the movement itself. It is the movement become self-conscious, seeking to concentrate and make politically effective the morality that is diffuse in the workers' own spontaneous institutions, while remaining democratically responsive to the movement. There exists the evident danger, Gramsci concedes, that this instrument will be bureaucratized and lapse into a centralized "Byzantine-Bonapartist" authority. (This was written as Stalin consolidated his power.) Yet that danger is less terrible than the menace of impulsiveness, fatuity, vanity and arbitrariness that attends undisciplined initiative. Gramsci devoted much time to this definition of the party's role, to its relations with the class's native institutions, and to the question of how far ahead of the masses it can go in trying to put their "real" interests above their "apparent" or short-term interests. In the end, all his formulations are unsatisfactory for those who do not share the faith in a "dialectical" interplay between a central authority of political leaders and the aspirations of a mass movement nor share the confidence that the will of a minority of technicians of the coup d'état can regularly coincide with the ethical aims of a mass faith.

At least the context of the problem is clear: the party is the cutting edge of a movement that seeks to realize (make real) a new morality, to translate it from speculation into a way of living. This is the sense in which various philosophies (though not philosophy itself) can be said to culminate:

> There is a point of passage of every world-view into the morality that matches it, of every "contemplation" into the "action" that depends on it, and of every philosophy into the policy that depends on it ... the point at which the world-view, the contemplation, the philosophy become "real" because they tend to change the world and to revolutionize practice. So you can say that this is the crux of the Marxist philosophy, the point at which it becomes actual, lives historically, that is socially, and no longer merely in individual minds, ceases to be arbitrary and becomes necessary-rational-real.

Moreover, that "point of passage" does not concern only sociologists, but philosophers too, because it constitutes the only test or "proof" of a philosophy. There could be no other "transcendental" criterion in Gramsci's absolute historicism. A philosophy that can, in this way, become effective historical reality is a true one. Croce had already said that philosophy was history, but Gramsci went further and specified that history was politics—so philosophy was politics. Robespierre was the "implication" of Kant and, conversely, when Lenin seized power this was "a metaphysical event."[16] A philosophy cannot shrink from such "implications," for by constitution it has a missionary spirit; it has to seek its proof by conquering mass support as a way of living. And at a crucial point in that effort it will need a Machiavellian Prince to incarnate the collective will that has opted for its morality.[17] The Marxist philosophy finds him today in that politician-philosopher, the Communist Party.

> The Modern Prince, the myth-prince, cannot be a real person, a concrete individual; it can only be an organism; a complex element of society in which the cementing of a collective will, recognized and partially asserted in action, has already begun. This organism is already provided by historical development and it is the political party: the first cell containing the germs of collective will which are striving to become universal and total . . . the Jacobins . . . were certainly a "categoric incarnation" of Machiavelli's Prince . . . an example of how a collective will was formed and operated concretely, which in at least some of its aspects was an original creation, *ex novo*. It is necessary to define collective will, and political will in general, in the modern sense: will as working consciousness of historical necessity, as protagonist of a real and effective historical drama. One of the first parts [of a study of modern revolution] ought in fact to be dedicated to the "collective will," posing the question in this way: "When can the conditions for the arousing and development of a national-popular collective will be said to exist?" . . . The Modern Prince must, and cannot but, be the preacher and organizer of intellectual and moral reform, which means creating the basis for a later development of the national-popular collective will toward the realization of a higher and total form of modern civilization.

Thus in this "idealist" revision of Marxism, a social voluntarism replaces historical determinism. Economic factors are not overlooked but they are no longer autonomous. They appear among the conditions for the operation of collective will, and among the means it must use to renovate civilization. In the notion of a Machiavellian political party that organizes a moral and intellectual reform Gramsci considers that he has wedded Croce and Lenin, and combined Sorel's theory of spontaneous proletarian morality with Stalin's practice of party dictatorship.

Philosophers will hasten to point out that in these generous identifications of history, politics, and philosophy, it is philosophy

that gets liquidated. We are left with (as the two con-
stituents of culture) the existing mass ideology (religion, naive
realism, materialism), and, on the other hand, the Machiavellian pedagogy of a party seeking to install a different mass
ideology. "All is politics, even philosophy and philosophies,
and the only 'philosophy' is history in action, that is life
itself."[18] Of course, philosophy was bound to meet some such
fate at the hands of an absolute historicist. Yet one must note
the supreme irony that these things were written by a prisoner
in Mussolini's jails—for what most resembles this "idealist
Marxism" is exactly fascism.[19] They may indeed be poles apart
as social programs, but on the philosophical ground that
Gramsci has chosen they are the twin and contemporary
product of a confusion of Marx, Sorel, Machiavelli, and
Italian neo-idealism.

Gramsci's anti-Croce, then, is a rather different achievement
from Marx's anti-Hegel. Croce, after all, had been a Marxist,[20]
which is why Gramsci could say that his Marxism-idealism
synthesis was at a "higher level" or in a later cycle than Marx's
own. Yet what Gramsci did was not so much to stand speculative idealism back on its feet as to recover its Marxist ingredients,
taking them back complete with their idealist wrappings. It
is understandable that communist theorists outside Italy should
fear that, in the process, it is Marx that gets stood on his head.
Their apprehensions are most justified in regard to Gramsci's
endeavor to purge the Marxism of his day of all its "crude
materialism," "naive realism," and "positivist incrustations,"
i.e., to incorporate it into an absolute, historicist idealism. Some
warrant for this program exists in Engels, though less surely
in Marx. Indeed, Croce had complained that Marx was
insufficiently historicist and showed "residues of transcendence." Gramsci made the same complaint about Croce, and
offered to get rid of all transcendence and all objectivity in a
socialist version of the most uncompromising Italian neo-
idealism. So he argued that not only is all social thought
historically relative (including Marxism itself, which thus is
destined to be surpassed), but natural science is too (not
excluding, it would appear, logic and mathematics). Science

is part of the ideological superstructure. The "nature" it claims to study is simply "the category of the economic," that is, an incident in productive technology. "Without the [economic] activity of man, the creator of all values, even scientific, what would 'objectivity' be? A chaos; that is, nothing; the void." Lukacs is chided for restricting the dialectic (which here means having things both ways) to history, when nature too is dialectic because it is in social history: "Matter, therefore, is not to be considered as such but as socially and historically organized for production; and so natural science [is] essentially an historical category, a human relationship."[21] The upshot is a complete relativism that goes well beyond Sorel's "*métaphysique ouvrière*" to become a "subjectivism of *homo oeconomicus*." As Gramsci puns, he has converted Gentile's "philosophy of the pure act" into a philosophy of the impure, or economic act.

Yet of course no relativism is complete, because that would be an unthinkable incoherency. Croce found residues of transcendence in Marx, and Gramsci did in Croce: and we can in Gramsci, for the good reason that they must always be present to make discussion possible. If all is historically relative, that statement would be too, and thus in danger of ceasing to be true tomorrow. So Gramsci will be found defending formal logic and "non-historical concepts." This creditable inconsistency is not mentioned to make a debating point, but to draw attention to that substantial part of Gramsci's work that consists in the defence and illustration of formal logic, classic culture, liberal education and disinterested enquiry. These activities are not, in practice, menaced by Gramsci's extreme and quite theoretical historicism, but they have been endangered by the movement to which he belonged.

That he combined attachment to them with a confused relativism that would make them impossibly ambiguous is, perhaps, no more odd than that he combined a libertarian view of culture with the doctrine of rigid discipline in a Machiavellian party. To the extent that he reconciled these incompatible notions, it was on paper and in prison. In practice and at liberty, the party he helped found has been less successful.

The Western Marxists

But if, as some signs suggest, it is entering on a phase of liberalization, it will find nourishment in Gramsci's work, nourishment of a sort that, for all its adulteration, is not available at all in most other communist thinkers.

4. Lukacs: the Restoration of Idealism

The reason for taking Georg Lukacs as a representative of communist culture is not that he was typical. His range and ability were too great to be typical. Rather, it is that his work over sixty years (Lukacs died in 1971 at eighty-six) expresses the gamut of intellectual attitudes sympathetic to communism—better, committed to communism. His intellectual and political career is the path that few others have followed from start to finish, but which all communist intellectuals have travelled for some part of the way.

The stages of that journey are these: a youthful, romantic longing for an anti-capitalist cultural revolution and for a life more heroic than that of the bourgeois; a sympathy with syndicalism, based on the hope that the working class, as the enemy of the bourgeois, will become the vehicle of that revolution, the bearer of the new heroic culture; an adherence to Marxism as the rational or even scientific version of that hope. This is immediately followed, however, by a Hegelizing of Marxism, so as to distinguish it, as a cultural theory, as the program for a cultural rebirth, from the "vulgar Marxism" and materialism of the Second International. Then comes the reception of the Leninist theory of the communist party as the Machiavellian Prince that will manage the cultural revolution because the working class is not doing so spontaneously. The Leninization of Marxism having produced Stalinism, there follows a rearguard action against "sectarianism"; that rearguard action having failed, there ensues a complete capitulation to Stalinism, as preferable to Hitlerism, even though this requires putting aside most of the original cultural interests. Then, as Stalinist terror is relaxed, comes the admission that the experience has been culturally null and profitless—

the phase of disenchantment. Finally, the renewed quest, made known perhaps only obliquely, for another vehicle for the cultural revolution. The snake of Stalinism having brought us back to square one, we set out again, still full of hope at eighty-five, looking for the ladder that must lead us up to the fully human society—looking for the troops or the prince that will force upon the world the cultural renaissance that the sensitive intellectual feels is necessary. At this stage, of course, it is the search for a life more heroic and worthwhile not only than that of the bourgeois world, but than that of European (Russian) communism as it exists.

These stages are not of equal importance in the career of every communist intellectual. Lukacs's own most striking contributions were made at the phase of Hegelizing Marx and then in the reception of Leninism in the West. Yet (and this is what I mean by saying his range and power are beyond the ordinary) he also gave memorable expression to other parts of the journey, to the longing for cultural rebirth, to the opposition to Stalinist dogmatism, and then, ironically, to the abject surrender to Stalinism, as well as to the ultimate disenchantment with communist culture. Lukacs's expression of the last phase, the search for a new alternative, was not as sensational as that of Herbert Marcuse or of the pro-Chinese communists, but local political conditions might account for that. It is easier to say what you mean in San Diego than in Budapest, at least if what you mean is that communism has failed as a culture. As Lukacs admitted years later to having so often disguised his real meaning, told tactical lies, and made insincere recantations, one is entitled to read between the lines of his statements in this last phase.

Before depicting each of these phases (which, if I were able enough, I would make you see as a series of pictures in a gallery, portraits of the communist intellectual at this point and at that), I should indicate briefly the main dates in Lukacs's biography. He was born in 1885 in Budapest, the son of a Jewish banker, director of Hungary's biggest bank and bearer of a title. (Georg himself signed his first publications "von Lukacs.") The

Lukacs: the Restoration of Idealism

German bourgeois and the Jews of Hungary were all city folk, barely assimilated into the feudal agricultural society that persisted there well into this century, and unloved both by the small urban proletariat and by the landed gentry and peasants. So it was normal that after preliminary studies in Budapest, Lukacs should receive essentially a German education in Berlin and Heidelberg and that much of his work thereafter should be published in German. That work was mainly literary scholarship. From 1908 Lukacs was publishing on aesthetic theory, where his ideas showed the influence of the neo-Kantianism he had imbibed in Germany; there his two most influential teachers were Simmel and Max Weber. Political interests appeared early, however, at first via the influence of Hungarian syndicalists and hence of Sorel, then by way of study of Marx. This meant that right from that point Lukacs began to see works of art in a relativist way, as reflections of a society at a given time.

More important, it led him into the Hungarian Communist Party at the end of 1918. The apparent suddenness of this conversion surprised some of his associates in a semi-religious talking society called "Spirit" *(Szellenkek)*, which included Karl Mannheim, Arnold Hauser, Béla Bartok, Zoltan Kodaly, Revai and Fogarasi. More surprising was Lukacs's meteoric rise to the top of the party within two months—at least this would surprise those who did not know that the communist movement had no base in Hungary at that time and that, even when it was supposedly in power, there were no soviets in the land, only one ruling soviet which consisted of Béla Kun's friends. When the revolution came, Lukacs was the communist regime's spokesman on matters of education and culture, from March to August 1919. Many of his friends from the Spirit Society, notably Mannheim and Hauser, received university posts while he was in office. Lukacs issued decrees about classics for the masses, fairy tales for children, and prefects in schools, and he inaugurated the Institute for Research in Historical Materialism in Budapest. None of this had any effect on the brief history of the Béla Kun adventure, and when it was swept away by the reaction and followed by the Horthy

107

dictatorship and anti-Semitic pogroms (Jews were heavily represented among the communists), Lukacs went underground and then fled to Vienna.

In exile he played a role in the faction fight that rent the illegal party, siding with the moderate Landler faction against the dominant, Moscow-backed Béla Kun leadership. This struggle went on from 1921 to 1928, with varying fortunes for each side. Lukacs weakened his position by publishing in 1920 an article against parliamentarism[1] which incurred a rebuke from Lenin, in *History and Class Consciousness* (1923),[2] solemnly condemned the next year by Zinoviev, and in 1928 a series of recommendations on political action inside Hungary[3] which was equally solemnly denounced as anti-Leninist and opportunist by the Comintern. Thereupon Lukacs quit active politics for fifteen years. He worked in the Marx-Engels Institute in Moscow in 1930-31, in Berlin as a party activist among literary men in 1931-3, and fled to Russia when Hitler came to power. From 1933 to 1944 he worked in the Philosophy Institute of the Academy of Sciences in Moscow and helped edit party publications. Returning to Hungary after the Red Army, Lukacs became a member of parliament, a notable in other party bodies and in the World Peace Council, and held the chair of Aesthetics and Culture Philosophy at Budapest University. He played a prominent and generally disgraceful part in the Cold War and yet, when Stalinism was in its last paroxysms in Hungary after 1949, Lukacs himself was recurrently attacked for right-wing deviations and was obliged to withdraw from public life in 1951. As the post-Stalin thaw began, Lukacs re-emerged as a sympathizer with the Nagy opposition and the Petöfi Circle, venturing his first public criticisms of Stalin. When the 1956 Hungarian Revolution broke out, he became a member of the Central Committee of the Communist Party and Education Minister in the Nagy government. Deported to Rumania, he survived and was freed, whereas some of his colleagues were shot or jailed. Back in Budapest, he lived in retirement, while still denounced periodically by the party of which he was no longer a member, and worked on a *magnum opus* on aesthetics. As the Kadar regime relaxed its grip over Hungary, Lukacs's position became more comfortable, though his work remained banned in some other communist countries. He was re-admitted to the party in 1968. He is understood to have protested against the invasion of Czechoslovakia by Hungary and her allies, though he did so privately, through correct party channels. Since the Kadar government was not happy about the Czech affair, the protest did Lukacs no harm; on the contrary, when a former admirer, Josef Szigeti, accused him of being a leader of an anti-party revisionist group, it was Szigeti who was reproved and sacked from his job. Then in March 1969, on the occasion of the fiftieth anniversary of the Béla Kun dictatorship (the first that Hungary could celebrate officially, Kun having been executed by Stalin), Lukacs was decorated with the Order of the Red Flag and was allowed to express his opinions freely in numerous interviews. He died in 1971 in odor, if not of sanctity, then of discreet glory.

Lukacs's communist career begins in a mood of ethical idealism and cultural romanticism. He had previously been a neo-Kantian practising the most arbitrary *Verstehende* analysis and exemplifying a pathetic, asocial outlook since identified as existentialist. When in his thirties he turned to social affairs, his first thought was for a revolt of the masses against the de-based ethical and aesthetic values of the bourgeois. David Kettler, who has reported on what Lukacs and Karl Mannheim were thinking during World War I, calls this line of thought the "revolutionary culture movement," and traces its lineage from the German romantics down to Marcuse.[4] These are the people who want to be rid of capitalism because they say its acquisitiveness has sullied spiritual life. The aim of revolution for them would be not so much to put an end to suffering and exploitation and to liberate productive forces obstructed by capitalism, as to install a higher culture. Lukacs himself summarized this attitude in an ordinance he issued while Commissar for Education in the Béla Kun dictatorship: "Politics is simply the means; the end is culture." Before that, the Spirit Society in which Lukacs was a leader had declared in its manifesto that it was against capitalism and positivism, against materialism and for a new idealism, a revivified spirituality and a fresh European culture.

The adepts of the cultural revolution usually are elitist, explicitly so when they are on the Right (for, of course, there is a tradition of criticism of ugly money-grubbing mass-welfare industrialism from the Right, one of whose best exponents in our time was Ortega y Gasset), but often implicity so when they are on the Left too, since their defence of the higher values usually entails rejection of bourgeois and democratic standards along with "mass society" and industrial civilization. At first, however, there was little of that in Lukacs's version of the faith; it was the mass of working people who were going to overthrow a corrupt and tasteless capitalism and display a native love of the higher values, a sterner morality, and a surer artistic taste.

Let me stress what is Platonist in this culture-communism. I mean by that the timeless argument against money-making that is set out in *The Republic*. Economics, the productive process itself, has debased morality and culture (complain both Plato and Lukacs), and the way to make culture and the ethical life free and pure again is to separate them from economics. Since there must be some economic activity to support cultural life at an acceptable level, it must be communized, i.e., limited, made into nobody's business and organized frugally and jointly. Culture must rule the economy and not vice versa. That vice versa—the economy determining culture—is what the Marxists called historical materialism, which they took to be a universal truth. Lukacs said it was a temporary and scandalous degeneration produced by capitalism. The task of the revolution was to make historical materialism no longer true. The revolution will be against the predominance of production and technology; cultural uplift or renewal will be the very content of socialism. All this is explicit in Lukacs at a time when he was already an official of the Hungarian soviet regime. There is no need to point out how far this cultural communism is from the proletarian socialism of Marx and Lenin, a movement concerned with the liberation of productive forces, and which seeks to put economic activities not outside public life but at its very center.

This is the source of many of Lukacs's recurrent difficulties with that movement, because its leaders could see that his Platonist, philosophical communism was at least as opposed to the socialist version of industrialism they were seeking to build as it was to bourgeois capitalist society. It is evident too that it would be quite uncongenial to working men, though in Lukacs's version they were to be the bearers of the new and purer civilization.

Lukacs chose the Left of the "culture movement," whereas others chose the Right. It sometimes seems to be a toss-up which way the cultural uplifters go, and there is nothing irrevocable about their choice: if one chosen vehicle disappoints them, they will start casting about for a new clientèle. This is the phase I suggest we see in Marcuse and, less patently, in the Lukacs of the 1960s. In 1918-22, however, his faith was with the working class, and he took it to its syndicalist extreme. The agent of the revolution was to be the workers' councils spontaneously set up by the masses as the direct, non-representative instrument of their power. Exactly like Korsch and Gramsci at that time, Lukacs saw revolution as an organic, independent activity of a class, much as Sorel and Rosa Luxemburg did. Indeed, his first reaction to the Bolshevik Revolution was hostile because it seemed to him undemocratic and it was led by a minority ready to split the proletariat's unity. He wrote in that sense in 1919 a paper that today is hard to find, but his reservations about a party-led dictatorship willing to terrorize part of the working class are evident for some time after that. Lenin reprimanded him in 1920 for these ultra-Left views when Lukacs wrote that once the workers could set up *soviets*— workers' councils—they should forget about parliaments and representative parties. And one of the deviations in the *History and Class Consciousness* book was that it reproduced, unseasonably in 1923, Lukacs's essays of 1920 insisting on the priority of workers' councils over the Communist Party. This enthusiastic sovietism was still evident in his 1924 book on Lenin,[5] quite incongruously, since the point of the book was to acclimatize the Leninist conception of the communist party in the West. Thus it contained an unresolved tension between the workers' councils and the party, between the former's direct rule and the latter's party dictatorship, i.e., between the dissolution of the state and its immense reinforcement. How to graft the voluntarist, elitist idea of the minority party on to the traditional Western idea of the revolutionary mass was to be one of Lukacs's preoccupations in the next phase, the Hegelizing of Marx. Though he solved this problem on paper (as Gramsci did), it was to return to haunt him in practice in 1956, when the government in which he was a minister was confronted by the workers' councils that sprang up spontaneously across Hungary. If the Russians had not liquidated them for him, his government would no doubt have had to do the job itself, as Gomulka did when workers' councils appeared in Warsaw factories.

In 1919 Lukacs began to see how heretical were the two notions we have mentioned: the primacy of culture over economics and of spontaneous workers' councils over the party. These two notions were utterly incompatible with orthodox Russian Marxism. Instead of simply abandoning these ideas, he chose to rethink them at the same time as he rethought Marxism. Significantly, the first essay in *History and Class Consciousness* is called "What is Orthodox Marxism?"—a question to which he gives an answer quite unfamiliar to the Russians as well as to the Second International. It is as though, having seen that his cultural preoccupations and his syndicalism were out of tune with communism, he decided that its orthodoxy would have to be revised as much as his own ideas. That rethinking of Marxism was to be Hegelian. It was set out, in quite poor German and in atrocious Hegelian jargon, in a book that can be understood—the proof is that it has had wide and persistent influence—and yet which cannot easily be paraphrased or summarized.

Writing in 1919-22, Lukacs did not have at his disposal the works of the young Marx, which were made known only after 1927; so he read off Marx's Hegelianism from the later work, particularly from *Capital*. Since he was obliged to disown his book soon after, he could not claim credit for his achievement when the young Marx's papers were published. But the fact that he could find, unaided, the Hegelian, existentialist Marx in

Capital is relevant to the debate about whether there are two people called Karl Marx or just one.

What he found, and what made his book the bible of Western Marxism and the secret doctrine of communist intellectuals from Berlin in 1930 to Prague in 1969, was the dialectic of totality. There are two ways of deriving this notion, one Marxist (drawing on the economic writings of the mature Marx), the other Hegelian (which nowadays can rely on the papers of the young Marx). The former is simpler and we shall follow it first, before restating the issue in Hegelian language. By running the two together one discerns Lukacs's peculiar achievement.

Marx said that behind each social form there was the action of a dominant class. It molded society the way it wanted, by force, fraud and education, and then sought to pass off that form as natural, as eternal. Force alone would not suffice to impose its way of living on others who suffered from it; there must be a formal science to make it seem normal, inevitable and unchangeable. Such fraud is not conscious; the dominant class comes to believe its own lie. Thus its theory and its practice conflict. Its theory says, "This is natural, science says so"; but its practice says, "This is how we want it and this is how it is going to be." The capitalists were the first to enforce a completely man-made, non-natural society, pushing back the boundaries of nature so that our whole environment becomes artificial, and yet they also produced, in economics, the most perfect science to disguise this force-engendered social form as a natural product. The proletariat being the worst and eventually the sole victim of this dispensation can, with Marx's help, come to see that capitalism (and hence all its clumsier predecessors) is not natural, and that its science, economics, is just a formal account of a temporary, arbitrary, though objective, situation. Thereupon the proletariat will have realized that all social forms are man-made, and it can propose to institute a new one on that basis, openly recognizing that it is artificial because the workers, being the vast majority, do not have to oppress anyone and hence have no need to fool anyone. Thus their theory and their practice will coincide. Their theory will be revolutionary in that it assumes that at any point man (exactly:

M

a class) can make his own history, can change the social arrangements and no formal science of natural laws can stop him. The
workers' theory will say, "Society can be revolutionized by a
mass of men," and their practice will consist in doing just
that.

To make this theory plausible one must take a unitary view of
society, envisaging a change in the whole social dispensation
more or less simultaneously. If any social domain (say, the
birth-rate or the source of technological inventions) remains
outside the all-embracing range of the class that is molding
society, then that domain would become a natural obstacle
subject to its own scientific laws. The class seeking hegemony
might wish to arrange matters in such and such a fashion,
but there might be too many babies and too few inventions
because demography and discovery had their own laws men
could not change. If man is to make his own history, he must be
able to make the whole lot and there can be no separate science
of parts of society, no economics, no demography, no history of
law, no aesthetics, but just one science, history, the story of the
global transformations of that concrete totality, society. Lukacs
does not simply assert totality; he cites scraps of evidence for
the claim that in social affairs everything depends on everything else, or, to put it another way, that there is a whole that
determines all the parts. These scraps come from Marx and
seem to me to refer only to economics; Marx was anticipating
equilibrium theory of the Walras-Pareto variety. But Lukacs
builds his vast superstructure on this narrow base.

The important point is to grasp the notion of a moving
totality, a whole social process within which everything is fluid,
nothing is fixed or hard, nothing obeys set laws of its own,
everything depends on and affects everything else, and the
whole lot consists of human activities and relationships between
men. If you can hold that vision in your mind, you will see
how all social science is the enemy of this dialectic of totality,
for a science amounts to saying that some part at least has its
own laws, not liable to change when a class molds the whole
anew. To treat society or part of it as natural, says Lukacs, is a
weapon of bourgeois ideology, in that it sets limits to total

change. Since each stage of the moving totality that is history is the product of one dominant class, that class is all the time trying to pass off bits of its arbitrary arrangements as natural. It wants no one, least of all its victims, to see the whole, to have the vision of the dialectic of totality (for that is a revolutionary view, recalling the arbitrariness and impermanence of social forms). Instead they are to see only the separate sciences, each one embodying the assertion: "Here's a part of the system that was not forced on us by the ruling class and which we cannot change, because it has laws which apply to many periods and many societies." Such natural solidified things no longer look to be human activities and relations between men. They become obstacles to revolutionary change. The most successful attempt to convert activities and relations into things is economics, which even manages to take parts of my personality, of my self-expression, that is of my work, and to convert them into goods subject to impersonal laws. This is reification, *Verdinglichung*, the turning of human activity into frozen objects, economic commodities—all the time with the purpose of subtracting them from the totality that men, organized as a class, can change. If the proletariat accepts that point of view, it condemns itself to continue to exist as mere merchandise governed by inhuman laws. So it must, for its own liberation from reification, take the dialectical, total view: repudiate every so-called fact and thing in favor of the whole that a class can revolutionize.

If the argument is beginning to seem too abstract, imagine what a communist trade union leader in the United Kingdom would say if you told him his men must accept a pay cut for the sake of Britain's balance of payments. His answer might be a faint echo of the case Lukacs is stating here. His opening remark, "To hell with the balance of payments," would then not be unpatriotic but philosophical, being a rejection of a supposed external fact to which he and others must bow, and he would, if he were revolutionary, go on to talk not about such parts but of the whole set of human activities, which he proposed to change. If, however, he went on to say the balance of payments was the boss's problem and his was only his men's pay, he would not be a Marxist or a revolutionary, because his attitude would be falling far short of the dialectic of totality.

Now all this can be got from Marx's later work if you look for it. What is less evident, and therefore more to the taste of intellectuals who want to be communist for superior reasons, is the Hegelian restatement of it. The moving totality of interlocking, conflicting, and interdependent (i.e., dialectically related) activities that makes up history may be called human Praxis. Its dominant form—which determines the whole and the parts, more or less, at each stage of history, and determines them quite completely at the capitalist stage—is the practice of a powerful ruling class. In history to date such classes have exercised power unconsciously: that is, without seeing clearly that the social dispensation they brought about (merely by going after their short-term interests, by generalizing their style of living and seeing to it that society was made safe for their sort of activity) was their own creation. They had to pretend, and pretended even to themselves, that it happened naturally. Thus, man was making his own history (there was nothing external to it, and nothing in it but human activities dominated by one ruling class; no natural objects or scientific laws). Yet he did not know he was making his own history. However, if the proletariat, the mass of the people and the victims of the system are to institute their sort of man-made social dispensation, they would have to be conscious of what they were doing. They could not merely generalize their practice, force their way of living on others, because that way of life was determined inside capitalism and was subhuman. They lived as mere merchandise. They would have to destroy themselves as proletariat, disregard their apparent and short-term interests, reach out consciously for their long-term interests, which are to return to human, non-reified stature, and then knowingly create a fresh, artificial arrangement in which no one had to be fooled and victimized by supposed natural laws. For the first time, man would be making his history and know he was doing so. Man would be both the subject and the object of history: the subject, the self-conscious molder of social arrangements;

and the object, since men *are* those social activities. You might say that history at last had come to consciousness in a self-conditioned subject-object. This is a fair description of the situation Marx imagined and it is couched in the terminology of a great philosophical tradition, that of German idealism. Marx came from that school of thought and—according to Lukacs—remained in it.

Translating the issue into Hegelian terms, we may recall that the goal of idealism (not just of German idealism) has always been to find the absolutely unconditioned or self-conditioned whole on which everything else depends, the whole that is the truth. In classic German philosophy this was narrowed down to the quest for a certain activity, the self-creation of reality, where the subject and object are one, and that in turn was narrowed down, from Hegel on, to the search for a certain historical activity which comes to self-consciousness. Find that and you will have located "that subject of the 'action' of which the concrete totality of reality can be understood as the product." And if we can then participate in that historical activity "we pose the world as thought, as a concrete meaningful system 'produced' by us and arrived in us to consciousness of itself."[6] Hegel thought he found it in the spirits of nations unfolding themselves in history, but Lukacs pointed out that in Hegel's theory the World Spirit worked *through* nations, so Hegel's moving totality, universal history, did not have a subject that was both immanent and free. (Nations are immanent to history but not free; the world spirit is free but transcendent.) Lukacs considered that Marx had found the free subject-object in the notion of society, social history, as one total act, the act of a class. Such social Praxis has been unconscious till now. But at the moment when *it* sets out to make history, the proletariat will know what it is doing. Some class or other has always been the unconscious subject, the real agent of history, but now for the first time a class realizes that history is made by a class and sets out to do the job in its own way, seeing through all that seems to be contingent, external, transcendent, inevitable, reified in history and taking complete mastery of the whole process.

Much more space would be required to make this a little clearer (it can never be made perfectly clear). But enough has been said to show that Lukacs had set Marxism in a "systematic framework quite different from and incompatible with that in which Engels had set it in the *Anti-Dühring*,"[7] till then the philosophy book of the Marxists. One of Lukacs's worst sins, no doubt, was to make no bones about Engels's comical dialectic. In the communist movement, as we know, one may ignore Marx, but one must never say a word against Friedrich Engels. In place of the dialectic of nature Lukacs set the dialectic of (social) totality, which is the common theme of the *Critical Theory of Society*[8] from Horkheimer and Adorno to Marcuse. It asserts the permanent possibility of total revolution, the fluidity and arbitrariness of even the most general categories of social thought, and it dismisses any scientific objection to revolutionism as reification and ideology.

Lukacs's direct experience of the failure of the Hungarian and German revolutions brought him to see a first weak point in this philosophical construction—and here we pass to the next phase, the reception of Leninism in the West. The weak point was that the working class did not become aware that it could— and in its long-term interests must—revolutionize society. It seemed to prefer to chase short-term apparent interests—like the trade unionist I mentioned earlier who, as Lukacs would say, is content to leave the worker mere merchandise but wants a higher price tag put on the commodity. That is a normal difficulty, said Lukacs, because whereas earlier classes just did what they wanted and thus unconsciously molded history to suit themselves, the workers have to destroy the working class in order consciously to make history human. Lukacs handles the difficulty by drawing on the "ideal types" of his teacher Max Weber. An ideal type refers to behaviour that perhaps no actual person exhibits but which all members of a class would exhibit if they went to the end of their ideas, lived completely consistently according to their lights. Thus the ideal type of capitalist is always rational and calculating, whereas it is notorious that real capitalists often are irrational, sentimental, patriotic. But social theory, says Lukacs, is not about what men actually think and feel but what they would have thought and felt if they had perfectly grasped their situation and the interests it implied. The workers' class consciousness is an ideal type. It is the awareness of the duty or mission of the class as outlined in the Hegelian-Marxist theory according to which the dialectic totality will come to consciousness in that class, even though many or most actual workers are not clear about this. It is not difficult to see where this specious theory is leading. If the workers will not see their duty, someone must see it for them and lead them to it—i.e., the party.

History and Class Consciousness is a series of essays written between 1919 and 1922 and one can trace the evolution from the spontaneity theory of Sorel and Rosa Luxemburg to the frankly elitist, voluntarist theory of Lenin, exactly as one can in Gramsci's work a little later. This is the famous, because ultimately insoluble, problem of the relations between working class and Communist Party, to which the only "solution" is that the party must be accepted as a "mystery of reason" (Merleau-Ponty). Gramsci's wrestling with this problem is finally, and necessarily, indecisive, but superior to Lukacs's on this vital point. Gramsci sees that between class and party must come the bureaucracy and so the whole upshot of the party's effort to educate the class into its historical vocation will depend on how educated the bureaucracy is, on whether (Gramsci says) it is Roman-Anglo-Saxon or Byzantine-Bonapartist.[9]

Lukacs, in contrast, reacts away from romantic, spontaneous mass revolutionism to the equally romantic notion of a tiny band of elite heroes who will impinge on the masses directly without the intermediary of a paralysing bureaucracy. He was, perhaps, the first (and certainly the first outside Russia) to take all the elements of the Leninist theory of the Communist Party and lay them end to end with a ruthless logic and a complacent delectation. I sometimes wonder whether this was not one of the unstated charges against him in 1924—whether his cold, brutal frankness about the superior minority that will manipulate the workers did not make even some communists feel uncomfortable. Certainly that was the source of the morbid fascination Lukacs's book exercised over certain intellectuals in Vienna in the 1920s and in Berlin in the 1930s. As Borkenau says,[10] Lukacs stated what was implicit in Lenin and carried the theory of the almighty central committee, against which Rosa Luxemburg had forewarned Marxists in 1904, to the last extreme. This full-blown and cynical Leninism can be found in Lukacs's book *Lenin* and in the last chapter of *History and Class Consciousness*. The working class is ideologically null and must be led to its real interests by a conscious active element, composed of strictly, indeed rigorously, disciplined intellectuals who have deciphered history's meaning and who recognize no good or bad, only the expedient; who are indeed ready for any zig-zag, any action legal or illegal. Their tasks are to manipulate the proletariat's changing allies; to fight the non-revolutionary workers' leaders; to oppose the whole working class when it fails to see its duty. The organizational problem is central, because the revolution no longer has anything to do with a class and its ethic but is all a matter of tactics over a constantly changing front, on which Kemal Pasha can become a revolutionary, whereas a great Western working-class party is declared reactionary. The unprincipled band is dedicated to installing the "reign of liberty." This is not the individual liberty that those corrupted by capitalism aspire to, but "true" liberty which begins with the renunciation of individual liberty and conscious submission to the Communist Party. Discipline in the party is the only way to authentic freedom. That party is distinct and separate from the working class; it is autonomous; it cannot grow out of the class but always arises as the self-conscious act of a revolutionary vanguard. These are all quotations from Lukacs, who freely admits that this theory had stuck in the throats of Western socialists and who consciously sets out to spread the Leninist idea in the West.

Lukacs himself was the first to fall victim to this monstrous creation. His book was condemned by Zinoviev on behalf of the Comintern in 1924, whereupon Lukacs disavowed it, refused to let it be reprinted for over forty years, and performed a long series of self-criticisms and recantations. Why was he condemned? He was denounced by Zinoviev, along with Graziadei and Karl Korsch, for the minor offence of reprinting earlier opinions he admitted to having given up, i.e., attachment to Rosa Luxemburg's ideas. For Zinoviev, it was a scandal for a communist to admit ever having had non-Leninist opinions. A rather more serious offence was that in 1923–4, just when the Comintern was drawing the moral of the failure of the German revolution, Lukacs displayed a quite unseasonable revolutionism, writing as though world-wide revolution was both imminent and necessary.

More serious even than that tactical error was another, more fundamental. One of the conclusions Moscow drew from the failure of the German revolution was that Soviet Russia must take over complete control of the world communist movement, and from 1924 begins the Bolshevization of the national sections. It would have been extremely dangerous then for the belief to gain ground that there was a crude Russian Marxism and a cleverer, more philosophical Western Marxism, exemplified in the books of Karl Korsch and Lukacs. It was intolerable that a Western communist should attack Lenin's crude representationist theory of knowledge or mock the naive dialectic of nature accepted in Russia as the ABC of communist philosophy. If Russia's writ were to run at the political level, it must have the right philosophy too—for had not Lukacs shown that a communist party's basic justification is that it has deciphered the philosophy of history which the short-sighted workers cannot read? So Western Marxism was condemned with a rare ferocity as a deviation from, not a development of, Marxism.

Lukacs has written one book, *Der junge Marx,* and another, *Der junge Hegel.* Some day someone will write a book, *Der junge Lukacs.* We at least are finished with him now, for Lukacs buried him in 1924 at the age of thirty-nine. The survivor, while bowing to the will of the party he himself had made the repository of truth, undertook the long struggle against the rising sectarianism that was to culminate in Stalinism. This is the period down to 1928–9 and concerns mainly the conflicting tendencies among the Hungarian exiles in Moscow, Vienna, and Berlin.

It is extremely intricate and its climax was the condemnation of the Blum Theses in 1929 by the Comintern ("Blum" was the name Lukacs had in the underground). In 1928 he submitted inside the illegal party an analysis of the failure of the Béla Kun dictatorship, his version of the development of Hungary under Admiral Horthy, and, finally, his recommendations on what the party should do. Unfortunately he made the mistake of anticipating the Popular Front line of 1935: that is, he drew the conclusion from the strength of fascism in Hungary that the workers alone—and even less the communists alone while denouncing other workers' leaders as "social fascists"—could not hope to overthrow fascism and install a proletarian dictatorship. Rather they must fight fascism first in the name of democracy and in alliance with, at least, the whole of the working class, under the slogan "Class against Class." The party must pose as *the* democratic party, seek a mass basis outside the working class and propose a "democratic dictatorship of workers and peasants." To that end it must criticize itself for the mistake of the Kun regime in refusing to give the peasants land. It must now promise land to the peasants and silence those communists who argued that land division was not socialism. In general, the Blum Theses are dogmatic communist stuff, and the democratic pose in particular is patently tactical. Still, they did take into account conditions inside Hungary and the needs of the anti-fascist struggle. They were condemned in the name of an abstract Stalinism which took account of neither.[11]

The Comintern replied that the Blum Theses were the work of a Rightist, an anti-Leninist, a half-social-democrat, a liquidator of the Hungarian Communist Party. Blum could not see that the social democrats had become social fascists, nor that the wave of the "third period" was swelling—and so this was the time for Bolsheviks to fight against democratic illusions. It was the moment for pure proletarian socialist revolution, and there could be no talk of the republic or democracy, even as a stage towards proletarian dictatorship. Not only could there be no proletarian alliance with the bourgeois; even an alliance with the peasants was impossible unless one category within the peasantry, the rich peasants, the *kulaks*, were excluded. The slogan "land for the peasants" was not specifically condemned but seems to have been set aside, which was in line with the policy Stalin was preparing in Russia itself. In short, Moscow was on a fanatically, ultra-Left tack. But it may well be that it was angry too because Lukacs's positing of a careful and generally sensible analysis of the Hungarian situation as the base for Hungarian party policy implied resistance to Moscow's domination, in the name of a national communism. Certainly, it was that aspect of the Blum Theses that was uppermost when they were revived—indeed, made available publicly for the first time—in 1956. Lukacs's ideas of 1928 were discussed in Budapest in 1956, as representing part of a tendency toward a more democratic national way to communism. But in 1929 he disavowed them after the blast from Moscow, performing a thorough act of self-criticism. He recanted that recantation in 1956, saying that Moscow had threatened that unless he withdrew his theses the entire Hungarian Communist Party would be expelled from the Comintern.

This was not the last nor the most humble of Lukacs's self-criticisms, for he entered now on the road to his long career as the complete Stalinist.

When he took refuge in Moscow after leaving Berlin in 1933, he performed (according to Morris Watnick)[12] "one of the most abject acts of self-degradation on record" before the philosophical section of the Academy of Sciences. Watnick suggests that Lukacs was reacting in horror from the shock he got in Berlin in 1933 when he saw some of his former fellow-students at German universities go over to Hitler, so that he now saw his youthful idealist philosophy as the seedbed of fascism. Lukacs himself said later that in those days you could not criticize Stalin without aiding Hitler and that he did carry on a sort of guerrilla war against Stalinism, getting books published by making fulsome references to Stalin but nevertheless holding to opposition views on Hegel. I am not of course concerned here to pass judgement. Suffice it to say that if this period were all there were of Lukacs's work, he would scarcely be worth talking about, for this is the type of communist intellectual most familiar to people of the pre-war generation. Its features are: fawning adulation of Stalin, acceptance of Lenin's amateurish philosophy (though Lukacs had specifically disproved the representationist theory of knowledge in his earlier work and could not possibly believe what he said about it later), and endorsement of the "dialectic of nature." To his credit, I do not know of his ever applying the "dialectic of nature." He just says it exists (he had earlier proved the contrary), but that took no more than half a line and Lukacs left it there. Finally, there was the customary defence of the Moscow trials and scurrilous abuse of Western socialists. Philosophical discussion for Lukacs in this period was just boasting: our philosophy is better than theirs, Lenin was a genius who foresaw all.

This was bad enough but it got worse during the Cold War, when Lukacs was back in Budapest. He then descended (in the words of Rusconi) to "cultural terrorism." His 1954 book, *The Destruction of Reason*,[13] could well be preserved as a monument to the debasement of communist intellectuals in the six years before that date. It has even been attacked as excessive in Moscow. Admittedly nothing was said against it in Moscow at the time, but after Lukacs had been expelled from the party for his activities in 1956, *Voprosy Filosofii* remembered that *The Destruction of Reason* had been a disgraceful racialist attack on the Germans. It did not recall that after each anti-German outburst in the book came the assertion that the Americans were no better, that General Ridgway and Senator Joe McCarthy were a new Goering and a new Hitler, and so forth.

Already, underneath this strident Stalinist propaganda, one could see Lukacs's disenchantment with communist culture, which was to find expression only after Stalin's death. The Stalinists were not fooled. They noticed that in the mass of literary criticism that Lukacs published in those years there was hardly a reference to Soviet literature, which Lukacs virtually ignored while he wrote about bourgeois writers like Thomas Mann. For this sin of omission, an attack on Lukacs was mounted in 1949 which became the aesthetic aspect of the Rajk Affair. Lukacs duly made several self-criticisms, which only enraged the Stalinists further because they were obviously insincere and incomplete.

These attacks came from the highest level, from the government, and eventually (in 1951) Lukacs lost his public offices and retreated to semi-retirement. The charge sheet against him said that he admired only Western bourgeois culture and had nothing to say for socialist realism. True, he said nothing against it but the Stalinists suspected the worst (correctly, as Lukacs later admitted). They complained that he hid behind quotations from Marx and Engels in praise of the bourgeois classics; but Marx and Engels had had no socialist art at their disposal, whereas Lukacs had and scorned it. Lukacs was challenged to come out into the open and say Soviet art was bad, instead of hiding behind the officially tolerated doctrine of "uneven development," which conceded that a society more advanced economically need not have, right away, a superior art, philosophy, or literature. The Stalinists at that time ruled that the superior economy must be superior in art and science. A saying of Lukacs's on that subject circulated in Budapest and was held against him: "Marxism-Leninism is the Himalaya among ideologies but a rabbit that lives in the mountains is not bigger than an elephant that lives in the plains."

Lukacs later said he could not state his real views on the nullity of Soviet art because for the literary critic opposition was physically impossible. That was no doubt true, but it was even more true for the artists themselves. So Lukacs was in an untenable situation. As a Stalinist propagandist he was defending, without being too particular in his choice of weapons, a regime that had made him a high priest of aesthetics although he had no freedom to express the opinion that this society had produced no art and left its artists no liberty. His open statements on the vacuity of Soviet culture,[14] when at last they came (after 1956), were devastating. One remembers that Lukacs had begun his career as a communist official a generation earlier with the motto, "Politics is simply the means; the end is culture." From 1956 on he repeatedly said things like

"We still do not have a Marxist psychology, ethics, aesthetics or logic"; "today there still exists no Marxist pedagogy, psychology or ethics"; "philosophy, economics and historiography have been stagnant for decades." Though problems of culture could decide the capitalist-communist rivalry in the age of leisure, communism has nothing to propose, no socialist way out for men left spiritually hungry by capitalism, and there is no socialist model for a better culture. The central problem of socialist ideology he now saw to consist in a *Bewältigung der Vergangenheit*, in explaining how Stalinism was possible.[15] As for socialist realism, all examples of it to date were dismissed as party propaganda, didactic naturalism, "literature as illustration," and trite revolutionary romanticism.

Lukacs had taken a long time to discover and longer still to admit what Gramsci foresaw: that the working people of their day lacked cultivation, almost by definition, and so their spontaneous culture would be crude, simple-minded, and tasteless. For after all what was Soviet art but what pleased the traditional conservatism of the Russian masses? What was it but the uneducated taste of the most ignorant and oppressed people in Europe—a taste that came to be consecrated by an outdated aesthetics, a century behind the times, and then was officially proclaimed doctrine of state and its respect enforced by the police? Thus, the prudishness, narrow-mindedness, and neurotic reaction to any new form of expression which had distinguished Victorian philistines came to be passed off as revolutionary thought. Lukacs's own conservative aesthetics has lent theoretical support to these attitudes. But whenever it came to actual works of art he has always preferred classic culture to works produced according to his politico-aesthetic recipes. For this he was periodically denounced (for example, in 1960 in very violent terms) as bourgeois, aristocratic, elitist, idealist, anti-proletarian, and counter-revolutionary.

This is plainly an unsatisfactory outcome for a revolution entered upon for culture's sake. Yet it did nothing to reconcile Lukacs to Western culture. The Stalinist attacks on his preoccupation with bourgeois writers might suggest this, but in fact Lukacs dates the decadence of Western culture from the successors of Balzac, Stendhal, Dickens and Tolstoy. With partial exceptions like Thomas Mann, he saw everything that has happened in Western art since 1848 as pathological symptoms of imperialism, Hitlerism, and American preparations for atomic war. Lukacs rejected, with what Fernandez-Santos has called "heroic incomprehension,"[16] everything modern, experimental, formalist, and surrealist in Western art. He vilified Kafka, Joyce and Schönberg in terms close to those used, regarding those same artists, by the Stalinists and Nazis. Typical is his pronouncement on Kafka: "no work of art based on *Angst* [anxiety] can avoid, objectively speaking, guilt by association with Hitlerism and the preparations for atomic war."[17] The rest of Western culture is "op art, pop art and mini-skirts," i.e., fads, foibles and fashions.

Lukacs's aesthetics deserves separate treatment and is mentioned here only to make one point. Since he saw the product of fifty years of communist art as a desert and since he rejected almost all modern Western art as a wasteland of imperialist decadence, this professor of aesthetics was still, at the end, waiting for the cultural revolution.

This brings us to the last chapter: the old man disappointed with the working class as a *machine de guerre* against capitalist culture and casting about for a new vehicle for the inevitable cultural revolution. In some communist intellectuals this leads to attachment to the Chinese communist cause; not so with Lukacs.

At the end of his long life, Lukacs thought that a new capitalist era had begun and that socialism consequently was going through a second childhood. It is back again where it was at the start of the nineteenth century, unarmed with any sound theory. This means that Marxism-Leninism is irrelevant to our present situation. "We need a new theory." Such a theory will be a protest against capitalist exploitation and oppression, which today are not what Marx knew but assume the form of manipulation of leisure time. The economic groundwork now exists for a free human life such as Marx envisaged in his 1844 manuscripts, and yet we are alienated in the industrial society because capitalism is stunting our cultural growth, limiting it to manipulated free time and to mere consumption. Marxism is helpless and has no solution to offer. The proletariat is not class conscious but democratic, and yet, because it is the mass, it could still provide a combat vehicle to turn on the manipulators, provided a revolutionary theory were brought to it from outside. The mass always needed outsiders to fire its revolutionary discontent; that is even truer now than in Lenin's time. The discontent, the emptiness are there; the challenge is to exploit them. "We need a new Lenin."[18]

We must set out to turn dumb discontent into open rebellion by convincing people they are not happy even when they think they are. To do that we must form a nucleus that will be in the nature of a political party in that it will have a structured organization. But it must not be dominated by East European style party secretaries. Rather than run the risk of a new Stalin or Rakosi it should be managed by a Kennedy-style brains trust. Its task will be to locate the issue that will get the masses moving till they can be brought to see their real interests. We do not yet know what the magic word will be that will cause the popular explosion and we must sift dozens of likely issues till we find it—our Dreyfus case. It need not be a socialist slogan that we find and need not even be directly related to our objectives. After all, Lenin seized the leadership of the Russian masses at the crucial moment with non-socialist slogans like peace, land for the peasants, and independence for the nationalities. Meanwhile, we must resist the temptation of *Praktizismus*, activism, like that of the angry young pro-Chinese ultra-Leftists who dash off to Bolivia or Somalia to fight imperialism. Lukacs had no sympathy with Régis Debray or Daniel Cohn-Bendit, a type he compared to the fascists, because he envisaged a more durable rebellion against the industrial society than the brief outbreaks they could spark off.

Against the "industrial society," not just capitalism. Speaking in Budapest, Lukacs was not free to say that this effort would be directed against communism as much as capitalism. Yet it is clear that his strictures on manipulation and reification apply to the system now ruling there too, which he denied was

Marxist socialism (and which he is said to have called "Stalinism without the camps"). Lukacs's Marxism implies opposition to any sort of rationally organized, specializing social arrangement in which economic, productive considerations dominate. In protest against the manipulation such a system is held to entail, the unrepentant intellectual adventurer still sought to arouse the assorted malcontents of both worlds. This Marcuse-like search for a clientèle for philosophers who hate everything about the modern world is at a considerably lower level than the theory of *History and Class Consciousness*. There, the subject of history—the social force whose ideology was to mold the whole of society—could only be a social class, a concrete universal, a totality, a collective Machiavellian Prince. Today that role is to be assumed by a few old academics and young firebrands plaintively scolding the masses for settling for less than the cultural millennium.

It is in these sands that one of the streams of communism peters out. Yet that does not mean the original source is of no interest. Enduring regimes—and the communist states seem to be of that sort—look back to their founding illusions, to the sources of inspiration long since run dry. Lukacs, *der junge Lukacs*, just because he was too extreme, too logical, too intellectualist in overstating the faith, is assured of a claim on the memory of the communist movement.

5. In the Shadow of Hegel: from Marx to Marcuse

In September 1914, when French and German working men under the commands of Joffre and Moltke were locked in decisive combat along the Marne, Lenin bought several school exercise books and settled down in Bern to annotate Hegel's *Science of Logic.* He found it heavy going. There are numerous complaints in his notes and in the margins about Hegel's obscurity. Still, Lenin found what he wanted, for there are just as many "N.B."'s and "Well said!!!"'s. The proletariat that was to make the revolution had fallen under the sway of social democrat parties and had been led into an imperialist war. Something had gone wrong, and the new way forward was to be found in a fresh reading of Hegel.

In March 1920, Lukacs, just out of a Viennese prison, wrote an essay, "Class Consciousness," containing, as he later said, "a Hegelianism more Hegelian than Hegel." (It was published three years later, along with some earlier essays written in the spirit of Rosa Luxemburg and some later essays in the spirit of Lenin, as *History and Class Consciousness.*) The communist revolution in Hungary in 1919, in which Lukacs had played a role, had failed and Bolshevism's effort to spread westward had been thwarted. Something had gone wrong, and the new course was to come from a re-Hegelizing of communist theory.

In February 1929, Gramsci began scribbling the 2,848 pages of his notebooks in the prison of Turi di Bari. In the third of his thirty-two notebooks he wrote: "It is necessary to effect on the philosophy of Croce the same reduction that [Marx and Engels] practised on the Hegelian philosophy. This is the only historically fruitful way to bring about an adequate renovation of [Marxism]." Gramsci had been condemned under Mussolini's laws of exception, along with other leaders of the Italian

Communist Party, to a long prison term and the whole Italian party had been wiped out by fascism. Something had gone wrong, and the way forward led via a new infusion of Hegelian idealism.

On 30 January 1933, Hitler became Chancellor and a Nazi apologist; Carl Schmitt said, "On this day, one can say, Hegel died." Marcuse, a refugee in Geneva, agreed that Schmitt spoke truer than he knew. Hegel and the labor movement that was his heir were indeed dead—so Hegel must be resurrected by a new reading. Marcuse proceeded to this, in essays published from 1934 in the expatriate *Zeitschrift für Sozialforschung*. The working-class movement in West Europe had come to grief. This could have something to do with the fact that Marx, Lenin, Lukacs and Gramsci had read Hegel incorrectly. If something had gone wrong, a new reading of Hegel would show the way forward.

That the history of Marxist theory in this century can be told as the story of successive re-readings of Hegel is not surprising, because Marxism began in the last century as a reading of Hegel. Indeed, Marx's was only one of a series of readings of Hegel, and one that depended on several made before it, notably on Feuerbach's. That people should go on for 140 years looking in Hegel's books for something that might more realistically be sought elsewhere (e.g., in the study of social movements) is due to two things. First, to the acceptance of Hegel's own claim that in his work all previous human thought culminated in a system that took up, corrected and preserved everything worthwhile men had ever thought on important questions. Now, to have the whole intellectual history of mankind in a capsule, even if it were such a mouthful as Hegel's books, would be a great saving of time and labor. Such a history, if it existed, would contain vital political lessons. Secondly, there is the fact that Hegel's philosophy is exciting but in many respects incomprehensible. What he says is so fantastic that he cannot mean all of it but it does sound portentous. For non-religious readers at least, it is a strange dream that challenges interpretation.

The Western Marxists

Some early attempts at interpretation were to the effect that Hegelianism was really about politics, about the need of a radical liberal revolution in Germany, but that Hegel became obscure and contradictory in trying to hide this, out of cowardice or conformism. The rational was not real but it ought to be and a radical revolution would make it so. These were the opinions of the Berlin *Doktorklub*, including Engels, and they were still alive after Marx's death, in Engels's *Ludwig Feuerbach*.

Feuerbach read Hegel very differently, in a way that is easy for us to understand because we have seen the rise of analysis first in the economic interpretation of history, then in psychoanalysis, later in the sociology of knowledge and in linguistic analysis. That is, we treat many utterances as symbols. When a person says something that we refuse to take at face value, we do not scold him for lying (which is what the *Doktorklub* did to Hegel). We say it *means* something else. It *stands for* an economic interest, or a sexual wish, or a class bias, or a disguised command —depending on which analysis we practise. Feuerbach started all this by saying that Hegel's cloudy philosophy symbolized a psychological condition: mankind's projection of its own virtues into an alien god. Marx saw the brilliance of the method but, adopting a suggestion of Moses Hess, he read off a completely different meaning. Hegelianism was not an allegory of religion but of economics. The adventures of Spirit, its passage via objectification back to itself, were a symbol of man's sufferings in a divided economy and of his eventual return to wholeness by the reappropriation of what was really his own but seemed alien, the economic process.[1]

Having decided this was what Hegel was about, Marx dropped him and spent decades opening up what he considered a new continent he had discovered for science: the study of economic history.

Although his intention and, to some extent, his achievement were scientific, there were traces in his work of the origin of his inspiration in a particular reading of Hegel. Of course, no one would bother going back to that source as long as they took Marxism for science. It was only when things went wrong that some people—those who do not look at social facts to explain disappointments—started to re-mystify Marx, working back to Hegel. Lenin adumbrated this *ricorso*, but Lukacs was the first to show how considerable were the traces of an interpretation of Hegel in Marx's work. Lukacs could demonstrate in 1922, in a clever exercise in re-mystification, that behind the notion of commodity fetishism in *Capital* one could detect not merely the alienation of young Marx but the "objectification" of Hegel's Spirit. Once the earliest writings of Marx had been published a decade later, anyone could do the same and there grew up a whole academic industry of that sort, *die Marx-beschäftigung*.

For the Second International, however, and for contemporaries who took Marxism seriously, none of this mattered yet. They were puzzled by the theological language Marx sometimes used to describe the commodity[2] and they were irritated by his "coquetting with the dialectic."[3] Still, these had clear meanings: mankind had a basic or real or proper set of wants, notably a need for psychological integrity or personal wholeness, which shortly would be satisfied in communism, a system that would put an end to commodity production for profit. The reason one knew it would arrive shortly was that capitalism was digging its own grave by using men as commodities. It was at this point that one could, if one wished, flirt with the dialectic by saying that capitalism's negation of proper, basic human wants was about to be negated. That figure of rhetoric was the only use Marx came to have for the dialectic of contradiction. It was a neat way of putting his main finding, that capitalism would be buried by its victims, the laborers whose pay was just what it cost to produce laborers, but they would maintain all of capitalism's productive achievements in a society that satisfied men's real wants.

As is well known, this did not happen. Most people looked at the social facts to see why not. The revisionists concluded that capitalism must have *other* laws of development, while Sorel drew the conclusion that revolutionary movements must have *other* modes of operation. In their various ways they stayed with Marx, studying the social facts. Lenin, the first of a line, went back to Hegel. He gave as his reason: "You cannot completely understand Marx's *Capital* and in particular its first chapter, without having studied and understood *all* the *Logic* of Hegel. So not one Marxist has understood Marx after a half a century!!"[4] Thanks to a re-reading of Hegel, Lenin will be the first man to understand Marx and to show how to "continue the work of Hegel and Marx."[5] One might deduce from the time he did it, however, that Lenin had other things in mind too. The working class which was, at that moment, marching to fratricidal slaughter on the Marne and which would soon be fed by the hundred thousand into the world's first mass death factory at Verdun surely could not be the "heir of the classical German philosophy," that sum of all humanity's wisdom that culminates in Hegel. It—or leaders acting in its name—had usurped that heritage. The first Marxist reading had produced a suicidal monster. A *new* reading of Hegel would decipher the *lettres de noblesse* of another revolutionary movement.

It was Lenin who said that philosophy was just politics carried on by other means,[6] so one must expect his philosophizing to be cavalier and practicalist and one must look to see what the political problem was that he was trying to carry over into philosophy. In September–December 1914 it was the collapse of the workers' international. As Lenin saw it, the Marxists had converted Marxism into a rigid metaphysics, into a historical astronomy dressed up as what Kautsky called "the science of social development." This scientist veneration for the laws of motion of society had led them into gradualism and a distaste for revolution. Incidentally, it also implied that agrarian Russia was no place for a proletarian expropriation of capitalism. Moreover, the workers' movement had fallen under an inadequate leadership that was politically incompetent because it did not have the sort of party Lenin had invented. The upshot was that the proper wants of the workers, those that could be satisfied only in communism, had been lost and perverted in a lot of false, short-term wants such as capitalism consented to satisfy in order to buy off the "aristocracy" of working men—at the expense of other workers and of their own proper wants.

Lenin opens Hegel's *Science of Logic* in the light of these issues. His method is the opposite of Feuerbach's and Marx's. Instead of analysing the whole dream, interpreting it as a single allegory, he dismisses some dream sequences as silly and accepts others as literally true. He condemns as obscure, mystical and abstruse all that does not suit his own book but endorses enthusiastically misunderstood snippets that do. For example, when he notes Hegel saying "Nature = submersion of the concept in exteriority," Lenin comments *"Ha-ha!"*[7] Marx did not laugh at this; he interpreted it to mean "Commodity = submersion of humanity in reification," i.e., personality is mutilated in the production of marketable goods. Lenin gives this account of his manner of reading:

> I am trying all the time to read Hegel as a materialist: Hegel is materialism stood on its head (according to Engels)—that is, I am mostly eliminating God, the Absolute, the pure idea, etc.[8]

The absurdity of reading a systematic thinker in this way was to be repeated later by those who "read Marx as an idealist," leaving out the bits about the proletariat.

What does Lenin's method yield? First, he copies out Hegel's attacks on evolutionism, writing in the margin *"Leaps!"*, *"Interruptions of continuity"* and then *"N.B."* next to Hegel's remark that gradual transition explains nothing without sudden jumps. Lenin is taking Hegel's criticism of the logic of pre-formation as support for his quarrel with gradualism in politics. Plekhanov had made careful note of these same passages and had not reached that conclusion; but Lenin wants to fracture Kautsky's "science of social development" with revolutionary leaps and surprises, so as to make room for voluntarism, beginning in semi-feudal Russia.

Secondly, Lenin copies out approvingly what Hegel says on the contradiction in things, endorsing such passages as: "All things are contradictory in themselves," "Movement is existing contradiction itself," and "Only in so far as something has contradiction in itself does it move, have impulse or activity." Lenin comments,

> Universal elasticity of notions, elasticity that leads to the identity of contradictories—that's the whole point . . . that's the dialectic.[9]

He overlooks the passages where Hegel speaks of the negation of that negativity, of the surpassing of contradictions. Whereas for Hegel selfcontradictoriness is a sign of the inadequacy of objects, of their inferiority and of their need of recuperation by the Idea, Lenin wants to hypostasize contradictions. Hegel means to surpass contradictions toward the Absolute but Lenin wants to wallow in them.[10]

From this incoherence Soviet philosophers are still trying to elucidate Lenin's "sixteen laws of dialectic"[11] but an anti-philosophical Leninist long ago saw what it really meant: suppleness of political tactics.[12] All Lenin cares for in Hegel's dialectic is "elasticity of notions" such as will allow one to hold contradictory opinions either simultaneously or in quick succession. Under the "mysticism and empty pedantry of Hegel" what Lenin sees is that:

> . . . human concepts too must be refined, worked up, supple, mobile, relative, linked one to the other, united in opposition, so that they can embrace the universe.[13]

Instead of the one big contradiction that interested Marx, when the working class "negates" capitalism, Lenin wants a myriad of daily contradictions in order to warrant a flexible political practice where alliances can change rapidly, where policies can be reversed overnight and where no force is permanently Left or Right but at once that and its contrary.[14] (That sort of dialectic was established on the political scene soon after the 1917 revolution, when the Bolsheviks declared Kemal Pasha a progressive revolutionary and the Western working class anti-revolutionary and reactionary.)

In the Hegelian mythology of the re-appropriation of things by spirit (which Marx saw as the symbol of the return from alienation, of the rehumanizing of the economic process) Lenin sees a pragmatist theory of scientific verification[15]—a curious pedigree to claim for his practicalist bias. Finally, Lenin wholeheartedly takes over Hegel's absolute idealism, the notion that everything is in touch with everything else in one vast moving totality.[16] This is that "total movement" that is to be so useful in Lenin's political writings. It is the overall picture, to which the party has privileged access, and in terms of which other people's political actions can be declared too Left, too Right or even (this has also happened) "too Center." The total movement of history is leading to the reconciliation of real wants and apparent wants, that is, to the point where workers actually demand communism. It passes by the exposure of those who pander to false, short-term wants, the social democrats. The Bolsheviks will float on this great current; everybody else is just drops of water in the river.[17]

Lukacs's new reading of Hegel was less clumsy, if only because he had been at it longer. He began as a Hegelian and, on becoming a revolutionary during the war, he sought, "essentially on Hegelian grounds, to synthesize Hegel and Marx in a philosophy of history."[18] That was because he was dissatisfied with Marx's reading and wanted another that would better advance the only revolution he was interested in, an anti-bourgeois cultural renovation.[19] Lukacs participated in Béla Kun's revolution in that spirit, as a syndicalist disciple of Sorel and Rosa Luxemburg, but its failure began his evolution toward Leninism. He was to reach that doctrine—indeed to surpass it in ruthless cynicism—in 1924.[20] *History and Class Consciousness* is an incident in that political evolution.

Because he wants an anti-industrial cultural restoration rather than an anti-capitalist industrial liberation, Lukacs must re-mystify Marx. Presented by Marx with the economic interpretation of the Hegelian dream, he must reconstruct the dream, clouds and all. Where Marx denounced the fetishism of commodities, Lukacs attacks reification *(Verdinglichung)*, including under that name not only the *"alienation"* of the youthful Marx (still unknown in 1920) but the objectification of Spirit *(Vergegenständlichung)*, that laying out of the Idea in objects that was Hegel's bizarre explanation of objectivity. As

Lukacs admitted later, "an historico-social problem is thereby transformed into an ontological problem." It is not only capitalism that is being attacked but all industrialism, and by implication all objective science, if not objects themselves.[21]

Drawing explicitly on Hegel, Lukacs magnifies Lenin's "total evolution of society," the grand movement of history, into an Absolute, compared to which all mere social particulars are relative, inauthentic, subjective and possibly counter-revolutionary.[22]

Isolated facts are nothing against the "destiny of global society," the social totality. Though this is presented as Leninism, Lukacs is actually anticipating Stalin, as when he says, "Only relationship to the whole destiny of the proletarian revolution makes an idea, a measure etc., right or wrong. Even to know whether an event is a victory or a defeat, one must know the whole 'historico-social development.' " Lukacs is explicit that only a few have such knowledge.

As a good Hegelian, Lukacs naturally throws out Lenin's materialist dialectic of contradictories. Engels, too, is castigated for this illogical talk of "fluid concepts." It was no doubt for this reason that Lukacs's book was pilloried by the Comintern. Wishing to play fast and loose with political rationality, the party needed a philosophical apology of self-contradiction and "fluid concepts." In contrast, for Lukacs the dialectic becomes once again what it was for Hegel, the movement of Spirit through alien matter back to itself—except that now the hero of this adventure, the subject that makes all objects out of itself, is not Spirit but the proletariat. In this neo-Hegelianism, all history comes to self-knowledge in the proletariat, the self-conscious agent of the total process. Lukacs insists that in this affair Marx was more Hegelian than he realized himself.

Though the party thus seems to lose the dialectic pretext for fluid concepts and elastic notions, Lukacs is preparing for it a more magnificent power. Revolutionary disappointment has taught him, what Lenin learned years before, that the prole-tarian God of History does not always know its real interests, its proper wants. The contrast of real wants and false wants is now conceived in a frankly idealist way, as an instance of the two levels of being. On the one hand, there is *essence*: proper wants, which are the goal of the total social process, known to the Communist Party. On the other hand, there are *phenomena*: false wants, the partial satisfactions of everyday life, which are pandered to by Social Democrats. Thus, the class consciousness of the proletariat, which is to be the self-consciousness of the God of History, is not "the actual empirical thoughts" of working men. It is not "the psychological consciousness of individual proletarians nor their general mass mind." There is a great distance between even the most revolutionary workers' level of awareness and genuine class consciousness. The latter is in reality an unconsciousness. It is Objective Mind. It is what the proletariat would want if it properly grasped its historical stituation, if it saw the total process.[23] So the Leninist party must be the mind of this day-dreaming god. The party will be the custodian of its real interests and proper wants, against the false gratifications of social democracy and neo-capitalism, for the party alone knows "all that is really at the base of [the masses'] unconscious actions and confused thoughts and feelings."

The restoration of idealism is complete. There is a sovereign absolute (history) reigning over dependent particulars (men). There are two levels of being: essential, authentic wants in the party and false inauthentic appearances among mere ignorant working men. Condemned by the Comintern, this was nevertheless to be the secret doctrine of the movement for decades to come because it offered to solve, in its dialectical dualism of essence and appearance, the problems that worried intelligent communists: party and masses, direction and spontaneity, Jacobinism and primitivism, theory and instinct, the party line and what the workers wanted. As Merleau-Ponty put it, "The party is thus a mystery of reason, as it were; it is that point in history where the meaning that exists [*le sens qui est*] understands itself, where concept becomes life."[24]

Gramsci turned back to Hegel because of the utter failure of Leninist strategy in Italy,[25] but also because of his anxiety about the rise of Stalinism, the "Byzantine-Bonapartist" bureau-cracy. He agreed that Marx had been too optimistic in thinking that "contradictions" in the economy would spark a revolution, so Lenin was correct to arm the workers with a Bolshevik party. Even then, the revolution in West Europe had been defeated because politics was not enough either. There were moral and ideological restraints preventing the workers from revolting; so the struggle had to be broadened to take in cultural questions such as had engrossed Gramsci (like Lukacs) before he became a Leninist, as well as ethical questions such as Sorel had said were fundamental for socialism. In that way, the revolution became a project for "moral and intellectual reform." This meant that tough-minded materialist jargon about the "real basis" and "mere ideology" had to be discarded. In particular, the distinction between essence and appearance in society was indefensible; it was nothing but political polemic, anyhow.[26]

The reason why world communism had failed was that it had been vulgarized and had become too "materialist," and the fault for that was Lenin's.[27] To overturn the capitalist state, one must first win hegemony in the moral and cultural insti-tutions of civil society. To that end, the movement needed new ideas[28] and they were to come from idealism and first from Hegelianism, that "world-historical movement of philosophical enquiry"[29] of which Marxism was a first reading.[30] To see more in civil society than economic life, to see its independent cultural institutions, was indeed to go back from Marx to Hegel: but there was no reaction here because Vico had shown how *ricorsi*, historical re-runs, could be progressive. This new reading of Hegel would be "at a higher level" and it would reinstate the workers as heirs of classic idealism,[31] an inheri-tance they had forfeited because Leninism had degenerated into that "materialist superstition" that comes naturally to the lower classes.[32]

Unfortunately, Gramsci's Hegel is a Neapolitan. In drawing his revivifying transfusion from the Italian neo-Hegelians, Gramsci contracts an extreme case of subjective idealism. Not only is his "moral and intellectual reform" a translation of Croce's "ethico-political history," but he insists that historical materialism is not materialism at all but absolute histori-cism.[33] That is, because culture is determined by the class situation of its producers at a certain moment in history, it is all relative and transient. Even science's assertions are subject to historical categories because science is related to human needs. Indeed, reality itself is merely the historical subjectivity of a social class.[34] Everything, literally everything, is for Gramsci what the simple-minded materialists had called "mere super-structure"—but he thinks there is no material substructure.

This looks to be the very opposite of Lenin's materialism. But where Gramsci innovates most is in rejecting the essence-phenomena dualism that had supported the dichotomy of real and false wants, and in restoring the autonomy of ideology, ethics, and culture. It is henceforth impossible to say the workers really want what the young Marx said they should want and what Lukacs said they would want if only they knew what the party knew, and that all other wants can be dismissed as false appearances. Wants, which form clusters called moralities, exist in their own right, all on the one level. The first question to ask about them is whose they are: whether they are the demands of isolated Utopians or the morality of a great mass movement.[35] If the latter, they will need coherent exposition by people belonging to the relevant movement, its "organic intellectuals." Above all, they will need political leadership if they hope to prevail, and to become the ruling culture. They will need a Leninist party,[36] one that can no longer dictate "real wants" but can simply exercise the specialized function of "directing spontaneity."[37]

Gramsci, then, is back with the problem of all the commun-ists, the relation between party and masses, between direction and spontaneity; but now it is an empirical question that can be handled all on the one level of being. The problem is how a set of wants makes its way, and specifically what Proudhon called *"la capacité politique des classes ouvrières."* The discussion therefore covers the dangers Sorel pointed out, about the mis-representation of new moralities by intellectuals and their betrayal in bureaucratized parties. In this nexus of problems, Hegelianism has once again been reduced to a turn of phrase:

the "rational" (an ethic) will "become real" (win power in the state) when it has fervid mass backing, an intellectual formulation, and determined political leadership.[38]

Although Gramsci is more liberal than earlier communists in not imputing "proper" wants to workers, he is still a communist. His party is a Machiavellian philosopher that is not content to put in words the dumb language of the workers' native institutions but seeks to educate the masses. In doing so, it risks getting more than "one step ahead" of them and becoming a patronizing elite.[39] Moreover, his relapse into subjective idealism leads him to assign an exaggerated role to intellectuals who then, as he well sees, have to be kept in line by the party.[40] Finally, the morality for which he seeks to secure hegemony is the "national-popular" culture, a solidarist ideology that at the very time Gramsci lay in prison was being put about by fascists and which, more recently, has been embraced by an Italian Communist Party anxious to share power with other political parties.

When a Nazi said that Hegel died the day Hitler came to power, he meant that this event marked the end of German illusions about the "ethical state." In concurring, Marcuse meant that

> it was not with Hegel's death but only now that the fall of the titans of classical German philosophy occurs. At that time [i.e., when Hegel really died] its decisive achievements were saved in the scientific theory of society, in the criticism of political economy [i.e., in Marxism]. Today, the destiny of the workers' movement, in which the heritage of that philosophy had been preserved, is uncertain.[41]

In other words, Hegelianism had been kept alive in Marx's reading as amended by the successive re-readings of communist theorists, all of whom had seen the working class as the demiurge of history and who saved appearances (i.e., explained the proletariat's failures to live up to that role) by reference to the Communist Party.

The triumph of Nazism, coming on top of the workers' other defeats since 1918, showed that Marx had been wrong to interpret "self-movement of the Idea" as "labor movement" and Lenin and Lukacs had been wrong to declare the Communist Party custodian of that essence of history that had so much trouble emerging in historical actuality. As for the sort of absolute historicism that Gramsci had made out of historical materialism (not that Marcuse could have read Gramsci himself) it had become a Nazi weapon—for if truth were relative to history and history consisted of politics, there was no objectivity, just political propaganda.[42] Moreover, as a Berlin Social Democrat, Marcuse must have seen the disaster that came from the dialectic of contradictories in communist hands. The political zig-zags it was meant to excuse had ended in the party's annihilation. It was August Thalheimer, one of the K.P.D. leaders of the 1920s, who had discovered such "dialectical contraries" as man and woman, day and night; suitably enough, he was himself eliminated by one of the Comintern's dialectical about-turns, several years before the whole party succumbed.

Hegelianism in that debased form having foundered, Marcuse proposed another reading. He had already essayed a vitalist-historicist reading of Hegel[43] under the influence of Heidegger, which means, in this respect, under the indirect influence of Lukacs. Now Marcuse recoiled from that line of thought, for the same reason as Lukacs repeatedly disowned *History and Class Consciousness* in the 1930s; because they now saw its fascist possibilities, become explicit in Heidegger. The Hegel that mattered now, after 1933, was the secretly, or at least implicitly, revolutionary Hegel imagined by the Berlin *Doktorklub*, the Hegel whose theory of essence was a program for revolution. This aspect of Hegel, said Marcuse, had been dropped by idealist philosophy[44] but kept alive by Marxism, for which essence signified a program, "the task of a rational organization of society to be achieved through practice that alters its present form." What Marxism had got out of Hegel and what Marcuse wanted to salvage from the wreck of the German Marxist movement was the notion of two levels of social being, real wants and false wants.

Here appearance and essence become members of a real antithesis arising from the particular social structure. . . . The essence of man and of things appears within that structure; what men and things could genuinely be appears in "bad," "perverted" form. At the same time, however, appears the possibility of negating this perversion and of realizing in history that which could be. . . . Materialist theory takes up the concept of essence where philosophy last treated it as a dialectical concept—in Hegel's *Logic*.[45]

Marcuse could hardly be clearer, given his training under Heidegger. He means that what is to be saved from the ruin of German communism is that doctrine to which communists had been forced by the failure of the working class to meet Marx's expectations: the doctrine of real wants as the essential motive force in history, as against the bad, short-term, false interests of everyday life. This is all Marcuse wants to save—not the working class as exemplifying those real wants and not the Communist Party as the custodian of them in times when workers do not exemplify them. True, as long as real wants are exiled from history, it will be all one-dimensional, it will consist of mere facts: "bad positivity," short-range interests of the sort Marcuse later denounced as superfluous consumption. But real wants will not always remain out of history. One day they will break into this ordinary world, despite the fact that no class feels them and no party promotes them. The problem is not, as Hegel thought, timeless but historical in the sense that essence will out, in revolution. One day, somewhere, somehow, Heidegger's "authentic life" (the true wants of Lukacs's absent-minded proletarian god) will burst into history. This is the neo-Hegelianism Marcuse proposed in 1936, and he has not varied from it since.

In 1934 Marcuse held that the workers' movement as the agent of essence (of essential wants) was in jeopardy. In 1936 he outlined the theory of real wants as a force in history and insisted that they must be incarnate in some social subject, but he did not mention the workers or any other group as a likely vehicle. In 1937 he declared that the workers' movement had been suppressed and defeated, yet he maintained that the theory of real wants, which it was supposed to exemplify, was still true. By 1938 he drew the implications of this even more crudely than Lukacs had:[46] the workers could not distinguish "between true and false wants and interests, nor between true and false enjoyment."[47] Consequently, the "gratification of the individual's needs and wants is abstract and incorrect as long as it accepts needs and wants as ultimate data in their present form."[48] There are so many dangerous and false pleasures about that folk think they are free and happy when they are not.[49] False interests, what people think they want, are decried in the name of their true interests in a "happier real state of humanity [against which] the interest of the individual is no longer an ultimate datum."[50]

This is the Lenin-Lukacs justification of the Communist Party, as against social democracy, living on without any party or working class. By 1941[51] Marcuse makes plain that the bearer of real wants is "reason" and that the fundamental, revolutionary principle of Hegelianism is: "What men think true, just, and good should be realized in the effective organization of their individual and social life." Hegel did not say this outright because, as the *Doktorklub* maintained before Feuerbach and Marx interpreted him, he compromised with German conservatism.

This replacement of the proletariat and its party by the proper wants of human reason was facilitated not only by the annihilation of the party by fascism but by some features of the communist theory Marcuse was taking over. The proletariat had been glorified by communists as "the universal class" which, as history-come-to-consciousness, lost all the empirical features of a social stratum (e.g., the characteristic proletarian culture and institutions that Sorel and Gramsci had described) to acquire the blank radiant face of man-as-such. This was already evident in Lukacs, but it became much plainer in Marcuse because in the meantime the manuscripts of the young Marx had been discovered. Indeed, Marcuse was one of the first to give an account of them.[52] Young Marx, before he came in contact with workers' organizations, was an adept of Feuerbach's humanism and man in the abstract. A little later, in *The German Ideology*, Marx specifically abjured all such essence-mongering, but Marcuse can work back to this "anticipated caricature" in humanism and still claim to be Marxist.

K

In fact, he was later to seek to mystify the whole history of the working-class movement as really aiming at the proper interests of "man, as man."[53] By 1941 the ripest product of communist theory—the notion of the hidden real wants of a social class as the motor of history—had been taken back into the mainstream of Hegelian idealism purged of such impurities as the Communist Party and the working class.

By then Marcuse had emigrated to America. The god immanent in man and alienated in men's false, short-sighted wants must suffer a sea-change. There was never a Marxist labor movement in the U.S.A., and scarcely a social democracy, so a doctrine drawn from Lukacs and Lenin would be hard to acclimatize. There was, however, a widespread infatuation with Freudianism. So the real wants of man, that once had masqueraded as Hegel's world-self and later had been incarnated in the working class and cared for by the Communist Party, were resuscitated as Eros.[54] The mixture of psycho-analysis and Hegelianism gave some people the uncomfortable feeling that Marcuse was prescribing Freudian therapy for the Absolute, treating its self-exhibition in objects as a case of sexual frustration.[55] In reality, the notion of proper human wants that had been read into Hegel and that had been elaborated in communist theory was appearing in a new guise.

Not that it was simply being served up *au goût du jour*. The new presentation had theoretical reasons. To invoke Freud helped one escape the paradox Lukacs was forced into when he maintained that class consciousness was really an unconsciousness, since the workers did not know what they should want. In Freudian terms it was easy to argue that proper wants were unconscious, even if Freud himself never said so. Secondly, one could explain why workers (or any other social group fit to incarnate those wants) never revolted. They were restrained not only by the economic motives Lenin had pointed to in his theory of the workers' aristocracy, and not only by the ideological forces Gramsci highlighted in his theory of hegemony, but by psychological factors. They were *repressed* as well as *oppressed*. The fault lay in their very instincts. Anyhow, they were unscrupulously manipulated by the psychological technicians of neo-capitalism so that their real wants were replaced by perverse false wants and substitute satisfactions. Moreover, in Freudian jargon one could explain why such attempts at revolution as did occur (in Soviet Russia, for example) failed: the revolutionaries carried their neurotic mentality into the new society.[56] There is here a blatant confusion of politics and psycho-pathology but it is held to be warranted because present-day society has no great social movements and is composed entirely of individuals, so it is justifiable to psychology.[57] Atomism, the claim that society consists of individuals who contain all their springs of action within themselves (over against a block called Civilization), is indeed one of the shortcomings of much Freudian literature, and Marcuse took it over uncritically.[58]

The metamorphosis of the imaginary working class into Eros led to an uneasy masquerade. I doubt if one can say that Marcuse, who indeed runs back to the Young Hegelians on so many points, was relapsing into their sexual obsessions too.[59] Embarrassed by misunderstanding among young followers, Marcuse protested that he was not preaching pansexualism. To be sure, he cannot find words harsh enough for mere "genital" sexuality. He was simply juggling with high-level entities drawn from Freud's meta-psychology and making an arbitrary choice among Freud's various hypotheses, in order to support a doctrine whose origin and purpose had little to do with psychoanalysis.

For example, he seized on Freud's unsupported (and unsupportable) speculation that repression had an economic origin, i.e., that children were curbed because the family could not afford to indulge their every fancy. Marcuse wants to argue that the family can now afford, on economic grounds, to relax repression. In fact, Freud had other and more plausible accounts of how sexual fantasy came to be bridled and channelled, but Marcuse ignores them. The impossibility of saying in Freudian language what he wants to say is nowhere plainer than when he advances the suggestion for a rationally acceptable measure of sexual repression which will accord with our

The Western Marxists

present economic possibilities and cause no psychological difficulties. As the psycho-analysts point out, you cannot forbid a child to run across a busy street (rationally justified repression) without grazing potentially serious difficulties about what motor-cars symbolize, about normal death wishes, about the effect of any parental prohibition whatsoever, and so forth. Marcuse's Utopia of a happily liberated Eros, with its *petit relent de bergerie*, finds no support in psycho-analysis.[60]

The reason is that Eros is just a reincarnation of the universal class, of the essence of man and the *Gattungswesen*. Its Freudian dress keeps slipping, to reveal such familiar avatars as "the integral satisfaction of total man," "the complete individual," "the metaphysical plenitude of total man," and the "realized concept of man." This resuscitation, from young Marx and Hegel, of the unitary theory of mind involves a serious retrogression from Freud, since Freud destroyed the monolithic notion of personality by showing the fact of conflict between motives. Instead, Marcuse revives the legend that all motives really seek the same thing—"gratification, fulfilment, peace and happiness."[61] This accords well enough with absolute idealism (all particular motives subserve the whole mind, just as all particular individuals must serve the totality of society), but it does not accord with the facts, which indicate that men and motives want different things, to the point of acute conflict.

The ill-fitting Freudian dress was cast off when the proper wants of man came to be described as not erotic but aesthetic and imaginative.[62] Marcuse still held that Utopia would arrive in history the day an exiled set of wants, borne by no class and promoted by no party, supplanted false satisfactions; but now he said that those wants were artistic, if not surrealistic. This entailed going back beyond the young Marx and Hegel to a writer who exercised a great influence over both of them—to Schiller. The epic dramatist was one of the first to complain that the division of labor in the new economy was crippling man's "whole nature." He added that politics would never restore the "lost totality" (he wrote this during the French Revolution) but that art could.[63] Marcuse's reading of Schiller is selective and constitutes no guide to the dramatist's meaning, but it gives Eros and the universal class their new name, Imagination, their new power, Beauty, and their new objective, to create "society as a work of art."[64] Yet there is more than a change of terminology involved because now the exiled wants take on a frankly irrationalist air that is foreign to the communist tradition Marcuse took over. The god that is betrayed by our false needs henceforth is art, the aesthetic imagination, and what it is rebelling against is not social democracy or sexual repression but "the dictates of repressive reason." And, of course, the art in question is not the classic art of Schiller but the post-surrealist anti-art of a hippie avant-garde. So the attack on technology and positive science in Marcuse's earlier works (notably *One-Dimensional Man*) is broadened into a revolt against facts. It is brute facts and mere objects that are an outrage to the imagination, that negating potential that lies imprisoned under them. There is obviously here a relapse to that "horror of objects" that Hegel's idealism was designed to cure, but Colletti is also correct to say that Sartre's *La Nausée* well represents Marcuse's attitude.[65]

By now one has come some distance from Lenin, who initiated this long *ricorso*, and yet the theme has not varied. There is a dispossessed god whose names are legion—Spirit, whole man, Eros, imagination—and who is wandering like a lost soul outside actuality, begging for a social subject that will please, please help it back into history. As its desperation mounts, any social subject will do—the proletariat, the Communist Party, Negroes, hippies, Vietnamese, students, Puerto Ricans, the New Left, artists, radical minorities[66]—anyone, so long as they will lead the god back into the one dimension, the only one that actually exists.

There is good reason to have no sympathy with this plight. The notion of *different* wants, of another set of needs than those at present obtaining satisfaction in society, is a liberating thought, for it suggests other ways to live and it robs established institutions of their supposed necessity. Naturally, such a thought at once raises Gramsci's question as to *whose* it is—whether it is the speculation of a lone Utopian or the moral criticism advanced by a social movement. If the latter, we then have the problem that Gramsci alone among the communist neo-idealists contributed to: the empirical, one-dimensional problem of how moralities make their way. In sharp contrast, the notion of *real* wants is an authoritarian thought for it asserts that there are things that it is illogical, improper, and inhuman not to want although they are not currently demanded by any effective social movement. So these wants need to be dictated or intepreted by suitably qualified people such as Leninists and other elites. Because this is the one doctrine Marcuse salvaged from the collapse of communist theory, he is inevitably tempted by the pedagogic dictatorship, the armed aristocracy that will usher in Utopia, and yet he always incoherently backs away from it.[67] Whether or not he draws consistent political conclusions, Marcuse's aristocratism is the leading feature of his criticism of democracy, of industrialism, and of the mass distribution of cultural works.[68] Thus he is at one with Right-wing critics of contemporary Western culture such as Ortega y Gasset,[69] except that in Marcuse familiar Rightist views are presented as Leftist, ultra-Leftist indeed, because they arose in a re-mystification of Marx, in a restoration of his "anticipated caricature" in Hegel.

The shadow of Hegel has not yet been exorcized.

6. Ideologists of the New Left

The New Left has been said to have not so much a political theory as "a political aesthetic" (the aesthetic of pop art and happenings, according to Norman Mailer) and to be interested in political figures *"above all* [for] *their aesthetic quality, their style* [and their] *new sensibility"* (Alasdair MacIntyre). Indeed, conservatives who have expected the New Left to spell out a traditional political ideology have found it, instead, to be "formless, *insaisissable"* (Charles de Gaulle) or "faceless, mindless" (Raymond Aron). Yet the New Left does have an ideology, and a fairly coherent one, even when it claims not to. After all, the slogan "No Theory!" has to be justified, explained and illustrated, i.e., set out as a theory; and the New Left does not always disdain theory, though it does often disdain disagreement and discussion. What its theory is will emerge by grouping typical utterances on logically connected subjects by its heroes.[1]

And that is the first point to note, that the New Left has heroes. The word is used without irony, for the men and the one woman it has chosen to adulate have shown notable physical courage and force of character (Rosa Luxemburg, Fidel Castro, Ché Guevara, Frantz Fanon, Régis Debray, Rudi Dutschke, Daniel Cohn-Bendit, Malcolm X, Huey Newton, Stokeley Carmichael) or at least more civic courage than is common amongst academics (Herbert Marcuse, Noam Chomsky, C. Wright Mills, Wilhelm Reich). Moreover, when the New Left draws ideals from men who have not shown courage, who have bowed to the authority of the Old Left parties, it forgets to acknowledge the debt (George Lukacs, Jean-Paul Sartre).

This admiration for heroism, for dash and daring and even for thoughtless defiance of anything "established" is connected with a theory: namely, that effective political action is always and everywhere possible, given enough courage, and any political theory that denies this is a cover for cowardice. In particular, it is charged, the Old Left, whether communist or socialist, has been made cowardly by its elaborate social theory. The taunt of cowardice will seem unjust when levelled at the survivors of the opposition to Hitler and Stalin, but from the immense suffering of the last generation the New Left draws the conclusion that sufficiently courageous action would have avoided it all (as do today's young Jewish activists who profess to despise six million docile martyrs). But it is not interested in such ancient history so much as in the activity of Leftist parties today.

Here it is plain (e.g., when one sees riot police deal with a communist-led workers' procession and then with a students' "demo") what is meant. Marxist theory, in whatever acceptation, bred in the Old Left a respect for the solidity of the social fabric, a feeling for timing and "ripeness" in political action and an awareness of responsibilities toward others (whether toward workers' families or toward Soviet Russia) that all seem to the New Left to be so many pretexts for inaction or compromise. Get rid of that theoretical burden and effective action becomes possible anywhere, any time. For example:

C. Wright Mills: We no longer need to accept historical fate. . . . These systems can be changed. Fate can be transcended.

Cohn-Bendit: Now put on your coat and make for the nearest cinema. Look at their deadly love-making on the screen. Isn't it better in real life? Make up your mind to learn to love. Then during the interval, when the first adverts come on, pick up your tomatoes, or if you prefer your eggs, and chuck them. Then get out in the street and peel off all the latest government proclamations. . . . Then act. Act with others not for them. Make the revolution here and now. It is your own.

Debray: Politico-military organization cannot be deferred. You cannot leave it to the development of the struggle to set it up . . . or else you will have to wait 2,000 years to begin the Revolution . . . insurrectional work is today the No. 1 political task . . .

Guevara: One need not always wait for the existence of all conditions favoring revolution; the insurrectionary nucleus can create them.

Castro: The duty of revolutionaries does not consist in waiting for the change in the correlation of forces. . . . Above all, it consists in creating revolutions.

Marcuse: We will begin with a commonplace: today any form of society, any transformation of the technical or natural milieu is a real possibility that has its place, its *topos*, in history. Today we can make the world hell . . . we can also transform it in the opposite direction. [This is] the end of utopia, that is, . . . of theories that in the past have cried "utopia" to rule out certain historical-social possibilities . . .
We cannot wait and we shall not wait. . . . I literally couldn't stand it any longer if nothing should change. Even I am suffocating.

Against Old Leftists who object that some thought must be taken before thus leaping into action (such disputes are known as "the praxis axis versus the action faction"), it is argued that ideology enough will be thrown up during the fighting itself. "They think that the ivory-towered men of ideas have cheated them, lied to them, and that action and spontaneous experience will show them the truth." Norman Mailer describes this mood: "You created the revolution first and learned from it, learned of what your revolution might consist and where it might go out of the intimate truth of the way it presented itself to your experience." Mailer mocks this as "the revolution as happening," but the heroes of the New Left are serious about it.

Guevara: Actual combat forges the ideologist as well as a fighter. A man may join the guerrilla group totally ignorant of ideology. His social conscience as a revolutionary must develop hand in hand with his military skill.

Debray: . . . The revolution is an indefinite process that has no stages you can break it down into, a process that cannot start out from a demand for socialism but leads to it inevitably when the revolutionary avant-garde sincerely represents the exploited classes; that seems to be the lesson of the Cuban Revolution. But the Cuban Revolution also teaches that the crux of the problem is not the initial program of the revolution [but] the very practice of the struggle, which you can never determine in advance but only by living it (therefore no endless theoretical discussions about the details of the future agrarian reform, which only serve to divide and delay . . .).

153

This notion that prior discussion is not only unnecessary but positively baneful is characteristic of the New Left heroes.

> Oglesby: S.N.C.C. and S.D.S. [Student Non-Violent Coordinating Committee and Students for a Democratic Society] wanted instead to go south and get their hands and their heads—their lives—into the dangerous, the moral and therefore the authentic. The instinct from the beginning was to discover the streets and there was nothing at all anti-intellectual about this. It embodied rather the refusal to tolerate the further separation of thought from its consequences: books argued with each other and lied and in any case did not make much of a difference; only direct experience was incontrovertible.

> Marcuse: The New Left is characterized by deep mistrust of all ideology, even socialist ideology, because people feel somehow betrayed by it, disappointed by it.

> Debray: I would not for all the world add to the senile liturgy of formulae, invocations and quotations of a socialism that has become a rite.

> Castro: We must end the deliberative vice.

Though thus opposed to theory, the New Left claims to be Marxist. Marcuse, Castro, Guevara, Debray, Dutschke and the West German S.D.S. all explicitly laid claim to the title. Yet, apart from objecting to political thought generally, all of them reject Marxism if it is incarnated by the working class, by communist parties, by Soviet Russia, by social democrat parties or by any other organization, not excluding Maoist China.

The proletariat, for a start, is dismissed as the kept woman of neo-capitalism.

> Wright Mills: To cling so mightily to the "working class" of the advanced capitalist societies as the historical agency or even as the most important agency . . . [is] a labor metaphysic . . . a legacy from Victorian Marxism that is now quite unrealistic.

> Marcuse: The New Left, moreover, again with the exception of small groups, is in no way fixed on the working class as the revolutionary class.

> Debray: The mountains make proletarians of bourgeois and peasants; the city can make bourgeois even of proletarians.

Lenin's description of the "workers' aristocracy" has been applied by the New Left to the whole proletariat. The populist faith once placed in workers is now transferred to peasants and slum-dwellers. The working class being jettisoned, "its" party gets short shrift: communist parties are assailed as ferociously as by the Right. For example, Guevara and Debray accused Latin American communists of hypocrisy, impotence and treason; they accused them of collaborating with local dictatorships, as when the Bolivian C.P. sided with Barrientos during Guevara's campaign. Fanon charged that communists were disloyal and conservative whenever involved in colonial struggles. The S.D.S. in West Germany has (until fairly recently, in its so-called "Spartakus" phase) been violently anti-K.P.D. and one of its factions put the K.P.D. "to the right of the Christian Democrat Union." Cohn-Bendit summed up New Left thought on the issue in his famous apostrophe, *"les crapules staliniennes!"*

Nor does Soviet Russia get greater consideration. Indeed, it is blamed for the degeneration of the communist parties.

> Oglesby: The U.S.S.R.'s self-containment, expressed finally as the doctrine of coexistence, could hardly have been a more explicit directive to revolutionaries *also* to coexist. A hard-fisted irony had closed: revolution needs the security of the U.S.S.R., but the security of the U.S.S.R. outlaws revolution. . . . Russia-firstism had been made insupportable by Hungary and then unintelligible by the Sino-Soviet split, well before Czechoslovakia was to make it grotesque.

Though Castro, for obvious reasons, has mostly but not consistently avoided criticism of Russia, Guevara, who met stiff Soviet opposition to his economic policies in Cuba, was to denounce Russian policy before Third World leaders assembled in Algiers in 1965.

One thing the New Left has taken over from communists is vilification of social democrats, whether British Labour, German Social Democracy or insecure experiments in Left-liberalism in Chile or Venezuela. In part, this rejection by supposed Marxists of any and every historical form of Marxism is due to mistrust of all parties, if not of all social institutions.

> Guevara: Notwithstanding the lack of institutions . . . the masses now make history as a conscious aggregate of individuals who struggle for the same cause.

Debray: The presence of an avant-garde party is not an absolute pre-requisite to starting armed struggle.

Neue Rote Turm: All traditional parties are bankrupt.

Cohn-Bendit: All revolutionary activity is collective and hence involves a degree of organization. What we challenge is . . . the need for a party. . . . If a revolutionary movement is to succeed, no form of organization whatever must be allowed to dam its spontaneous flow.

Marcuse: The aim is not to seize central power—to occupy the Pentagon —but to bring about some kind of diffuse and dispersed disintegration of the system, in which interest, emphasis and activity is shifted to local and regional areas. Such action must not be party-political, for all is corrupt in that universe . . .

  I simply said, relying on my own experience, that I expected nothing to come of a radical transformation of the big parties and my pessimism on that score is exactly forty years old.

Though couched in general terms, the anathema is directed at the Old Left parties. The New Left, says Marcuse, "is the nightmare of the Old Marxists," i.e., it is an internal affair of the Left. The Old Left complains of this by saying that the New Left does not study the Right or society generally, devoting all its time to abuse of earlier Leftists. That is why it has no social theory of its own, no new economic theory, and no political analysis.

  Indeed it is true that the New Left is content with the sketchiest sociology. Even its leading theorist, Marcuse, is notoriously vague about facts and cases. His authority on social affairs seems to be Vance Packard, the causes he espouses resemble those of Ralph Nader and yet he builds on this slender base a towering structure of prophecy. Debray and Fanon too have been criticized at length by the Old Left for neglect of political analysis. As for economic theory, seemingly the New Left accepts without examination the theories of John Kenneth Galbraith, notably that the "new industrial state" can avoid slumps, has bought off discontent with consumer goods, only awakens demands it can satisfy, etc.

  Neglect of all social, economic and political analysis is a scandal in the eyes of the Old Left, which it ascribes to indolence, immaturity or to the misconception, common to Max Stirner and the existentialists, that instant political agitation can be used as a sort of group-therapy for the cure of personal psychological difficulties. In reality, the New Left has a theory to justify its scorn of analysis. It holds that the only practical *and theoretical* attitude to take toward our society is total rejection. You must *not* analyse it, take it bit by bit, because that is already reactionary.

> Marcuse: This opposition . . . is sexual, moral, intellectual and political rebellion in one. In this sense, it is total, directed against the system as a whole; it is disgust with the "society of abundance," the vital need to break the rules of a crooked bloody game—to have no further part of it.

> Dutschke: Every radical opposition to this system must necessarily assume a global dimension today . . . we are not bound together by an abstract theory of history but by an existential disgust.

The claim that scientific analysis of society, or any separate social science, constitute in themselves philosophic error and political surrender has seemed wild to the Old Left. Yet it is deduced from the most subtle and ultra-philosophical variety of Marxism, namely, the application of absolute idealism to Marxism by Georg Lukacs in *Geschichte und Klassenbewusstsein*. This doctrine was taken up by Marcuse in the 1930s and later popularized among the New Left in his attacks on positivism and empiricism.[2]

Lukacs had argued that society was a concrete, dialectic totality that had to be taken, and could only be changed, as a unit. To isolate facts or to set up separate sciences (economics, law, or demography) would be to fall into a bourgeois trap because it would lead to admitting that there were some things in society you could not change, things that had their own laws. You must avoid just such "fetishism," such "reification of human relations" if you meant to understand or to change society. You must keep your eye always on the big picture, the total dialectic system, which you could then aspire to revolutionize at one fell swoop. This notion founded the "critical theory of society," a philosophical school of sociology. It was adopted by Marcuse in the essays later resurrected under the title *Negations* and it re-appears in his condemnations, e.g., in

One-Dimensional Man, of all partial, empirical, positive social studies, which simply distract attention from the whole and thereby encourage timidity and surrender.

It is the same theory that Marcuse uses to condemn tolerance and to justify violence in his influential essay "Repressive Tolerance": "According to a dialectical proposition, it is the whole which determines the truth . . . in the sense that its structure and function determine every particular condition and relation. Thus within a repressive society, even progressive movements threaten to turn into their opposite to the degree to which they accept the rules of the game."

Fanon used the same theory to argue that nothing could get Algerian patients to be specific at medical consultations, nothing would persuade Arab families to listen to the radio nor Arab women to abandon the veil—until immense revolutionary violence came to change all those little facts, and many others besides, in one total transformation.

It is because it accepts this theoretical view that the New Left holds that the only way to deal with a system is systematically, the only way to study it is dialectically, and the only thing to do with it is to reject it utterly in favor of the totally new.

Carmichael: I'm a political activist and I don't deal with the individual. I think it's a cop out when people talk about the individual. . . . I want to talk about the system.

Dutschke: Using all the means at its disposal, the existing system strives to prevent us from introducing those conditions in which men can live creative lives without war, hunger and repressive work . . . the globalization of the revolutionary forces is the most important task of those who are working for the emancipation of the human race.

Fanon: The struggle is, from the start, total, absolute. . . . [There is] refusal of gradual solutions, a scorn for "stages" that interrupt the revolutionary torrent and rob the people of their unshakeable will to take everything into their hands right away so that everything can be changed.

Since it is a totality the New Left wishes to deal with, its ambitions are total, nothing less than what Guevara called *"the sacred cause of the salvation of humanity."*

André Gorz: This dictatorship [of capitalism] is economic, political, cultural and psychological at the same time: it is total. That is why it is right to fight it as a whole, on all levels, in the name of an overall alternative. A battle which is not from the beginning waged on the cultural, "ideological" and theoretical fields as well as on the main battleground would be vain. . . . The cultural battle [is] for a new conception of man, of life, education, work and civilization.

Dutschke: Those of us who have understood what there is in this world . . . have had a stunning revelation: a totally new world is being hidden from us, refused us. That is why the individual must take up a stance of total opposition, not as representative of a class, but as representative of the species, against a system that threatens to annihilate the species. He must carry on total opposition for the salvation of the human race and for its emancipation. That salvation is possible today.

Fanon: The revolution in depth, the real one . . . changes man and renews society . . . creates and orders a new humanity.

Marcuse: A new, fundamental experience of being will totally modify human existence.

Since one is dealing with social wholes and since one's purpose is to provoke a sudden mutation from one of Spengler's "cultures" to another such "culture" within which everything will have a new meaning, it is obviously idle and certainly distracting to bother with detailed political analysis. The whole society hangs together dialectically so you do not need to seek the one best point at which to apply your force. Action on it anywhere is action everywhere.

May Day Manifesto: In fighting anywhere we are fighting everywhere.

Dutschke: Vietnam is coming closer. In Greece the first units of the revolutionary liberation front are starting to fight. In Spain the conflict is coming to a head. After thirty years of fascist dictatorship a new revolutionary force exists among the workers and students organized in a united front. The secondary school pupils in Bremen have shown how in the politicalization of immediate demands of day-to-day life—the fight against a fare rise—subversive explosive power can be developed.

It will seem strange to put high school children's protests against increased bus fares on the same plane as the war in Vietnam. Yet Lukacs, the author of this theory, spent time when he was a minister in Béla Kun's beleaguered regime in Budapest drafting instructions on fairy tales to be taught in kindergarten. Since Hungarian society was a dialectical totality, *that* was fighting too. The same doctrine produces among New Left activists the conviction they are participating in one vast universal combat.

> Castro: For the Cuban revolutionaries, the battlefield is the whole world.

> Guevara: There are no frontiers in this struggle to the death. We cannot remain indifferent to what occurs in any part of the world.

> Dutshcke: The under-privileged of the whole world constitute the historical mass base of liberation movements.

> Malcolm X: It's impossible for you and me to know where we stand until we look around this entire earth. Not just look around in Harlem or New York or Mississippi or America. . . . You can't understand what is going on in Mississippi if you don't understand what is going on in the Congo.

Revolutionary ecumenicity had unexpected consequences that disturbed its prophets. Students sought to install "socialism on one campus" by using the guerrilla tactics of Guevara and Debray; U.S. blacks like Carmichael invoked Fanon as "patron saint." As a black leader said during the 1967 Chicago riots, "Every brother on the rooftops can quote Fanon." Seeing the absurdity of applying the same tactics in every part of the supposedly single struggle, Guevara, Debray, and Fanon all expressed doubts about the use of their authority in Western cities, slums, and universities. Fanon explained that his universalist utterances expressed Pan-Africanism and could not even be extended to the whole Third World. Debray said his theories were for Latin America, not for Asia or Africa, while their reckless extension to the West could lead to romantic pantomime. Guevara, too, was concerned with Latin America, and his failure in the Congo presumably convinced him his doctrines could not find ready application elsewhere. Still, he was reluctant to part with the vision of one vast global battle:

> May a true proletarian internationalism develop . . . let the flag under which we fight be the sacred cause of the salvation of humanity, so that to die beneath the banner of Vietnam, or Venezuela, of Guinea, of

Guatemala, of Colombia, of Laos, of Bolivia, of Brazil . . . would be equally glorious and desirable for an American, an Asian, an African and even a European.

Although Guevara's list of banners under which to die omits the pennant of Columbia University and the coat of arms of the city of Paris, this incantation has been widely influential. An all-embracing internationalism has been one of the most visible consequences of the totalist doctrines of Lukacs and Marcuse.

The totalist doctrine has had another and less engaging consequence, a penchant for what looks like undiscriminating violence, not only in the eyes of the authorities but of other Leftists who excuse occasional resort to force. If the political organization, the society, on which one hopes to act is a dialectic totality, if it is all of a piece and so closely knit that (as Marcuse explains) it is compromising even to protest peaceably within it, then the only possible attitude to it is the Great Refusal. And the only way to bring into existence another, totally different totality is to provoke a mutation by the external application of ruinous force.

Guevara and Debray insisted that this force must be external, that it have no political connection with the society to be transformed, and thus it can be administered by foreigners who do not even speak the local language (as Guevara could not speak to the Bolivian Indians) and do not know the local geography (Guevara's band spent much of its time getting lost).

The first rule, said Guevara, for the revolutionary is mistrust. He must be wary of the peasantry, while of course he must have no truck with corrupt urban folk like workers or Leftist politicians. Thus he is, at first at least, an apolitical, asocial force as different as could be from the Maoist revolutionary who moves among the masses "like a fish in water." The reason is, as Debray and Marcuse explained, that the society to be overturned is a unity and it will corrupt opposing forces and "turn them into their opposite," e.g., turn protest into approval. Only violence can create a zone of instant conversion to a new culture, and that zone then spreads rapidly.

161

L

Guevara: The peasant base is not developing yet; still, it seems that by planned terrorism we shall secure the neutrality of the mass; their support will come afterwards. . . . The Army announces the arrest of all the peasants who collaborated with us in the Masicuri region: now comes a stage when terror over the peasantry will be exercised from both sides, though in different ways; our triumph will signify the qualitative change necessary for the leap toward development.

Debray: So it is useless to create anti-bodies inside existing political organizations; the opportunist infection, far from abating, will be aggravated and exacerbated. It is proven today that certain political and ideological debates, certain public disputes, have just retarded the decisive engagement of the masses. . . . A successful ambush, a torturer shot down, a load of weapons captured, these are henceforth the best answers to velleities of reformism. . .

Fanon: Violence alone, violence committed by the people, violence organized and educated by the people's leaders, makes it possible for the masses to understand social truths and gives the key to them. . . . At the level of individuals, violence is a cleansing force.

Marcuse: The minority must go beyond discussion and writing, to local and regional direct action, riots, ghetto rebellions and so on.

Malcolm X: You've got to take something in your hand and say, "Look it's you or me." And I guarantee he'll give you freedom then. He'll say, "This man is ready for it." I said something in your hand. . . . I don't mean bananas.

A group that sees itself as external to the society it proposes to transform is an elite. Elitism is characteristic of the New Left even when its language is populist and "neo-primitivist."

Appeal from the Sorbonne: We alone can refuse [this society] because we are privileged in not yet being fully integrated into this infernal cycle of consumption. No one will help us because no one can. . . . Progress will be what we want it to be. . . . Our [revolution] will be social and cultural so that man can become himself.

Debray: Strategically, they [the revolutionaries] gambled their all to win all; they deserved to get all, in the end. . . . [The revolutionary group] is the "little motor" that starts up the "big motor" of the masses. . . . This little group, if it wishes to survive, cannot stay still, alone. It gambles everything it has. *Patria o Muerte*. Either it dies, physically dies, or it conquers, saves the nation and its own skin.

In addition to the ideology that emerges by combining the views so far illustrated, one finds more or less prevalently on

the New Left certain emotional attitudes or styles that are left
to individual taste. Political ideologies generally have these
aurae. Opponents will try to argue that the aura is specially
significant or revealing, as when British Conservatives are held
to have a taste for blood sports, whereas Labour militants are
suspected of vegetarianism. In its turn, the New Left is accused
of (and some of its heroes indeed exhibit) coprophilia, primitivism, bucolic romanticism, peasant populism, anti-urbanism,
Bakunist destructiveness and, finally, nympholepsy.

Lewis Feuer[3] is a typical hostile critic in taking such things
to be general and important, though of course he also notices
many of the elements of the New Left ideology I have set out
above. Now, Guevara showed a cheerful acceptance of filth
and discomfort, which occasionally seemed a positive preference
for them and it is possible that this endeared him to some. The
iconolatry now practised on the photograph of his bearded,
unwashed corpse (although a doctor, he boasted of going over
six months without a bath) may, for some, be connected with
the widespread reaction against cleanliness. And certain New
Left extremists seem to glorify the "sub-proletariat" exactly
for what is ignorant, maimed, and pathological in its miserable
condition rather than for what shows through its disabilities
as human or promising.

Detestation of cities and urban culture, and the prejudice
that peasants have retained virtues apt to found a new civilization, are attitudes (very far removed from Marxism and the
social tradition) that one finds adopted by several heroes of the
New Left. They revive, apparently without knowing it,
Bakunin's credo: "I believe exclusively in the peasant community and in the educated community of irreconcilable
youths." It was Guevara's faith that, under the leadership of
educated folk like himself, "the armed peasants will conquer
the countryside until the cities tumble like rotten bananas into
their laps." In practice, he found that in the Congo his peasant
allies were "butchers and cannibals" and he came to despise
the Bolivian peasants as *animalitos* (little animals). In the last
pages of his diary one sees desperate anxiety to get back into
contact with urban Leftists. Debray believes the city corrupts

and softens whereas the bush can even make a man and a revolutionary of an intellectual.

Dr Marcuse has toyed with this bucolic romance, though, to be sure, the implied scene of his erotic idyll is a well-kept park rather than the jungle. It was Fanon who was most explicit about the moral and revolutionary superiority of wretched peasants who have been fortunate enough not to live in the cities built by imperialists in their colonies and who have preserved autochthonous culture and primitive virtue in the bush.

Bakuninist destructiveness is not in fact common among the New Left, though Guevara, Debray and Fanon are enthusiastic about the morally bracing side-effects of violent destruction. What really interests them, however, is the new culture that will replace the one destroyed. Admittedly, when revolutionaries are vague about what that culture will be like, when they condemn any effort to prepare it beforehand, and when they insist that anything at all would be better than what exists, then Bakuninist nihilism is not far away.

The nympholeptic metaphysics of Marcuse tends in that direction, as when he says, "The true positive is the society of the future and therefore beyond definition and determination, while the existing positive is that which must be surmounted." In the 1930s he put this in the assertion that essence, the real truth, is negatively inside the "merely" existing, and it will out, come true, by destroying what is. In the meantime, "What is, cannot be true."

I mention this Young Hegelian tenet here among the emotional attitudes of the New Left rather than among its theories because it cannot be stated coherently enough even to serve as ideology. And it mainly shows up as a restless striving for the ideal and unattainable, as the conviction that everything worthwhile is *elsewhere*, that is, as violent Quixoticism. Guevara's last letter to his parents began: "Once again I feel Rosinante's bony ribs between my legs." Marcuse has never dismounted from that metaphysical nag.

Although the New Left has no detailed utopia, its heroes throw out many hints on the better society. They can be summed up in the slogan: No Mediation! For example, the cumbersome representative mechanisms of modern polities, democratic or not, are rejected for the vision of a society where interests have direct access to what concerns them, without intermediaries. This faith in spontaneous organization has revived the anarcho-syndicalist ideas of workers' soviets. Hence a new veneration for Rosa Luxemburg and, in another variation, the sudden re-appearance of the Industrial Workers of the World (the "Wobblies") on mid-west U.S. campuses.

The West German S.D.S. wanted soviets and one splinter group (the Baader-Meinhof band which went underground in 1970–72) organized itself as the "Red Army Faction"; Marcuse speaks of concentrating political activity "on local councils of manual and intellectual workers' soviets." And even Lukacs was carried back by the New Left ferment to the syndicalist faith of his youth, declaring to *Der Spiegel* some time before his death, "Workers' soviets are inevitable." The related notions of workers' control and participation, slogans of May 1968 in France, also express this refusal of mediation. Therefore they are combated vigorously by the traditional Leftist intermediaries, the parties and unions.

The economic doctrines of the New Left, if they can be honored with that name, express little more than the refusal to use the mediation of money, to travel the round-about paths of heavily capitalized production and in general to adopt any tool or technique that risks being alienated from its transparently instrumental function. Guevara's economics for the "love generation" gave confused expression to this. It was succinctly put in the Sorbonne Appeal: "We reject the consumer society but in part we are wrong. We do wish to consume —but only to consume what we have decided to produce." Of course, if it is the same "we" that consumes and decides to produce, the economy is limited to such unmediated activities as small farming and *khaddar* spinning.

In looking at the influence of the New Left in its first decade one is struck by the small number of its activists and the large number of its occasional sympathizers—and by the youthfulness of both. Its heroes sing paeans in praise of youth and of the unreflecting action and impatience that are held to go with it. Debray notes that only the young could apply his doctrines and Guevara's, for they would tax the very physique of a mature man, however revolutionary his spirit. "It's useless to talk to people over thirty," said Parisian students in 1968, and the Sorbonne Appeal declared, "Let us count only on our youth, our 'immaturity,' our lack of responsibility . . ."

Curiously, Marcuse did not at first notice that his best audience was the youth. He did not include them among the potentially revolutionary as late as 1964. It is only since 1967 that he has praised young men, and achieved world fame—principally for the illiberal views set out in "Repressive Tolerance." It is only odd at first glance that that essay should also have been printed and distributed by the Government of Generalissimo Franco. It is an excellent statement of the philosophy of Spanish integrism. Still, its widest influence has been among the Cids of the American New Left, as Paul Breines shows in an interesting essay.[4]

Debray and Fanon, though writing for Latin America and Africa, also found their audience among the blessed of the earth, American students, and U.S. blacks. Ché Guevara, in contrast, has joined Saviour and Saints in the popular iconography of Latin America. Fidel Castro says it was European intellectuals who invented the Ché myth but that this myth provided the point of convergence for the forces of the Third World, ghetto blacks, and rebellious students.

In so far as that improbable alliance exists, it is at the sentimental, hero-worshipping level and Guevara is indeed its emblem. In California, adulation of Guevara became a debased religion for drug-takers, in which the dirty jungle guerrilla figures as a Satanic Christ, killing savagely for love of the poor and hoping to attain crucifixion thereby. Debray provided a more respectable, highly intellectual statement of Guevara's doctrines in a book that has sold a million copies in a dozen languages, making it one of the best-selling political tracts of the day.

One measures the influence of the New Left by seeing where it stops, and that is at the line drawn by the other Leftist forces.

Taken by surprise on their left during a period of decadence and discouragement, the communists have had telling arguments but ho heroes to set against the New Left. Communist officials have described Marcuse and Cohn-Bendit as "werewolves" and "C.I.A. agents." The French party insisted rather heavily that both were German. The Italian party has been better inspired in seeking to limit the ravages of the New Left by hastening the canonization of Antonio Gramsci, the Marxist saint of the Old Left in the peninsula. Gramsci's beatification had begun with the quest for a "national way to socialism" when Togliatti forced polycentrism on Moscow. Now Gramsci has proven useful not only by being Italian but by providing in advance devastating criticism of the New Left's anti-intellectualism, spontaneist romanticism, and contempt for political parties.

Chinese communism, having a hero and a young ideology of its own, has provided effective opposition to the New Left, from Italy to Latin America. Despite superficial resemblances between their doctrines, both sides have been clear on the blank contradiction as to the main point: rejection of party-political leadership by the New Left. Cohn-Bendit and Debray were explicit that the Maoists for them were no better than the rest of the Old Left.

The social democrats and American radical liberalism have suffered worst from the advance of the New Left, and they have sought to set against it, not heroes, but a characteristically pedestrian ideology. However, critics from the Old Left like MacIntyre[5] and Holz[6] go beyond that when they show up all that is pre-Marxist in the New Left, its running back to the Young Hegelians, its innocent rediscovery of exploded Utopian illusions, and its discarding of all the social and political knowledge acquired by the socialist movement in a century of struggle.

A non-party critique of New Left ideology would concentrate on exposing the ravages of absolute idealism in social thought, on the Left today as on the Right yesterday. It would show that the totality posited by Lukacs, Marcuse and *epigoni* does not exist, that there is no "single systematic web of interconnections by means of which each part of society is dominated in the interests of the total system" (MacIntyre). Once that bogus totality goes, we are again able to draw distinctions (e.g., those Marcuse denies between fascism and liberalism); we secure ground for opposition without compromising ourselves irremediably; and we find more productive things to do than the Great Refusal. We cease to spurn everything short of the absolutely unconditioned (which is what the totality is supposed to be). We accept the necessity to pass via mediations in quest of benefits that are qualified, conditioned, and even delayed.

7. From the Associated Producers to the Flower People

The apparently sudden and certainly widespread resurgence after a period of 120 years of the social doctrines of young Marx (along with those of Fourier and some minor "utopian socialists") is a puzzling phenomenon for which the intellectual and sociological reasons are still being sought. It is relevant to that enquiry to notice that these utopian and proto-socialist doctrines have re-appeared in a peculiarly perverted form. Before 1848 they were associated with a robust faith in science and industry—so that they could be readily incorporated into the ideology of a proletarian socialist movement that boasted it was "scientific" and that went on to found in Russia a new polity obsessed with industrialization and scientific achievement. In their second coming these doctrines are, in contrast, marked by distrust, not to say detestation, of industry and its products, of science and indeed of logic itself. A doctrine once dedicated to the "associated producers" who would master nature with science and with a jointly planned division of labor has been transmuted into the faith of "flower people" who denounce the ravages of industry, the domination of science and the absurdity of any division of labor in a free-form existence.

Admittedly, as both Hegel and Marx noted, ideas that get a re-run usually are grotesquely, even comically, misunderstood the second time around. So one would not expect Pop Marxism, Zen Marxism, Fourierist Marxism, existentialist Marxism, and phenomenological Marxism to be exact reproductions. In their case, however, one can pinpoint the moment at which the scientific-socialist faith in industry changed into a rebellion against "capitalist" science and technology (rather than capitalist property relations). This occurred in Germany under the Weimar Republic, amid a pullulation of irrationalist doctrines that prolonged the "revolt against science" of before World War I and which eventually blossomed into Nazism and irrationalist Marxism. If this is correct, the problem is not to account for the mysterious revival of young Marx's ideas after a long interval but to explain the world-wide acceptance in the 1960s of a variety of Marxism imagined just a few years before by men who are still alive today. In other words, the rising from the dead of young Marx is actually the apotheosis of the Critical Theory of Society, which Max Horkheimer, T. W. Adorno, Herbert Marcuse, Jean-Paul Sartre and others made out of the ideas of Lukacs and Heidegger.

That only defines the intellectual problem more exactly; its sociological explanation is yet to be found. For some, the reception of utopian ideas today is a romantic throwback, *le passé, rien que le passé*.[1] Atavism may be a social phenomenon but it is not an explanation. For others, ideas that were wildly utopian in 1840—and scarcely less so in the Weimar Republic —are today, at last, simple good sense. Abundance is about to overtake us in the West and we face the problem of what to do with our growing leisure, so it is natural that folk should look back to the utopians and young Marx who prophetically foresaw this as the inevitable outcome of industrialism.[2] This suggestion would be more plausible were it not precisely the traditional assertion of utopians for the last two millennia. For utopians and philosophical communists, abundance is always possible *now*—given certain assumptions about voluntary restriction of demand, assumptions that contemporary utopians never fail to make.[3] Nor, since Francis Bacon first based a science-fiction utopia, *The New Atlantis*, on a reference to unspecified marvellous inventions, is the enthusiastic mention of automation and nuclear power a new argument. The claim that these inventions foreshadow plenty still lacks an economic base, so that those who say that the utopian ideas had to wait 120 years before coming true risk having to wait another 120 years before the economists agree with them.[4]

More plausibly, it is suggested that the re-appearance of such notions is due to an analogy of social situation between workers in early industrialism and students or young intellectual workers in our contemporary economies. For that reason, chiliastic faiths that arose in the industrial slums in 1840 will serve, *mutatis mutandis*, for the new oppressed on university campuses. Adopting a theory of J. K. Galbraith's—that intellect is now the scarce economic factor and that therefore "the educational and scientific estate" must assume social leadership[5]—the New Left has felt entitled to take over socialist classics and put scientists and students in the historic place of the proletariat. Right or wrong, those who have done this have been successful (in Marcuse's case, successful beyond his own expectations) in putting their finger on discontents that others had not even suspected or had underestimated. In adopting for the "new working class" of intellect the pathos of utopian socialism, they put forward criticisms and demands that turned out to have considerable backing. In replacing the labor theory of value with an intellect theory of value, they voiced pretensions that took all political parties by surprise. In denouncing prosperity and welfare, they revealed de-stabilizing forces unleashed by the neo-capitalist system itself. Lukacs was willing to take this worker-scientist parallel to the point of suggesting that the start of the latest "late capitalist" era has carried socialism back to its "second childhood," so that outbursts of opposition to technology among the youth are comparable to Luddism—machine-smashing—among workers a century and a half ago.[6]

Jules Monnerot has tried to work out the parallel with some precision.[7] Large numbers of young people admitted to a higher education that was once the door to an upper-class culture find that, by their very numbers, they cannot readily be assimilated and that, besides, the admission tests to which they must submit are out-of-date. Rejected at examinations, or successful but still not admitted to the ruling class they aspired to, they feel they have a right to participate in something that is being denied to them. Thrown together on immense campuses the way landless peasants were in industrial slums, they have the same feeling of being uprooted from a way of life they cannot go back to, and the feeling of being shut out from another for which their family traditions have not prepared them but to which their own exertions entitle them. They have in common with the workers of yesterday their youth, impatience, and ignorance. The traditional Left having at just this time admitted its bankruptcy, their recourse is to the utopianism of the first industrial workers.

> Against the dreary excesses of Bolshevik and post-Bolshevik "realism," the unrealism of the Marx of the 1840s, which Marx himself covered over with the economic researches that followed, had the effect of a breath of fresh air in the 1960s.

Monnerot, in adding that many of the teachers of these students are Marxists, links whatever truth there may be in his sociological theory to my own contention that what was in fact gaining ground was a theory prepared by certain Marxist intellectuals of the generation immediately preceding.

It was this generation that discovered (in Lukacs's case, anticipated) the work of young Marx. The anti-scientific and irrationalist reading they gave of these documents has become so widely accepted that it is almost worthwhile recalling that the first reader of the young Marx was the mature Marx—and *he* was so far from being "anti-scientific" that in working out the ideas of his youth he thought he found a new science fit to rank with chemistry and biology. So I shall seek to state briefly the main points of young Marx's doctrines, making no effort to conceal their utopianism and unreality but underlining also their respect for science and industry. I want to indicate then what the Critical Theory of Society made of this when the texts were first published in the heyday of German irrationalism and what the New Left in turn has deduced from that. Finally, I hope to identify the turning point at which Marxism was forced into alliance with irrationalism.

Rephrasing a distinction as old as the one the Greeks made between *physis* and *nomos*, and which had become familiar since Saint-Simon as the contrast between labor and property, Marx in the earliest drafts of an ambitious work he never wrote set the free activity of men in society over against the frozen, reified forms of social institutions. Since gods and other superhuman influences had no part in social life, there was nothing in society but men's relations one with another; and yet some of those relations—some of the things men made, some of the arrangements they entered into for their mutual convenience—solidified, hardened, and became obstacles to continued free activity. An example would be the state, which arose because men had certain common interests and yet which hardened into something distinct from, and even opposed to, their interests. It came to stand over them and instead of it being "theirs," they became "its." This state of affairs is what Marx called, among other names, alienation: things we do turn into objects that start doing things to us, using us, leading a life of their own. The case that most scandalized Marx was capital which (as the classical economists taught him) was nothing but accumulated labor and yet it set itself up as an autonomous force that used labor, and used it in the 1840s none too tenderly. Man's main activity, work, which should express his whole personality, turned into something objective, separate, indifferent, unfeeling, independent both of workers and of capitalists, legally autonomous, and a juridicial person: capital.

Nietzsche, who held that a commonplace of German thought and one that marked it off from Latin philosophy was the preference for *Becoming* over *Being*, would perhaps say that Marx was here illustrating his point very well. There is in the Paris Manuscripts a sort of outraged protest against the circumstance that the ongoing, the fluid reality of social life, namely productive labor and personal relations, should come to be dominated and cruelly used by things that were just thrown up in the day's work—such things as the inevitable division of our tasks and mutual help, which solidified into a thing called the Market, or such as the social utility of our exertions, which gelled hard into a horror called Money.

Physis, the natural and proper, was self-expression in useful work, whereas *nomos* was the artificial and inhuman institutions that crystallized out from our working relationships. Yet Marx was not being nominalist about institutions like the market, capital, money and the state. They existed quite objectively and the proof was that they hurt. It was their priority over ongoing activities, even their independence of them, that was an absurd reversal of things. The way back to a normal human society led via the liquidation of these objects that dared set themselves up against men's ever-changing creativity. And *that* process was called dialectic. Marx used this sadly over-worked word variously, vaguely, even inconsistently. Sometimes it meant the liquefaction of artificial, man-made obstacles to human activities, the re-absorption of *Being* into *Becoming*, the return from alienation. At other times, truer to Hegel's usage, it meant the whole process in which the living and ongoing (which for Marx was productive labor) expressed itself in certain necessary, objective arrangements (association, division of tasks, machines, factories, rules, planning), and then subverted those arrangements to invent new ones better suited to evolving needs. On this view (and this would be a third usage of the term) the relation at any given moment between an individual and an institution—say, between a worker and a factory or between a citizen and the state—would be a dialectical relation, meaning that the social thing was "predicate" (the attribute or instrument) of the person and yet a necessary one because without it he could not express himself. The person (not this or that man, but what is social in each person) and the institution were, as the logicians say, mutually constitutive: they made each other. It was the person that always had priority over any one institution because he and his fellows could sweep it away and replace it by another.

Marx said this in 1844.[8] He was still saying it thirteen years later.[9] Labor must, like Hegel's Spirit, necessarily objectify itself in solid, perfectly real things and arrangements like machines, work rosters, and factories; but it did *not* have to alienate itself in any one given set of arrangements that claimed to be permanently and absolutely necessary conditions of production, such as the capitalist economy. On the contrary, any dispensation of progressive creativity, any social thing thrown up in the day's work, no matter how "objective," was transient and self-cancelling. Nor did Marx change his mind as he worked out his theory in painstaking, empirical detail in *Das Kapital*. The capitalist market set relative values on commodities, yet all it really had to deal with was "a jelly of labor," bits of human personality split off ("abstracted" is Marx's Hegelism) and bandied about as though they were things.

> We are concerned only with a definite social relation between human beings, which, in their eyes, has here assumed the semblance of a relation between things. To find an analogy [adds Marx, recalling what he had heard decades before from Bruno Bauer and Ludwig Feuerbach] we must enter the nebulous world of religion. In that world the products of the human mind become independent shapes, endowed with lives of their own and able to enter into relations with men and women. The products of the human hand do the same thing in the world of commodities. I speak of this as the *fetishistic character* which attaches to the products of labor, so soon as they are produced in the form of commodities. . . . Such religious reflections of the real world will not disappear until the relations between human beings in their practical everyday life have assumed the aspect of perfectly intelligible and reasonable relations as between man and man and as between man and nature. The life process of society, this meaning the material process of production, will not lose its veil of mystery until it becomes a process carried on by a free association of producers, under their conscious and purposive control.[10]

In his preface to the second edition of *Capital*, written in 1873 almost thirty years after the Paris Manuscripts, Marx repeated that this revolutionary dialectic—the doctrine that objective social dispensations are transitory and self-destroying arrangements always subservient to human need—was a contribution to positive social science. It was an aid to our understanding of our world, as well as a contribution to human productivity, because it undermined stifling restrictions on creativity.

> In its rational form [the dialectic] is a scandal and an abomination to the bourgeoisie and its doctrinaire spokesmen because, while supplying a positive understanding of the existing state of things, it at the same time furnishes an understanding of the negation of that state of things, and enables us to recognize that that state of things will inevitably break up; it is an abomination to them because it regards every historically developed social form as in fluid movement, as transient; because it lets nothing overawe it but is in its very nature critical and revolutionary.[11]

On this presentation, then, Marx's earliest views, although they are quite unrealistic about the *resistances* to change in any society, are continuous with his later views, which were so firmly dedicated to science and industry as to be attacked as

"scientistic" and coarsely "materialist" by many critics. Yet
when those early documents were recovered, they were interpreted in a very different sense by the founders of what I have
called "Western Marxism" and of the "Critical Theory of
Society." Horkheimer and Marcuse in Frankfurt absorbed the
new Marx material into a theory they had already begun to
build on the ideas of Lukacs and Heidegger. That interpretation
was then carried over, in their exile, into their teaching and
writing in Switzerland, France, and the U.S.A. Some of the
extreme developments of their line of thought appeared in
English in New York and London during and immediately after
World War II and then in a series of works by Adorno and
Marcuse since the war. Very similar ideas were brought back
to France by Sartre from his stay in Germany in the 1930s and
published after 1945. Meanwhile, the reconstituted Frankfurt
School resumed the teaching of Critical Theory in the West
German Federal Republic, although now abated by a measure
of American sociological empiricism. When one considers the
volume and dispersion of this material, one is less surprised that
the New Left, after the usual lag of several decades, should
have translated it into doctrines ready for popularization in
many countries.[12]

The Critical Theory of Society generalizes Marx's revolutionary dialectic into the assertion that, since there is nothing
in society but our activity and its ephemeral products, it is all
totally plastic and liable to instant revolution at almost any
moment we wish—if only we would wish. There can be no
natural obstacles or resistances to our overturning all social
relations, because what seem to be so will turn out on closer
examination to be mere reifications, alienations of our own
activity. So they can be liquidated by a different activity.[13] The
dependence of social *things* on productive *activity* to which
Marx drew attention in his dialectic is reformulated in a way
characteristic of German idealism. Activity becomes the totality,
the one general process that is going on in history, and all
social things become its dependent particulars or manifestations. This living, moving totality can be revolutionized, utterly
changed—but only by itself, not by some merely partial

manifestation like, say, the proletarian socialist movement. It is the self-moving subject-object of the German idealists, the all-embracing activity that has no external relations but does have a myriad of internal manifestations. At unfortunate moments of history, like in the Germany of Hitler's day or in contemporary America, this totality can be totally bad and then we must wish for the utter negation of it, a state of affairs we need not specify beyond saying that it would be *wholly other*.[14]

What began in Marx as the critique of political economy (i.e., the demonstration that economic laws, though true, concern only the alienations of our productive labor and are backed by capitalist domination) becomes in Critical Theory the rejection of all the social sciences as mere instances of reification and domination. There is nothing in society that is not man-made and man-dependent;[15] so anything natural (repetitive, law-abiding) discovered there by a social science would be a fair target for the revolutionary dialectic, which would soon re-absorb its usurped *Being* back into the eternal *Becoming* of man's activity. That re-absorption is called de-alienation, meaning the replacement of reified institutions (such as money, the market, or political representation) by consciously controlled instruments. Indeed, on this theory, all social things and arrangements are, or should be, simply our instruments. That is why they can all be revolutionized at one blow. They are, after all, merely extended bits of our personality. They are the ways we objectify or express ourselves. So they all hang together, as do our personalities, forming a system that we can change when we like. The whole point of them is to express our personality totally—not, of course, what is idiosyncratic in each one of us but what is properly human and representative in all of us. The goal of a radical overturning of a system that no longer did this would be the peace, happiness and fulfilment of the properly human part of us, together with a completely conscious control of history which became, once again, transparent to us all.

To this point, one can recognize in Critical Theory a quite uncritical and uncautious extension of views Marx held when

M

young and which he later interpreted restrictively in the direction of realism and positive science. One can, at the same time, recognize many of the characteristic dogmas of the New Left (which we examined in the last chapter), notably of Marcuse at a time when he had become a hero of the students. The rejection of everything established, for it is based on domination; the Gnostic belief that the whole present world is the work of the Devil; the yearning for the wholly Other; the faith in instant revolution; the preference for expression of the whole personality over any specializing occupation; the feeling of shame and personal responsibility at the sight of institutions that should be our instruments doing things we do not approve (making war in Indochina)—all these can claim to find their rationale in Critical Theory and, to the extent it is an idealist development of young Marx, in Marx's revolutionary dialectic. Even Ché Guevara's economic theories (which brought Cuba to the brink of ruin and led to strenuous Soviet objections)— the abolition of money-accounting inside an economy conceived as a single centrally-controlled activity—have their origin here.[16]

Yet on a series of other points there is a sharp contrast between Critical Theory and anything Marx wrote when young, let alone later as a spokesman of the proletarian socialist movement. These concern the status of science and technology. For Horkheimer in 1937 science is an instance of reification. It is reified ideology with no claim to general validity, because it is just another branch of the capitalist division of labor. Scientific statements and concepts are in a class with money or commodities in being artificial and improper solidifications of the fluid, ongoing reality. Technology, echoes Marcuse, is no better, for it, too, is a "vehicle of reification" and an "apparatus for control and domination." Broadening the attack, the Critical Theorists reject all objectivity, in the sense of independence of the observer, because all facts and objects are products that properly belong under human control. To credit them with independent status is to be slavishly conformist, says Horkheimer; and Marcuse adds darkly, "The power of the given facts . . . is an oppressive power." Formal logic, too, belongs with the capitalist division of labor, and it consists of a series of improper solidifications that a dialectic logic will dissolve. Dialectic is "irrationality against dominating reason," for reason too is domination and reification. The concept, the principle of identity, the law of the excluded middle—these are all tools of domination. They are arbitrary, and static things set against the fluid reality.[17]

Now Marx from the start, to say nothing of the various socialist movements that invoked his name, was all for science and technology. Apart from sharing in the respect for science that was almost universal among educated people in the middle third of the last century, Marx saw in science and technique the tools for rational self-expression in work—and he regarded work, productive activity, as the mark of humanity. Marx held it to be one of the frauds of bourgeois society that it made science *seem* capitalist to the workers, when in fact it was a general human achievement. The "associated producers," after they had liquidated capitalist alienation, would *still* be using machines and distributing work rationally.[18] With later socialists these beliefs grew into the veneration of labor and science that is to be found in Soviet ideology. Yet, supposedly from Marx's own work, Critical Theory and the New Left argue to the conclusion that science *is* capitalism and technology is enslavement.[19] Therefore, freedom must lie with the "flower people," or in schizophrenia[20] or in surrealism.[21] Scientific objectivity can be left behind as "a churchy dogma,"[22] as mere ideology.[23]

Such views have, I suggest, a very different origin. They come from a line of thought that also made use, but in a quite distinct sense, of the *physis-nomos* contrast. At the turn of the century there occurred a "revolt against science" that achieved its *succès de scandale* in Henri Bergson's lectures at the Collège de France and scored scarcely less notable triumphs in the Germany of Rickert and Simmel, in Italian futurism and on the fringes of American pragmatism. The general argument was that *physis*, the real, was a ceaseless flux, a fluid *durée* of Becoming, of which genuine knowledge could be had only by feeling and participation. In contrast, *nomos* was the merely practical, arbitrary and abstract cuts made into this continuum by the practice-bent scientific intellect. Intellect, for the purposes of *homo faber*, froze, fixed, and coagulated movement into static concepts.[24] It invented "things" that were nothing but the product of *chose-ification*, as Bergson said, meaning in French much the same as *Verdinglichung*, or reification. This artificial world of hard facts and useful concepts was the domain of the solid, dead, and inert—of the "practico-inert," said Sartre half a century later, with the air of one coining a phrase. It was the sphere of our power over nature, that is, of industry. Bergson insisted that causality "expresses the very mechanism of our industry." Culture and freedom, on the other hand, were to be won in the struggle against automatism and "solidification"—by implication, in the rejection of science and industry.[25]

This implication became explicit, as Colletti has noted,[26] in German theorists like Rickert and Simmel. The denunciation of the reifying concepts of science was taken up into a discussion going forward at that time among German philosophers about *Kultur* (a romantically conceived organic culture) and *Zivilisation* (rationalistic society). The latter, civilization, was identified with industrialism and technology; as, of course, science had been by the Bergsonian vitalists. So science, industrial civilization, big business (just then getting very much bigger), and capitalism could be run together. In the end, behind a pathetic critique of modern capitalist "mass" society could be passed off a vitalist attack on intellect and causality. Colletti notes ironically, "The 'tragedy' of modern society is that it is a public sphere, an *objective* world: the place of *Allgemeingültigkeit*, that is, of that universal and *impersonal* validity that is common both to the assertions of science and to the behaviour and 'rules' of life in society."[27] In short, science is a betrayal of Life, that single organic totality, and it is incarnate in big business and other bourgeois institutions.

As will be recalled, Bergsonism was an extraordinarily popular but quite brief fad. It was only in one country, Germany, that there persisted well into the 1920s a widespread intellectual movement committed to biological metaphysics and irrational pragmatism (i.e., a pragmatism that *condemns* reason because it is "merely" pragmatic, as contrasted with disinterested feeling). That fact is of historical importance, since the Nazis only had to specify that the scientific-bourgeois mentality was "Judeo-Western," over against the organic totality of biology and of race, to have all the "philosophy" they needed to launch their onslaught on the "dirty-Jew" aspects of civilization such as science, rationality, moral codes, and capitalism.

It was in this situation that Georg Lukacs, a former pupil of Rickert, sought to reformulate Marx's social theory in the language of absolute idealism. In doing so, he in turn ran together two lines of thought that no one had previously imagined to be related: (1) the criticism of the fetishism of commodities in *Capital*, which, as we have seen, derives from Marx's youthful account of reification of productive activity in capitalist society; and (2) the denunciation of the reification of fluid reality in scientific concepts and in intellect generally, which derives from irrationalist vitalism. In fairness to Lukacs, it might be recalled that at that time he had not seen the young Marx manuscripts. When he did see them, years later, he at once realized that he had made "a gross error"[28]—the error, namely, of arguing that the culmination of fetishism was scientific objectivity, of seeing the scandal of reification and alienation to consist in the mere existence of a given, natural world alien to subjectivity. It was Lukacs who first generalized Marx's critique of classical political economy into a rejection of all social science on the grounds that the supposed facts of such sciences were fetishes of bourgeois thought that needed "historico-dialectic treatment" to integrate them back into the social totality.[29] Productive activity, which for Marx had a fairly simple and *almost* common-sense meaning, became for Lukacs the totality, "the fundamental category of reality"— i.e., the onward-rolling Whole of History that cannot be analysed by such "weapons of bourgeois ideology" as social science.[30] It was the whole social process (what contemporary idealist Marxists call "Praxis") and it had nothing outside it, so it was the combined subject-object that German idealism had longed to find.[31] Objects of experience could be grasped only as elements of this whole.[32] *Becoming* was the truth of

Being. Process was the truth of things, and evolutionary trends enjoyed a higher degree of reality than mere facts of experience. To take facts, or even laws, as distinct was to show the static, fixed character of reified thought, for they were only frozen bits of process, of the "authentic and superior reality."[33]

By the time Lukacs's book was taken up into the first part of Heidegger's *Sein und Zeit* and was adopted by Marcuse, Horkheimer and Adorno, the Critical Theory of Society was well launched on the course that has led to the contemporary alliance of Left thought with absolute idealism and anti-scientific irrationality. Why this process should have begun in Germany in the 1920s, coeval with Nazism, is a question of origins which, like others of the sort, is probably insoluble.[34] Lukacs himself may unwittingly have made a helpful suggestion in 1948 when he named as thinkers who formed the fascist ideology several who figure among Critical Theory's antecedents: Nietzsche, Bergson, Simmel and Heidegger.[35] What is intended in such comparisons, I should emphasize, is formal resemblance rather than any substantial community of spirit between political movements. Still, that is enough to account for the frequently noticed "fascist" style of New Left reasoning. To put it briefly, once Marxist thought takes "Praxis" as its sole subject, and Praxis turns out to be the experience-matrix in which subject and object are one and of which all particular social phenomena are the ephemeral alienations and manifestations, then *that* Marxism is going to be mistaken for other species of totalizing irrationality which call their evolving whole "race" or "popular soul" or what-have-you.

This later became clear to Max Horkheimer and T. W. Adorno (though not to Herbert Marcuse). When the West German A.P.O. (extra-parliamentary opposition) wanted to apply their doctrines of the 1930s, they warned that their ideas could have no such political application, least of all in the changed world of the 1960s. Adorno's objections to the New Left were emphatic but of little force because in the last years of his life (he died in 1970) he would make them to any political activity whatsoever.[36] Speaking jointly on their behalf, Horkheimer in 1968 said that he and Adorno now realized that thoughtless application of Critical Theory assisted dictatorial forces and that Western democracy, with all its faults, was still better than dictatorship. Violence merely jeopardized the survival of culture, including indeed Critical Theory itself.[37] The dogma of totality had by then lapsed to the politically conservative use it has in the doctrines of Lenin and Mao Tse-tung: correct political action presupposes knowing the total situation, i.e., knowing everything about everything, so of course oppositional forces can be dismissed as partial, abstract, and wrong.

It was not, apparently, for this bathos that the Institute of the Frankfurt School was repeatedly occupied, devastated, burned and flooded by demonstrators of the New Left and that the latter-day Critical Theorists were insulted as *scheisskritische Theoretiker*. The school had already, a decade before, become inconsistent and eclectic by taking over American-style (and, in some projects, American-financed) sociology. The Critical Theorists by the 1950s had seen that the *physis-nomos* contrast in twentieth-century German thought had ended in the opposition of Aryan-German *community* and Judeo-Western *society*, in the clash of organic totality and positive science. So they abandoned the revolutionary dialectic for social statics, for the study of "groups" and pseudo-totalities like cities.[38] That is, they surrendered what remained useful in Marx's thought, the reference to the challenge that dynamic oppositional movements and their innovating moralities present to supposedly natural institutions and pre-ordained arrangements.

Even with the detection of that fateful point at which the denunciation of reified institutions was confounded with the denunciation of reified concepts (so that opposition to capitalism became opposition to science), it would still remain to ask whether Marxism was not from the start exposed to this confusion. This is a question that men of the Old Left, such as Colletti, cannot afford to ask because it puts in doubt assumptions that pervade all of Marx's work. Philosophies (and they are not only "German," as Nietzsche thought, but "Latin" too, as Bergson and LeRoy showed) which contrast the fluid "superior" reality with its temporary solid instruments are bound to take an illogical attitude to the latter, an attitude one might call instrumentalist. This applied to Marx. True, he insisted that the reifications he described were objective.[39] But he felt they were absurd, that they were instruments that had rebelled from their function. Thus, money is real enough but its role as a mediator "external to man" is a scandal, and indeed the "heights of slavery," because it makes money the real master of man. Again, exchange happens objectively, just the way economic science says, but it is "the contrary of a social relation" and men who exchange are not truly men. Credit and banking likewise are objective phenomena, but they are an immoral infamy in that they reduce man to a credit-risk, to an object. All such instruments of interpersonal relations should have remained "affirmations of individual existence" and should express no more than the "distinct and exclusive personality" of producers. Instead, mere intermediaries had become tyrannical principals, the authors of slavery, brutality, and the devaluation of man.[40] Although capitalist institutions were his main target, Marx did say that all previous institutions in human history had also failed to remain subservient instruments—all objectifications had become alienations, as he said in his characteristic Hegelian way.[41]

Reflection suggests that this was bound to happen. If we regard things as our instruments merely, we fall into the delusion that all their characters, all their fit and proper characters, are exhausted in the list of those of their aspects that serve our purposes. Any other quality they exhibited would make them bad instruments, and hence untrue to themselves, alienated. Yet the native characters of things will out. They keep surprising and disappointing us. Though we have demoted them to a second-class existence, they insist on revealing independent ways of acting, not all of them useful to us. The instrumentalist logic that recognizes the objectivity of things, but allows them only a *relative* existence and just as much reality as is convenient, is exemplified in Marx's approach to social studies. That is true not only of the Paris Manuscripts but also of his final theory of capital and the market. Because social things have relations with individuals (e.g., in their origins and in their uses) Marx thinks their characteristics should stop at that. They should never get to behave independently of individuals as though they enjoyed, like people, a full measure of objectivity; for that would entail alienation. For example—and it is an example that concerns the foundations of Marxism—because labor originates capital, capital should forever remain, like labor, "a manifestation of human activity" and never a "fetish," i.e., another thing with its own ways of operating.

As against that, to vouchsafe things their own independent characters does not mean surrendering to them; but, on the contrary, it is the necessary first step toward discovering which of their operations, if any, are in fact susceptible to our intervention. Simply to deplore, as Marx did, that social things like capital, markets, and states do have independent and characteristic ways of behaving is an emotional obstacle to any such discovery. Worse, it will tempt others—in Marxism's history this happened with Critical Theory and the New Left—to conclude that such things are illusions, that they do not really have a fully independent existence but can be reduced to their purely instrumental function by any hasty intellectual *putsch*. If their Being is usurped and spurious, it can be liquidated by any sufficiently resolute challenge, or even just by the Great Refusal; ignore them and they will wither away. For this reason, the notion that social science's concepts are improper "industrial" reifications of a fluid process—and the claim that our institutions are unseemly "capitalist" reifications of the free-form existence of love and anarchy—cannot be completely criticized without a re-consideration of Marx's life-long prejudice that *all* social things are scandalous alienations of work and personal relations: of the one true reality.

I turn now to that final problem.

8. *The Irrational Totality, or the Life and Death of Reason*

In capitalist and communist societies alike, great store is set today by maximum economic efficiency, by the utmost application of economic rationality. This is far from being an exclusive concern in either, but it is ostensibly the highest official preoccupation in both. One of the points in dispute between them, in fact, is whether socialism is more rational than capitalism or whether the market is not a more rational way to allocate resources than a plan. To ask which is the more rational way of being committed to economic rationality is to raise an objective issue, though one that is usually settled by appeal to non-economic (but still rational) considerations, such as equality or freedom. The importation of these non-economic considerations into the debate about comparative economic rationality is frowned upon by many authorities because it is one of their assumptions, often, that economic rationality is rationality *tout court*. That is, they would argue that the only reasonable way to arrange matters is to strive for maximum material returns from effort. Then, the more rational system would be the one that gave the greater returns, without appeal to non-economic considerations. "As long as there are individuals who suffer a sub-human standard of living and style of life, maximum efficiency imposes itself. . ." That remark of the economist, François Perroux, would be widely accepted as the simple rational basis of economic rationality.

Yet there exist many forms of critical opposition, in both capitalist and communist societies, to this pre-eminence accorded economic rationality. There are numerous activities in which people can turn away from economic preoccupations and disregard the relation between work and the return in material benefit. They do this when they indulge, for instance, in art, or learning, or sport, or the religious quest for eternal salvation. Still other activities are not simply uneconomic but positively anti-economic, such as militarism or, nowadays, ecological care for the environment, and there is no need to emphasize how influential at least the first of these has been in societies supposedly dominated by economic calculation. There is, then, constant conflict between activities governed by economic rationality and other activities, each of which has its own rationality, its own calculation of the relation between ends and means. Fortunately for them, the casuistry of economic rationality is infinitely resourceful and most of these other activities can be accommodated into the loose social unity in which economic considerations are uppermost. This is done by interpreting, or excusing, them as *special* types of economic activity. They can be presented as essential pre-conditions of production (e.g., national military security), as very slow-maturing investments (learning, immigration, natalism), or as covered by the specious notion of social costs (care for the environment or for public health).

The originality of the social challenge of the New Left and of the philosophy it draws from the young Marx's work is that it cuts across the debate about the comparative economic rationality of capitalism and socialism. It brushes aside the casuistry that enables non-economic activities to rub along with the official insistence on maximum material returns. The New Left holds that the rationality of such societies is a piecemeal, short-sighted rationality that leads to an over-all irrationality. Each particular economic calculation is reasonable, but the totality of economic calculations issues in total unreasonableness. Any piecemeal effort to improve the rationality of such societies, to reform them by doing this or that more reasonably, not only stabilizes the whole system but could actually contribute to worsening its total irrationality. To use a comparison that might sound caricatural but which is surely implicit in Adorno and Marcuse, economic societies resemble a Nazi death factory that is periodically inspected to ascertain its productivity, to ensure that its output of dead persons is optimal in relation to the input of poison gas, to the cost per square metre of concentration camps, etc. Any effort to improve the rationality and efficiency of such an enterprise, or to accommodate other activities to it as compatible or contributory, would only heighten the over-all lunacy.

Economic rationality, on this view, has been improperly generalized to *all* activities, so that what started out as the initiative and enterprise of the bourgeoisie has led to social automation, to the domination first of nature and then of man, to "total administration."[1] In such a society, the generalization of economic and technological rationality (the "performance principle") leads to the identity of productivity and destructiveness. The more productive it is in detail, the more it destroys wholesale. Partial rationality having led to total irrationality, any effort to recast or reorganize bits of the system (especially if that meant even further application of technological standards, as "social engineering" would) would exacerbate the total unreasonableness. It is in this sense that, in Adorno's words, *das Ganze ist das Unwahre*, the whole is untrue. The parts, in contrast, are innocent and it is no use fiddling with them. The general irrationality of the system will defeat any partial purpose, however well intentioned. That is why such societies become one-dimensional—in the sense that they contain no effective force that can act on the whole but only forces that are integrated against their will, forces whose short-sighted rationality only worsens total repression and destructiveness. Since the absurdity of the society appears only at the most general level, in its totality, it is *there* that the remedy must be applied; it is there that irrationality must be combated in the name of reason. Only total revolution can lead to a wholly reasonable society, whereas partial rationality reinforces the wholly unreasonable.

Though the spirit of this indictment can be traced back (and has been) to ancient Gnosticism, it is a characteristically modern theory. Its first social context was the period of the Stalinist Five-Year Plans, as these were contrasted by German intellectuals with the folly of Nazism and with the absurdity of the great Depression that had issued from piecemeal, pre-Keynesian economic rationality. In its first presentation, that theory could serve as a "philosophical" rationale for a specific social action: i.e., joining or collaborating with the Communist Party. That party proposed a rational whole, the Plan, to replace the multiple, capitalist rationality that had ended in absurdity.

Revived a generation later, the theory then had to reject Stalinism too, because total planning in Soviet Russia had led to a society that was at least as "irrational" and destructive as capitalism, especially a capitalism that had in the meantime acquired from Keynes a global, or at least less piecemeal, approach. However, this theory could not lead to any specific organized social action, for there was no party to join which offered a reasonable totality as against the ultimately nefarious economic rationality both of communist and capitalist societies. Quietist conclusions were drawn from this by Adorno and Horkheimer. The whole is senseless but there is nothing to be done about it. Marcuse, on the other hand, continued to cast about for some social vehicle that would bring in the wholly reasonable totality. His lack of success at that political level is what gives his work its incoherence and its "metaphysical" air, for once the reasonable whole is no longer the communist economic Plan, it lacks concrete social significance. This metaphysical vagueness, however, could now claim to be characteristically Marxist. It could even be taken to be a Marxist philosophy, because Marx's earliest rejections of all forms of economic rationality had by now become generally known. If Marx in 1844 had scorned not only the market but money and monetary calculation too (and possibly the division of labor itself), then surely one was being quite Marxist in rejecting any sort of economic rationality, whether capitalist or communist.[2]

Many activities, as I have already noted, deny or disregard the priority of economic rationality. But, on the totalizing theory, these are all guilty of complicity, if not of actually contributing to and stabilizing the over-all irrationality produced by economic activity. If one wished, therefore, to avoid guilt and complicity, there seemed to be three lines of conduct that were consistent with the doctrine of the malignant totality.

The *first* (which was probably a misunderstanding such as metaphysical theories frequently provoke) was to reject not only economic but all rationality by opposing to piecemeal rationality a piecemeal, everyday irrationality. If one had not the wit to be surrealist, one could "drop out," take drugs, or join mindless, sporadic agitation of the sort that came to be known in the West as "Maoist."

The *second* (which shaded off into the first but was essentially different) was to seek to liberate from the constraints of economic rationality a fundamental human nature that would reveal itself to be naturally reasonable, free, and pacific. This was the paradoxical program for a Freudian libido released from the "reality principle" and dedicated wholly to the "pleasure principle," as well as for a type of thinking that would be free of the domination of logic. Of course, this primary substratum could never be exhibited. How indeed could one show what human nature had been before it began to reckon with external necessity, or what thought had been before logic? One could not point to any moment at which a pristine human nature first fell under the domination of rationality, i.e., first began to calculate the proportion of means and ends, nor to any moment at which non-logical thinking had first succumbed to the tyranny of logic. Plans to liberate the undefinable and to inaugurate for it a life without conditions rapidly sank into incoherence. If this were to be remedied by *ex cathedra* definitions of what was proper or true humanity, it became too obvious that *someone* was dictating what people *should* want.

A *third* conclusion, also drawn from the theory of the malignant totality that issues from piecemeal rationality, was more logical but, alas, less original. It was to replace the mindless domination that supposedly rules economic society by a reasoned, non-economic plan. This is the age-old proposal of philosophical communism, which one has known ever since Plato's *Republic*. Instead of society being the upshot of a host of partial, reasonable calculations (for that upshot is said to be irrational), it should be the outcome of one general act of rationality. The house will be built from the roof down or, as Hegel liked to say, society will be made to march on its head, i.e., to depend on Reason. This rationality will supersede economic rationality because material wants will be restricted to frugality if not to subsistence and then economic preoccupations can be pushed from the center of social life. Meticulous plans that were literally thousands of years old thus came to be presented as the last word in Left thought and as prefigurations of "post-industrial society."

Now, economic rationality is not rationality *tout court*. One is entitled to oppose to economic reasoning objections based on different and equally rational considerations. Economists have a way of formally defining their subject which blurs this. When they say that economics is the science of human behavior seen as a relation between (a) ends and (b) means that are scarce and that have alternative uses, this is tantamount to claiming for economics the study of every sort of rational behavior, including those varieties studied in other subjects, such as ethics, military science, and so forth. On that view one would have no way of distinguishing economic goods from ethical goods or, for that matter, from the materials of other kinds of rational enquiry into practice. To illustrate. A perplexed mother who wants to know how many kitchen pots she can let a child play with if dinner is to be cooked is not practising economics, though on the formal definition just cited she would be. Nor is a general who wonders how many tanks he can spare for his left flank while his center is under attack. We can be rational and logical about collecting shells that give prestige in the tribe or about acquiring additional wives, just as we can about wealth and welfare. Although structuralist anthropologists have sought to draw some bizarre ethical and political conclusions from that fact, the logical point is certain.

In order to delimit the subject of economics, one must go beyond a simply formal definition that claims for it the whole field of rational conduct. One must specify a certain set of materials to which rationality has to be applied before it is economic rationality. Unfortunately, it is rather more complicated than that, because economics is not only about goods but about services too. So in addition to a set of materials, one must specify a certain *aspect* of human activities.[3] What those materials and aspects are, i.e., how wealth and welfare are described, is the task of economics. The important point is that it has a delimited subject and is not rationality in general. It follows that one can decline to be particularly interested in that subject, or at least refuse to give it priority, without ceasing to be rational.

This is so true that the notion of the priority of economic rationality only appeared in human history at a certain moment, after millennia of civilization; so that it was not a "praxeology" deduced from human nature. On one influential theory, indeed, it appeared in close association with a singularly irrational theological doctrine, Calvinism. Whether Calvinism was one of the causes of the very origins of capitalism[4] or whether it simply gave a powerful impetus to a movement that had other causes (to be mentioned below), the fact is established that what led many of the founders of the modern world to apply rationality primarily to the economic domain was an irrational choice of the soul. The traditional Catholic world they rejected was, according to its lights, eminently rational. In it the commonest ostensible concern was to get to heaven by the performance of certain precise actions or, when they were not performed, by meticulously calculated penances and intercessions. Against that, the Calvinists asserted that a relentless god was hidden behind an utterly corrupt world and that salvation lay in endless, irrational *effort*—as Franz Borkenau put it, "irrational in a threefold sense: in that it bore no relation to heavenly salvation [which was predestined] nor to success in work nor, above all, to personal happiness."[5] This is no matter of mere historical interest, for the continued association, over centuries, of capitalist enterprise and certain of the least rational of the Protestant sects (especially in the United States) continues to confirm that this particular application of rationality can have irrational motives.

Karl Marx knew nothing of that theory, but he had another that is no more respectful of economic rationality. He held that it was associated with, if not identified with, a religion he despised, namely, Judaism. His first statement of the view that economic rationality came to the world in its "dirty Jew" form was extremely coarse because Marx was rejecting that sort of mentality with something like horror. It is the repudiation of a certain rational attitude, the calculation of material advantage in monetary terms, rather than anti-Semitic feelings towards its supposed practitioners, that marks these passages:

> What is the secular basis of Judaism? Practical need, self-interest. What is the worldly cult of the Jew? Bargaining. What is his worldly god? Money. Very well! Emancipation from bargaining and money, and thus from practical and real Judaism, would be the self-emancipation of our era. . . . The Jew has emancipated himself in a Jewish way not only by acquiring financial power but also because, with him or without him, *money* has become a world power and the practical Jewish spirit has become the practical spirit of the Christian nations. The Jews have emancipated themselves insofar as the Christians have become Jews. . . . Indeed, the practical domination of Judaism over the Christian world in North America has achieved . . . clear and common expression. . . . Money is the jealous god of Israel before whom no other god may exist. Money degrades all the gods of mankind—and converts them into commodities. . . . The god of the Jews has been secularized and has become the god of the world. The bill of exchange is the Jew's actual god. His god is only an illusory bill of exchange. . . . The social emancipation of the Jew is the emancipation of society from Judaism.[6]

Attempts to edulcorate these observations[7] are mistaken if they detract from Marx's assertion that economic rationality came to the world as the work of an irrational religious minority. As opposed to Max Weber and Franz Borkenau who specifically denied that capitalism arose from money capital acquired by trading and money-lending[8] (once typically Jewish occupations), Marx held that economic rationality first appeared as monetary, commercial, and Jewish. Mention of the Jews was to disappear later, when Marx realized that a perpetual danger to socialism was that it would degenerate, in Engels's words, into *"un antisémitisme à grandes phrases."* Nevertheless, Marx's theory about the origins of capitalism, as given in *Capital*, was still that usury and commerce (the domain of "circulation") first produced large sums of capital which were then applied to production. This theory, which puts the origins of capitalism several centuries earlier than do Weber and Borkenau, has secured much later support.[9]

N

Marx later overcame the juvenile horror of economic rationality he showed in 1844. He even expressed admiration of some of its works but he never varied in the opinion that it was a contingent historical product, associated with the irrational, probably religious, choice of a minority and thereafter generalized by force. It was therefore no incarnation of reason, and yet, for all that, it was not to be abandoned. The capitalist sort of economic rationality was to be superseded by a more rational socialist sort. This latter could not make its way by sweet reason, either, but would have to be imposed by force: by revolution.

Marx's development on this point is of less interest than the evolution within the socialist movement, which followed a similar course. As a reaction to the imposition of capitalist economic rationality, socialism contained various strands. First, there was the act of setting everyday irrationality against capitalism's piecemeal rationality, as in Luddism, anarchism, and banditry. Secondly, there was the Romantic fantasy, which we have seen in the young Marx, about liberating a "true" human essence from all economic constraints. Thirdly, there was a pullulation of plans for subjecting economic rationality to the control of a totalitarian non-economic rationality, that is, utopian proposals (and some experiments) for colonies of philosophical communists. Fourthly (and most important), there was the lineage of socialism that stemmed from Saint-Simon, the socialism that accepts economic rationality but proposes to apply it *in fellowship* rather than piecemeal, i.e., in a national plan. Far from rejecting all economic rationality, this sort of socialist argues that it cannot be completely and coherently applied within the restrictive capitalist framework and that only socialist society will be utterly economically rational.

Nineteenth-century socialism was a generous confusion of these strands, but it was the last that came to pre-eminence as working-class support increased—without, however, the anarchist, Romantic, and utopian objections to economic rationality ever being quite disowned. Lenin carried the decantation of these disparate elements a stage farther. On the eve of the

Bolshevik Revolution, Lenin had paid lip-service to some of the most utopian doctrines of anti-economic communism; but within a few years of taking power he was ready, in order to repair the ravages of enthusiastic departures from economic rationality,[10] to restore even its capitalist variety, in the New Economic Policy. With Stalin, the commitment to economic rationality, in its socialist sense of production in fellowship, took the form of the Five-Year Plans, which sought to replace capitalism's piecemeal economic rationality (coordinated by the market) by the total rationality of a plan. Production in fellowship came to mean (it is hard to see how it could mean anything else in modern nation-states) bureaucratic economic rationality. As the bureaucratic ethos became more evident and the insistence on economic rationality harsher ("overtake and surpass the U.S.A."), the Stalinist form of planning—which had been described as the recovery of a lost totality by its metaphysical supporters in the West—was bound to alienate those participants in the socialist tradition who had never been interested in economic rationality or in any form of the "performance principle" and had thought that the commitment to socialism was a profound protest against such things. In point of fact, of course, it is only philosophical communism, i.e., the organization of consumption, that offers scope for such a human protest; socialism, in contrast, is a variety of the industrial movement and, like capitalism, is marked by a producers' morality.

The disillusionment of these elements was to be complete in 1956, when a new regime in the Kremlin admitted that the new application of economic rationality had indeed led to an aggressive, imperialist, and "irrational" society. Once the Russian Revolution had been shown in its true colours as less the rejection of economic rationality than a mere alternative way to modern industrial power in societies that had refused "Judaism" and "Calvinism," it was ready to be outflanked on its Left. The nineteenth-century amalgam broke up as the romantic, utopian, and anarchist *gauchistes* ceased their fellow-travelling with the communist parties. The communists remained loyal to the commitment to economic rationality not only in the backward countries but also in those Catholic societies of Europe that had never admitted the predominance of economic over other considerations. In France and Italy, for example, large communist parties, though smarting under *gauchiste* attacks, held to a role that they conceived as comparable to that of the Protestant Reformation[11] in that it proposed economic rationality (in its planned rather than its market form, naturally) to societies that had always regarded it as "money-making," as something best left to "Yids, Yanks and the H.S.P.," i.e., to Jews, Americans, and the Haute Société Protestante.[12] Communism in its unashamedly economic-rational form, as far as it bore any resemblance to the Reformation, was naturally irrelevant in countries where Calvinism (Marx would have said "Judaism") had triumphed, such as Britain and Holland and their cultural offshoots, notably the U.S.A.[13] Those countries had achieved a far superior economic efficiency by means of decentralized units of production coordinated in a market that, though regulated, still distributed profits and losses. Yet the *gauchiste* attack on every form of economic rationality was unleashed in those countries, too, by the final break-up of the socialist amalgam. The New Left raised its protest as vehemently there, against the market, as in countries where its main target was the communist doctrine of bureaucratic economic rationality.

This protest took much the same forms as a century and a half earlier. There was, first, piecemeal irrationality; secondly, the defence of a true human nature against social domination; and thirdly, the call for the total submission of the economy to a utopian philosophical communism. The coincidence that this rebellion took place during the period of the Cultural Revolution in China—which, since it was labelled "cultural," was taken to be anti-economic and did indeed for a time entail neglect of economic concerns while urgent political problems were being settled—led to the brief illusion that it was Maoist. In fact, Maoism remained the ideology of industrialization in a backward country, as adapted to a new national situation.

As a retreat from that enveloping, all-conquering economic rationality, the latest protest gave itself the airs of a philosophy, in the vulgar sense of a "spiritual" protest against "materialism." The similar protest at the height of the Industrial Revolution had coincided with the heyday of Romanticism and had taken the form of a retreat into Art, or rather into aestheticism. In our day, Marcuse also sought to revive that attitude, from Friedrich Schiller, announcing that art would provide the new totality. Outside narrow circles with a taste for paradox this had little appeal, though it did have some entertainment value. For an art to provide the unifying, reconciling force in a divided and irrational society, it would have to be popular art, an art for all. Hence the deliberate cult of vulgarity in the New Left's enthusiasm for pop art, camp, comics, spaghetti westerns, and happenings. Yet such art was not vulgar out of innocent bad taste or ignorance but because it was assigned a social, revolutionary role; it represented the creation of an elite vanguard. Hence the paradox just referred to: "mass culture for the select few—folk art for small cliques."[14] The sense of ridiculousness that comes over participants in these attempts to convert art, by way of a revolt against style, into what Marcuse pompously calls in an English text a *"gesellschaftliche Produktivkraft"*[15] only spared those who made small fortunes at it; others became aware of the "unhistorical consciousness" that presides over such futilities. What little social force Art may have is not to be increased by turning it into anti-art, into deliberate bad taste; and yet as long as it does not yield to vulgarity it has no relevance to the political purposes the New Left set itself. The notion of Art as the restorer of the human integrity that had been lost in everyday rationality remained patent escapism, exactly as it was when Schiller and the Romantics set it against the "horrors" of early industrialism.[16] So the protest against economic rationality was more successful as a philosophy, and specifically as a Marxist philosophy drawn from the young Karl's humanism (i.e., individualism): the defence of Man's True Essence from the arbitrary rationality of economics.

What is most original, then, in this rehash of Romanticism is the argument that piecemeal rationality can lead to over-all irrationality and that any attempt to be more rational within the system only exacerbates its total destructiveness. In another common formulation: technology produces domination, first of nature but then of men, and more technology can only produce more domination. Or again: greater productivity leads to greater destruction.

A first difficulty with this theory is to specify the social location of the domination that is so destructive and irrational. Is it some ruling class that is exploiting the economy for its own ends, so that when each one of us goes about his task reasonably we are working against our own interests and for the benefit of that ruling class? If so, we have the situation long denounced by the Old Left as "capitalist exploitation," except that the exploiters might have changed a little in their more modern roles as managers or technical specialists. Could one safely say that such a system was *totally* irrational, since it does, after all serve the interests of the ruling class? If it seems utterly reasonable to them and at the same time it is accepted as reasonable in detail by the exploited, this is surely not a case of rationality producing irrationality. It would, rather, be a case of rational exploitation at the top taking advantage of the fact that the subject agents are letting themselves be robbed. Would it not be better to say of it, as of a serfdom ruled by a tsar pursuing long-term expansionary aims abroad, that it was a case of piecemeal irrationality producing an over-all rationality?

Or is it, perhaps, that the ruling class itself, as far as one can be said to exist, is also dominated by technology and economic rationality, so that its piecemeal rationality turns against *its* interests too? This might be nearer the situation of rationality in detail producing total irrationality. Everybody in the society in question would be doing the reasonable thing and yet everybody would be working against his own and everybody else's interests. However, this, as François Perroux remarks indulgently, is "an obscure notion."[17] For my own part, I must distinguish it from a comparatively clear one that is not here in question. It is well known that individual enterprises have what are called social costs. Each entrepreneur might build and run his plant in the way most profitable and rational from his particular point of view, and yet society in general could be suffering damage and left to meet overheads that appeared in no individual's reckoning. This is, to be sure, something that economic rationality has taken into account and that governments have long legislated about. Such accounting and such legislation would be denounced in the theory we are examining as yet further examples of that reformist, piecemeal rationality that does not change the whole but merely stabilizes it and prolongs its evil.

It is striking, because it suggests the difficulty of the argument, that Marcuse has never been able to make up his own mind between these two possibilities. In being economically rational, are we being manipulated by an occult ruling class? Or is everyone, leaders and led, under domination, and no one ultimately advantaged by technology and production? When explicitly challenged on the point, Marcuse has opted for the former answer, saying that it would be "technological determinism" to imagine that the "apparatus" could be a self-managing monster. "In fact, however, I consider the 'apparatus' an instrument of domination in the hands of the ruling class ..."[18]

Yet that sacrifices the originality of his argument, which is better seen in the following quotations:

> The increasing rationalization of power seems to be reflected in an increasing rationalization of repression. In keeping individuals in the role of instruments of labor, in forcing renunciation and work upon them, domination is no longer defending only or primarily specific privileges but is defending also the whole of society on a wider and wider scale ... the rule of the father has been broadened to become the rule of society.[19]

Or again:

> These star leaders, together with the unnumerable sub-leaders, are in turn functionaries of a high authority which is no longer embodied in a person: the authority of the prevailing productive apparatus, which, once set in motion and moving efficiently in the set direction, engulfs the leaders and the led—without however eliminating the radical differences between them, that is, between the masters and the servants. This apparatus includes the whole of the physical plant of production and distribution, the technics, technology and science applied in this process, and the social division of labor sustaining and propelling the process.[20]

The Western Marxists

Or finally:

> The individual reproduces in his deepest self, in his instinctual structure, the values and ways of behaving that serve the maintenance of domination, while domination becomes ever less autonomous, less "personalized" and ever more objective, more generalized. What really dominates is the economic, political and cultural apparatus that social work has built and which has become a monolithic block.[21]

This is the version in which Marcuse's case coincides with that of Adorno[22] and of his own exegetes.[23]

There is no way of reconciling a blank contradiction but one might take the case to be at its strongest if presented in this way. There *is* a ruling class in industrial society but it suffers, too, from economic rationality and technology, even if it suffers rather less than people subject to its domination. After all, to say that there were no ruling classes in industrial societies, whether capitalist or communist, would be to fly in the face of facts. There are obviously people who consistently exercise more authority and derive more benefits than others. In pluralistic Western societies, as against totalitarian dictatorships, these power centres might be multiple and even occasionally in conflict and none might exercise power so great as to deserve the name domination. Still, one would need to be blind to overlook them. Yet this is what the New Left theorists do, in so far as they differ from the Old Left. After acknowledging that ruling classes do exert an influence, they go on to say that what "really" rules, however, is faceless Society. It is Technology which dominates, and not this-or-that group of technical specialists. It is economic rationality which enslaves and exploits, and not these central planners or those owners of capital, these managers or those decision-makers. And one *must* argue this way if one is to show that piecemeal rationality produces over-all irrationality.

Confusion is engendered by the vague notion of "technological domination," which is a ragbag of views on logic, science, technology, capitalist interests, and authoritarian dictatorship.[24] It was prepared by the act of confounding capitalist reification with scientific conceptualization, which was studied in a previous chapter. Only the illogical confusion of *commodity* and *concept,* taken as twin forms of alienation, allows the Western Marxists to mix up the protest against political domination and economic exploitation with irrationalist attacks on science. Marx said workers were dominated and exploited when they produced commodities, that is, when they accepted as reasonable the point of view of capitalist economic rationality. The Western Marxists say we are dominated and exploited when we produce concepts, that is, when we accept any sort of rationality, whether it be capitalist or communist economic rationality or scientific and technical rationality. In Western societies, resentment of the exploitation supposedly suffered in the act of producing commodities is no longer a live social force; so the old Marxism is largely irrelevant. But the application of economic and scientific rationality has made giant strides and this enables neo-Marxism to transfer the old-fashioned socialist pathos to an anti-scientific irrationalism. Only by oscillating from one of these levels to the other can it generate the illusion of political domination without a dominator, economic exploitation without an exploiter, or the flickering vision of a faceless irrational force that rises above whatever ruling exploiting groups are admitted to exist.

Domination and exploitation remain, for all that, transitive notions and, as applied to politics, they must mean that someone is dominating and exploiting someone else. Hence the standard Old Left complaint has been that by denouncing an *activity* such as science or production as inherently dominating and exploiting, the New Left is closing its eyes to groups that are using that activity as their instrument of domination— and, incidentally, blaming the victims for complicity. Whatever force there may be in that complaint, it is sure that the denunciation of activities in the name of individuals, who are held to be enslaved just by participating, is the customary humanist objection to politics. It amounts to making the discovery that activities have an impetus of their own, that they enlist individuals but have a longer life. Societies, as clusters of more or less compatible activities, breed true: they go on reproducing consistent and compatible activities, and they oppose

o

resistance to basic change. To complain that in order to do this they manipulate and model individuals (by a technique that psycho-analysts called "introjection" and which is misunderstood as a sort of white terror) is to miss the point that unless they did this there would be no society and identifiable culture to talk about. If a society constantly—instead of only very rarely—bred "instinctual structures" that were incompatible with its main components, it would disappear with every new generation of adolescents. That societies have a certain inertia and that social activities tend to persist in their nature would only be instances of domination if one started from atomic individuals, each whole and complete before any encounter with enslaving civilization. That there can be criticism of, and resistance to, any given set of activities is plain; but they will come only from other activities, and not from pure, pre-social individuals.

The upshot of the productive rationality of modern society is held to be not only dominating but destructive. That contemporary industrial production entails a measure of pollution, environmental damage, unreckoned social costs, and waste of resources has long been argued by conservationists and liberal reformers. In doing so, they have been urging a *more exact* economic rationality that would take into account certain calculable costs hitherto overlooked; or else they have been setting other rational considerations against economic ones. In neither case have they had to maintain, in order to secure the very considerable practical legislative gains they have made, that economic rationality was inherently self-defeating and destructive.

That latter assertion was said to draw some color in our day from a necessary connection between the course of American industrial development and the U.S.A.'s involvement in the Vietnam war. Exposure to economic and technological rationality was alleged to produce tensions within individuals that found an outlet in systematic destructiveness, channelled by the ruling class toward some faraway foreign culture. Such claims are worth little without demonstration of the mechanism that could link two such remote social phenomena. They are worth less, for example, than the more obvious fact that involvement in what became a hopeless war was due to mis-calculations of a political, military and strategic sort distinct from—and on many points opposed to—economic rationality. In any case it would be worth noting that during the years of the Vietnam war considerably greater destructiveness was seen in Biafra, Indonesia, and Pakistan for reasons that had little or nothing to do with economics and technology, but much to do with tribalism, religion, race, and general political narrowness. For all that technology in the past thirty years has placed an immense power of destruction in the hands of certain interests in societies dedicated to economic rationality, they have used it in that period to cause rather less devastation than was provoked by people in Africa and Asia with other predominant concerns. That they have used it at all, or in the ways they did, has awakened some opposition and much criticism; but these would hardly have been as effective as they have been if they proceeded from the false postulate that technologically advanced societies are peculiarly and necessarily destructive.

Finally, such societies are held to be not only dominating and destructive but irrational, for all their piecemeal rational-ity. At the risk of seeming to make a debating point, one would at once concede that they are indeed not rational, in the sense that no society is. Rationality concerns the adjustment of means to ends, and societies do not have any one end to be rational about. Even if one agreed with Max Weber that in addition to rationality about an end *(zweckrational)* there existed a rationality about values regardless of any achievement of ends *(wertrational)*, one would still note that societies had a plurality of "values" and were thus not accountable to any single over-all rationality. That would need to be pointed out only to people of a totalitarian bent; but it is useful to recall it here because utopians usually are fanatical monists, convinced that a whole society can be given one governing objective.

More commonly, however, the complaint of over-all irrationality comes from critics who concede that a plurality of objectives or values is a feature of any society, but who go on to argue that in economically rational societies one particular form of activity has come to overwhelming dominance despite the fact that it cannot produce its rational credentials. That is to say, economic rationality cannot reasonably justify its choice of a particular domain in which to be rational and so its pre-eminence is usurped. This deserves a less abrupt answer than the monist objection to diversity.

It is an answer that grants the objection but adds that it has no force. The choice of which end to pursue and what goals to be rational about is not itself deduced, and is never irrefutable or final. Any such choice will remain open to competition and criticism from other sorts of rationality. None of these competing or successive applications of reasonableness and discipline can produce an absolute warrant, and none could establish a claim to be the only rational way to live. This circumstance that ways of life are neither deduced nor proven opens no gate to irrationality, however, for in order to be ways of life or social movements they must consist in the creation of institutions, laws, moralities, and coherent world-views. That is, they must be reasonable.

To ask capitalism, or communism, or any other variety of economic rationality, for its scientific credentials is, then, to ask for something it cannot give. One would not think of making that request of social movements long since passed into history because, from within our particular culture, the arbitrariness or contingency of other ways of life is only too obvious. In contrast, capitalism and communism seem to have a special claim to reasonableness, or else a special duty to justify themselves, because they have made so consistent a use of science, reason, and calculation. Or, at least, so it seems to us, who are their products and participants, though it will not necessarily seem so to our descendants. To these latter it will be clear, without the effort we need to make, that the vast use that capitalism has made of science has not made *it* scientific. Nor can we grant that communism can be identified with science and reason. One can easily imagine societies in which science (in the sense of the study of the systematic connections and qualities of things) flourished without any special emphasis being placed on the perpetual increase in living standards, as we define them, nor on maximum material returns from effort. Nevertheless, even granted that they are not uniquely scientific and that neither of them is the one rational society, capitalism and communism are not, for all that, "senseless"— unless this means that all ways of living and all applications of rationality to institutions, law, and morality are contingent *sub specie aeternitatis*. There are various ways of living reasonably. They can be studied in the history of social movements. They can be, and are, criticized with the intellectual weapons of other equally creative social movements.

The difficulty of the case is made palpable by the fact that Max Weber, who made invaluable contributions to just that study of social movements, fell into the error we are pinpointing here. He took capitalism as so peculiarly rational and calculating that he thought it had gradually, despite its irrational origins, come to be identical with social rationality. Apart from leading him into a rather stuffy German conservatism, this had a consequence that all his Left critics have fairly jumped upon. They contend that if for Weber rationality simply is capitalism, then it is one social form or world-view among others. In which event, they argue, Weber has fallen into irrationalism: reasonableness is just one arbitrary and transient attitude to life among the indefinite succession of other attitudes. After going to great pains to distinguish facts from values, Weber comes to imply that an interest in facts is just one value among others. As one such critic writes:

> Science, that is, falls to the level of just one sort of human behavior, something individual and arbitrary like any other subjective faith. In the best of cases, it is nothing more than "the way of perceiving life and reality" proper to one epoch among so many others, specifically to the capitalist-bourgeois epoch.[24]

Left critics are anxious to make this point in order to defend socialism as another variety of economic rationality, but their argument has the same force when it is opposed to any sort of economic rationality at all. There has been reason in *all* the creative, institution-building movements, which is why

Hegel could speak of them grandly as successive forms of Spirit. If science and calculation have made immense and unprecedented progress in association with the latest of these movements, that has merely led to discoveries which henceforth can be used for other human purposes—but used only, as ever in history, by rational, creative institution-building movements that will express new laws and new moralities to contain men's eternal fatuity.

When we distinguish (though we cannot separate) rationality from capitalism (and, incidentally, from communism) and when we argue that there is a plurality of rational ways of living, we do not thereby restore Max Weber's distinction between facts and values. Indeed, it was just the reduction of social movements and ways of life to "values" and "intentions" and to other such personal attitudes as "calculation" that led Weber astray. It is not mere values and intentions that provide the variety of ways of living but social movements; and these consist in the public cooperative creation of institutions and laws, that is to say, in something as remote as could be from personal fantasy and the satisfaction of the "libido." Of course, private fancy, personal valuations, and the "choice of the soul" do exist. There are quaintly individual opinions about society; there are Swedish Buddhas, Bantu Voltaires, and Californian hippies; there is a lunatic fringe around any institution. But they are not social forces. It is social movements that put up the only effective criticism of opposed ways of life, and they do so not just because they are the big battalions but because they express their criticism in rational, self-sustaining institutions.

This brings me back to the Marxist humanists. Their repudiation of existing society has shocked only conservatives, and their critique of economic rationality has most dismayed those who mistook economic rationality for the one rationality. It is their attack on rationality itself, not only in the theoretical form of the concept but in the practical social form of institutions and discipline, all in the name of the individual, that has betrayed that they are not what they hold themselves to be, the rising force, the coming movement. One ancient Asian

The Irrational Totality, or the Life and Death of Reason

people had a god who was always with his divine ear to the sacred ground, listening for the footsteps of the future, and there are some students of social movements who resemble him. What will the movement be that will supersede economic rationality? This is an obsession with them. Some thought to hear its footsteps in the tumult of the New Left; and they discerned a new morality in the revolt of the Marxist humanists. It seems more probable, in view of past social movements, that the new force, when it comes, will be rather different. It will not present itself as setting outright irrationality against the reason of the day, nor as proposing to defend the human essence from the domination of reason in general. It will, I suspect, propose a new law and a new discipline, and a view of life and history about which mankind can once again be rational. It will appear as a project for a new set of institutions and a different morality which will require as much disciplining of personal fancy as the old moralities did. Pathetic defence of the self and its libido from "a world I never made" is no more a social program than the promise of individual peace, joy, and contentment. Yet acceptance of that ready-made world is no obligation either, as Marx explained in his social interpretation of Hegel's dialectic and as Sorel showed in his revolutionary analysis of history. There are new worlds to be made, but they are only to be made by creating reasonable institutions in fellowship.

Notes   1. **The Remystification of Marx**

¹ S. Talamo, *Rivista internazionale di scienze sociali e discipline ausiliarie* (January 1899).

² G. Sorel, "L'Ethique du socialisme," G. Belot *et al.*, *Morale Sociale* (Paris, 1899), p. 141.

³ G. Deville, *Philosophie du socialisme* (Paris, 1886).

⁴ In *Wage Labour and Capital* (1849), Marx distinguished productive forces and productive relations in these terms: "The social relations within which individuals produce, the social relations of production, are altered, transformed, with the change and development of the material means of production, of the forces of production. The relations of production in their totality constitute what is called the social relations, society, and, moreover, a society at a definite stage of historical development, a society with a unique and distinctive character." The translation (minus Marx's abuse of italics) is that of T. B. Bottomore and M. Rubel (eds.), *Karl Marx: Selected Writings in Sociology and Social Philosophy* (New York: McGraw, 1964; London: Penguin Books, 1970).

⁵ K. Marx, *Capital*, tr. Eden and Cedar Paul (New York: Dutton, 1930; London: Dent, 1930), p. 873.

⁶ On Hess's influence over Marx at that time, see David McLellan, *The Young Hegelians and Karl Marx* (New York: Praeger, 1969; London: Macmillan, 1969), pp. 154–8.

⁷ See, for example, H.-J. Krahl, "Bemerkungen zum Verhältnis von Kapital und Hegelscher Wesenslogik," *Aktualität und Folgen der Philosophie Hegels*, ed. O. Negt (Frankfurt, 1970). On this interpretation, Hegel's essence becomes the exchange value of goods, and his appearance their use value; the spiritual force superior to men becomes capital; the self-identity of the absolute refers to the reconstitution of capital by profit; and so forth. Krahl adds: "The Hegelian logic is, according to Marx, the self-movement of capital. . . . Capital is the actual phenomenology of mind, it is real metaphysics. . . . Hegel is the metaphysical thinker of capital. He is the first that takes up the viewpoint of the logic of capital; his philosophy is the idealistic and metaphysical disguise of [capitalist] production."

⁸ By 1937 Marcuse had already resurrected Young Hegelianism: "When reason has been realized as the rational organization of mankind, philosophy is left without an object. For philosophy . . . has drawn its life from reason's not yet being reality . . . the creation of a rational society. The philosophical ideals of a better world and of true Being are incorporated into the practical aim of struggling mankind, where they take on a human form." *Negations* (Boston: Beacon Press, 1968; London: Allen Lane, The Penguin Press, 1968), pp. 135, 142.

⁹ Compare the translation given in L. D. Easton and K. H. Guddat (eds.), *Writings of the Young Marx on Philosophy and Society* (New York: Doubleday, 1967), p. 264.

¹⁰ Ibid., p. 415.

¹¹ M. Merleau-Ponty, *Les Aventures de la Dialectique* (Paris, 1955), pp. 85–7.

¹² A. Labriola, *La Concezione materialistica della storia*, ed. B. Croce (Bari, 1953).

¹³ K. Marx, *Capital*, p. 873.

¹⁴ Ibid., p. 874.

[15] H. Arvon, *La Philosophie allemande* (Paris, 1970), p. 90.

[16] W. van Dooren, Marx en de ontwikkelingen in het huidige marxisme, *Actueel marxisme*, ed. A. G. Weiler (Bussum, 1969).

[17] A theologian declared van Dooren's suggestion to be "a *dangerous* undervaluation of Marx as philosopher" (my emphasis) and insisted that if it was hard to make philosophical sense of Marx, that was a sign of his "greatness," a sign seen also in Plato, St Thomas Aquinas, and Hegel (A. G. Weiler (ed.), *Actueel marxisme*, pp. 25–9). But then this theologian (it was B. Delfgaauw, who wrote *De jonge Marx*) has even found similarities between Marx and Teilhard de Chardin.

[18] On how West German Catholics and idealists can no longer have a good philosophical congress without the "salt" of some Marxist presence, see W. R. Beyer, *Tendenzen bundesdeutscher Marxbeschäftigung* (Cologne, 1968), pp. 16–17, 25.

[19] Chapter 5, "In the Shadow of Hegel: From Marx to Marcuse."

[20] O. Negt, "Zum Problem der Aktualität Hegels," *Aktualität und Folgen der Philosophie Hegels*, ed. O. Negt, p. 16.

[21] For criticism of these shifts see G. Harmsen, "De continuïteit in het denken van Marx," L. Goldman *et al.*, *Dialektiek en maatschappikritiek* (Meppel, 1970), pp. 9–47.

[22] Instead of thirty years' hard work, "a few pages and a few weeks would have sufficed to complete the existentialist analysis of the human condition under capitalism," if that had been Marx's aim, notes R. Aron in *D'une Sainte Famille à l'autre: Essais sur les marxismes imaginaires* (Paris, 1969), p. 119.

[23] K. Korsch, *Marxisme et Philosophie*, tr. Orsini (Paris, 1964), pp. 110–12.

[24] H. Marcuse, *Philosophie et Révolution*, tr. Heim (Paris, 1969), pp. 87, 106. The original dates from 1932.

[25] K. Kosik, *Dialettica del concreto*, tr. Pacini (Milan, 1965), p. 188.

[26] A. Gramsci, *Il Materialismo storico e la filosofia di Benedetto Croce* (Turin, 1955), pp. 25, 78–89, 232–4.

[27] Ibid., p. 217.

[28] Ibid., pp. 93–4; K. Korsch, *Marxisme et Philosophie*, p. 175.

[29] A. Gramsci, *Il Materialismo storico*, p. 87.

[30] L. D. Easton and K. H. Guddat (eds.), *Writings of the Young Marx*, p. 324.

[31] He said ironically in *The German Ideology* that he was using it only "so that the philosophers can follow." See L. D. Easton and K. H. Guddat, (eds.), *Writings of the Young Marx*, p. 427.

[32] For an excellent discussion of the confusion of alienation with objectification see F. Perroux, *Aliénation et société industrielle* (Paris, 1970). Perroux exactly recalls Marx's meaning by saying that to be alienated is to be "lost in things," whereupon they seem dead and inhuman and that the escape from alienation is to see those things—be they machines, monuments or social rules—as unfinished, subject to collective intentions and objects of a dialogue. Perroux even repeats Marx's error of monism, by holding *all* machines, monuments, and rules (even the bureaucracy) as subject to "our" intentions so that "at the limit" there is the possibility of unanimity, of agreement between all groups and of a common social project.

[33] I. Meszaros, *Marx's Theory of Alienation* (London: Merlin Press, 1970), p. 186, gives this unwitting definition of life without conditions: "Freedom

is thus the realization of man's own purpose: self-fulfilment in the self-determined and externally unhindered exercise of human powers."

[34] See Chapter 6, "Ideologists of the New Left."

[35] As is shown in J. Habermas, *Theorie und Praxis* (Neuwied and Berlin, 3rd edn, 1965), p. 168.

[36] "Under the conditions of late capitalism and given the impotence of the workers before the apparatus of oppression of the authoritarian state, truth has taken refuge in admirable small groups, decimated by the Terror . . ." M. Horkheimer, "Traditionelle und kritische Theorie" (1937), reprinted in *Traditionelle und kritische Theorie* (Frankfurt, 1970), p. 52.

[37] J. de Graaf, *Moraal, marxisme en ethiek in de Sowjetunie* (Hilversum, 1966), p. 47.

[38] G. Lukacs, *Geschichte und Klassenbewusstsein* (Berlin, 1923), pp. 39–40.

[39] Ibid., p. 136.

[40] Ibid., p. 198.

[41] H. Marcuse, *Negations*, p. 70.

[42] R. P. Wolff, B. Moore and H. Marcuse, *A Critique of Pure Tolerance* (Boston: Beacon Press, 1965; London: Cape, 1969), p. 97.

[43] See Czech, K. Kosik, *Dialettica del concreto*, pp. 43–69; Yugoslav, M. Markovic, *Dialektik der Praxis*, tr. Urban (Frankfurt, 1968).

[44] K. Marx, *Grundrisse der Kritik der politischen Oekonomie* (Berlin, 1953), p. 189.

[45] G. Lukacs, *Geschichte und Klassenbewusstsein*, p. 26. The gratuitousness of exploiting such references to economic equilibrium for the ends of absolute idealism has been pointed out also by H. Fleischer, *Marx und Engels* (Freiburg and Munich, 1970), p. 174.

[46] See M. Rodinson, "Sociologie marxiste et idéologie marxiste," *Marx and Contemporary Scientific Thought*, UNESCO Symposium (The Hague, 1969), pp. 67–92.

[47] G. Sorel, "Y a-t-il de l'utopie dans le marxisme?" *Revue de métaphysique et de morale* (Paris, 1899), pp. 164–70.

[48] M. Markovic, *Dialektik der Praxis*, pp. 124–7.

[49] I. Meszaros, "Lukacs's Concept of Dialectic," *Georg Lukacs*, ed. G. Parkinson (New York: Random House, 1970; London: Weidenfeld & Nicolson, 1970).

[50] F. Fanon, *Sociologie d'une révolution* (Paris, 1968).

[51] R. Zahar, *Kolonialismus und Entfremdung: Zur politischen Theorie Frantz Fanons* (Frankfurt, 1968).

[52] H. Marcuse, *Negations*, pp. 97–8.

[53] See L. D. Easton and K. H. Guddat (eds.), *Writings of the Young Marx*, p. 408.

[54] I. Meszaros, *Marx's Theory of Alienation*, p. 288. In real revolutions, needless to say, when the "radically new ethos of work" fails to appear, the new ruling class first pleads, then threatens that unless it appears, force will be applied. For an illustration, see an address to the Hungarian workers by Lukacs in 1919 during Béla Kun's communist dictatorship, "Die Rolle der Moral in der kommunistischen Produktion," *Schriften zur Ideologie und Politik* (Neuwied and Berlin, 1967), pp. 75–81. If the workers did not at once and spontaneously adopt work discipline and increase productivity, said Lukacs, the proletariat would have to "apply its dictatorship to itself,"

i.e., institutions would be created to force workers to do so. So, he concluded, perhaps to the puzzlement of the workers, Marx and Engels had been right. After the proletarian seizure of power, the reign of liberty began immediately, for then at last the workers were *free to choose*—between harder work and political tyranny.

⁵⁵ *Capital*, p. 873. See John Anderson, "Marxist Philosophy," *Studies in Empirical Philosophy* (Sydney, 1962), p. 302: "That Marx remained committed to the representational theory with all its defects is shown in his statement . . ." and there follows a version of the passage quoted in the text.

⁵⁶ See L. D. Easton and K. H. Guddat (eds.), *Writings of the Young Marx*, p. 431.

⁵⁷ Ibid., p. 415.

⁵⁸ G. Lukacs, *Geschichte und Klassenbewusstsein*, pp. 222–3. Later, after performing various self-criticisms and becoming a Stalinist hack writer, Lukacs accepted Lenin's theory of the reflection; see G. Lukacs, *Existentialisme et Marxisme*, tr. Kelemen (Paris, 1961), pp. 237–90.

⁵⁹ L. D. Easton and K. H. Guddat (eds.), *Writings of the Young Marx*, p. 414.

⁶⁰ For orthodox version see R. Garaudy, *La Théorie matérialiste de la connaissance* (Paris, 1953), and M. Raphael, *La Théorie marxiste de la connaissance* (Paris, 1937).

⁶¹ G. A. Paul, "Lenin's Theory of Perception," *Analysis*, 5, 5, 1938, pp. 65–73.

⁶² See G. Planty-Bonjour, "Ontologie et dialectique dans la philosophie soviétique," *Revue internationale de philosophie*, 91 (Brussels, 1970), pp. 80–89.

⁶³ B. Jeu, *La Philosophie soviétique et l'Occident* (Paris, 1969), pp. 165–78.

⁶⁴ Arturo Labriola, *Karl Marx*, tr. Berth (Paris, 1909), pp. 35–54.

⁶⁵ The First Thesis runs as follows: "The chief defect of all previous materialism (including that of Feuerbach) is that things, reality, the sensible world, are conceived only in the form of objects of observation but not as concrete human activity, not as practical activity, not subjectively. Hence in opposition to materialism, the active side was developed abstractly by idealism, which of course does not know real, concrete human activity as such. Feuerbach wants sensible objects really distinct from objects of thought, but he does not understand human activity itself as objective activity. Consequently, in the *Essence of Christianity*, he regards the theoretical attitude as the only genuine human attitude, while practical activity is apprehended only in its dirty-Jew form. He therefore does not grasp the significance of 'revolutionary,' 'practical-critical' activity."

Marx's meaning here is the same as in a passage in the *German Ideology* written at about the same time: "Feuerbach admittedly has a great advantage over the 'pure' materialists in that he realizes that man too is 'concrete object'; but he sees man only as 'concrete object' not as 'concrete activity' because he remains in the realm of theory. . . . He never manages to view the sensible world as the total, living, concrete activity of the individuals composing it." See the version given by L. D. Easton and K. H. Guddat (eds.), *Writings of the Young Marx*, pp. 418–19.

⁶⁶ S. Hook, *From Hegel to Marx* (1950, new edn, Ann Arbor, 1962), p. 274.

⁶⁷ Ibid., p. 275.

⁶⁸ Ibid., p. 281.

[69] Thesis Five runs: "Feuerbach, not satisfied with abstract thinking, wants empirical observation but he does not conceive the sensible world as practical, concrete human activity."

[70] S. Hook, *From Hegel to Marx*, p. 294.

[71] Ibid., p. 299.

[72] The last Thesis says: "The philosophers have only interpreted the world in different ways; the point is to change it." Hook's radical misunderstanding of the Theses puts him in a bad way because he says (p. 273), "I believe that Marx's critical theses on Feuerbach represent *in nuce* a turning point in the history of philosophy . . ."

[73] For a correct reading of the first Thesis, see H.-J. Krahl, "Bemerkungen zum Verhältnis von Kapital und Hegelscher Wesenslogik," *Aktualität und Folgen der Philosophie Hegels*, ed. O. Negt; and G. Lukacs, *Geschichte und Klassenbewusstsein*, pp. 32 ff.

[74] That is the meaning of Thesis Nine, which runs, "The highest point attained by that materialism that only observes the world, i.e., that does not conceive the sensible world as practical activity, is the point of view of isolated individuals in bourgeois society." Bottomore and Rubel (p. 84) make nonsense of this sentence by translating it as, "The highest point attained by that materialism which only observes the world, i.e., which does not conceive sensuous existence as practical activity, is the observation of particular individuals and of civil society." Hook (p. 299) bent it to his purpose by rendering it as: "The highest point which can be reached by *contemplative* materialism, i.e., materialism which cannot grasp the fact that sensibility is a practical activity, is the point of view of single individuals in 'civic society.'"

[75] That is the sense of Thesis Ten, which runs, "The standpoint of the old-style materialism is bourgeois society; the standpoint to the new materialism is human society or socialized humanity."

[76] See L. D. Easton and K. H. Guddat (eds.), *Writings of the Young Marx*, p. 418.

[77] See Chapter 4, "Lukacs: the Restoration of Idealism."

[78] M. Horkheimer, *Traditionelle und Kritische Theorie*, pp. 27–8.

[79] Ibid., p. 46.

[80] F. Schiller, *On the Aesthetic Education of Man* (Oxford: Oxford University Press, 1967), pp. 31–43.

[81] On the differences between these two stages, see Chapters 12 and 13 of *Capital*.

[82] *Capital*, pp. 525–7. In saying that this was the direction taken by the productive forces, that it was the logic of the modern economy, Marx still maintained that it was being obstructed by old-fashioned productive relations, i.e., that the capitalists were defending the old and excessive specialization of tasks, which could only be got rid of by revolution. Economic development has not provided any support for this contention, though it has shown numerous instances of trade unions defending an outdated division of labor against the versatility required by managers.

[83] Duly picked up and repeated by Marx, *Capital*, p. 385.

[84] K. Marx, *Texte zu Methode und Praxis, II: Pariser Manuskripte 1844* (Reinbek bei Hamburg, 1966), p. 175.

[85] Cf. Easton and Guddat, *Writings of the Young Marx*, pp. 424–5.

[86] Marx, *Texte zu Methode und Praxis*, p. 16.

[87] Z. A. Jordan, "Socialism, Alienation and Political Power," *Survey*, 60 (1966), pp. 131–2.

[88] K. Marx, *Capital*, pp. 9–10. The passage Engels added in the text, in brackets, read: "Nor does it suffice to say that he produces 'for others' without further qualification. The medieval peasant produced cense-corn for the seigneur and tithe-corn for the priest; but the fact that they were produced for others did not make commodities of cense-corn and tithe-corn. To become a commodity, a thing must pass by way of *exchange* into the hands of the other person for whom it is a use-value."

Engels explained in a note, "I add the passage in brackets to clear up a common misunderstanding. It has often and wrongfully been supposed that Marx regarded as commodities all products that were consumed by other persons than the producers."

[89] Ibid., pp. 6, 47.

[90] Ibid., p. 63.

[91] Ibid., p. 45.

[92] Ibid., pp. 381–2. Marx quoted the second phrase approvingly from Storch.

[93] Lucio Colletti, *Ideologia e Società* (Bari, 1969), p. 224. That Marx was indeed opposed to the division of labor as such is the principal theme of R. Tucker, *Philosophy and Myth in Karl Marx* (New York and Cambridge, England: Cambridge University Press, 1961).

[94] That is to say, economics is one subject among others and economic considerations are on a level with other considerations. In contrast, most neo-Marxist diatribes about, for example, the "commercialization" of art come down to regrets that aesthetics and economics are different subjects. Since they are, there is nothing mysterious about the circumstance (which is far from being invariably the case) that bad art can have a bigger *market* than good.

[95] Since Lukacs holds (p. 111) that the newspaper is the "culminating point of capitalist reification" because it commercializes ("prostitutes") subjectivity itself, let us take that case. If a newspaper consisted of the solidified, materialized self-expression of journalists, then to commercialize it, to treat it as a commodity and to wrap fish in it might be as wounding to them as it would be to a young girl to tear from her diary a poem she had written and wipe one's razor on it. On the other hand, if the value—in any conceivable sense of "value"—of the newspaper, and its very existence, depended on a variety of factors of which journalists' self-expression was only one, then complaints about the outrage done to journalists' egoes by the mere fact of a market in news and comment would be beside the point. Of course, however we look at it, the journalists' labor and personal involvement are *in* the newspaper and therefore will be affected by the way it is produced and marketed. But the problem then becomes the terms on which journalists consent to cooperate with the owners of presses, with printing labor, with suppliers of credit, with advertisers, with controllers of postal rates and other newspaper subsidies and, in general, with all the factors which contribute to a newspaper's value.

[96] Though Marx mocked Proudhon for "personifying society," he did it himself (in a passage already quoted) when explaining that under

communism "production as a whole is regulated *by society*" (my emphasis). According to his own standards, such an expression is a meaningless evasion.

97 Shortly before he died Stalin wrote (or caused to be written) a promise of the coming time when each citizen would blossom out fully, each choosing freely a profession without being bound by the division of labor to follow it forever. Trotsky, in *Literature and Revolution* (University of Michigan Press: Ann Arbor, 1960) had envisaged the transformation of men under communism into omnicompetent universal geniuses whose average level would be above Goethe, Aristotle, and Marx. At least the politicians had the modesty to put this in the future tense.

In contrast, Lukacs in 1935 proclaimed that the division of labor, and notably the separation of mental from physical labor, had already been overcome—in the Stakanovite movement! See *Contributi alla storia dell'estetica*, tr. E. Picco (Milan, 1966), pp. 91–2.

Whatever lip-service these communist pronouncements pay to Marx's (and Fourier's) fantasies, by installing the "community as universal capitalist," the communist states fail to meet a more important requirement set by young Marx.

98 K. Marx, *Grundrisse*, p. 89.

99 T. B. Bottomore and M. Rubel, *Karl Marx: Selected Writings*, pp. 259–60.

100 I. Meszaros, *Marx's Theory of Alienation*, pp. 212–14.

101 This combination also characterized *surrealism*, which was the quest for, firstly, a style of existence that would not be given ready-made but would be invented or agreed, and, secondly, an "absolute event" in which all man's possibilities would be revealed.

102 See Chapter 5, "In the Shadow of Hegel: From Marx to Marcuse."

103 "Socialized humanity is not only a classless but also a stateless, lawless, family-less, religion-less and generally structure-less collectivity of complete individuals who live in harmony with themselves, with each other, and with the anthropological nature outside of them. It hardly needs pointing out that this society without social structure is not a social order in any meaningful sense of that term. Speaking in the younger Marx's vein, it is an un-society." R. Tucker, *Philosophy and Myth in Karl Marx*, p. 201.

104 Marx was so sure that man's "true nature" was shown in social, productive, other-directed activities that he maintained the paradox that an egoistic man was being untrue to himself. *Pariser Manuskripte*, p. 175.

105 Adorno puts it less pithily than Sartre's character: *Radikale Vergesellschaftung heisst radikale Entfremdung*.

106 John Anderson, "Marxist Ethics," *Studies in Empirical Philosophy* (pp. 323–4), points out that in rejecting abstractions such as History in favor of "real living men," Marx spoke the "language of individualistic utilitarianism . . . the question is always of the survival or otherwise of persons, of the needs of 'life' . . . and not of the rival forms of activity, which might occur in the same person, and the survival or non-survival of which is, in any case, quite a different matter from the survival or non-survival of persons."

107 As François Perroux argues against Marcuse, who is similarly engrossed with the securing of private satisfactions. See *François Perroux interroge Herbert Marcuse, qui répond* (Paris, 1969), pp. 103–19.

108 H. Marcuse, *One-Dimensional Man* (Boston: Beacon Press, 1964; London: Routledge, 1964), p. 4.

[109] H. Marcuse, *Eros and Civilization* (Boston: Beacon Press, 1955; London: Sphere, 1968), Chapter 9.

[110] H. Marcuse, *Psychoanalyse und Politik* (Frankfurt, 1968), pp. 48–9.

[111] H. Marcuse, *Negations*, p. 73.

[112] H. Marcuse, *An Essay on Liberation* (Boston: Beacon Press, 1969; London: Allen Lane, 1969), pp. 5–10.

[113] No cars, aeroplanes, television or tractors, nor economic growth, but only "fundamental human needs," as defined by himself.

[114] Plekhanov made this objection to Antonio Labriola, as soon as the Italian advanced the saving hypothesis of latter-day Marxism: the workers did not see the tasks that confronted them. Plekhanov replied that ignorance explained nothing when it was ignorance of a social reality that did not yet exist. Labriola had nevertheless adumbrated the ideology of Western communism. *Fundamental Problems of Marxism,* tr. Katzer (London: Lawrence & Wishart, 1969), pp. 123–30.

2. Georges Sorel: Alienation becomes Violence

[1] "This relation [of labor to capital] is already an aberration: the thing becomes a person and the person becomes a thing. For what distinguishes this form [of the economy] from all preceding ones is that the capitalist does not dominate workers by virtue of some quality of his person but only to the extent that he is 'capital.' His domination is solely that of materialized work over living work, the domination of the worker's product over the worker himself." Karl Marx, "Notes sur l'aliénation," in *Cahiers de Marxologie* (vol. 2, no. 12, December 1968), p. 2424.

[2] As Henri Poincaré wrote about this time: "Laymen are struck by the brief life of scientific theories. They see them abandoned one after the other after several years of popularity; they see ruins piling up on ruins; they feel that the theories that are fashionable today will soon enough collapse in their turn, inevitably, and they conclude from this that such theories are totally vain. This is what they call the *bankruptcy of science.*" Henri Poincaré, *La Science et l'hypothèse* (Paris, 1935), p. 128.

[3] G. Sorel, *Matériaux d'une théorie du prolétariat* (Paris, 3rd edn, 1926), p. 58.

[4] The Sherman Act against U.S. restrictive trade practices dates from 1890, but the campaign against the "monopolies" occupied the first decade of the century and culminated in the Clayton Act of 1914.

[5] Notably in R. Hilferding, *Das Finanzkapital* (Berlin, 1910).

[6] André Philip, *La Gauche: mythes et réalités* (Paris, 1964), pp. 62–3.

[7] G. Sorel, *Le Décomposition du marxisme* (Paris, 1908).

[8] Poincaré said of Maxwell's theory of the ether, "One would think one was reading the description of a factory with its gears, its shafts transmitting movements and bending under the strain, its governors and conveyor belts." Duhem exclaimed of Lodge's treatise on electricity, "In it there is nothing but strings which move around pulleys, which go through pearl beads, which carry weights. . . . We thought we were entering the tranquil abode of reason but we find ourselves in a factory." Quoted from Abel Rey, *La Théorie de la physique chez les physiciens contemporains* (Paris, 3rd edn, 1930), p. 148. For the industrial origin of models in physics from the age of mine pumps to that of the steam engine, see A. Rey, *Le Retour éternel et la philosophie*

de la physique (Paris, 1927). Sorel's earliest essay on the philosophy of science sought to show the connection between theoretical models and industrial machines: "L'ancienne et la nouvelle métaphysique," 1894, published as *D'Aristote à Marx* (Paris, 1935).

⁹ The separation of ownership from management in the joint stock company (to be rediscovered several decades later as the "Managerial Revolution") was already, from the time of Walter Rathenau's *Von kommenden Dingen* (Berlin, 1918), being treated as another instance of the impersonal product becoming independent of, and superior to, the personal producer. The corporation becomes an active person and its real owners, the stockholders, become passive objects. This can be described in the same language, and (if one takes pity on the "ensnared small shareholder") with the same pathos as Marx used for the case of labor and capital. If, instead, one sees in these facts the rise of a new social entity with its own ways of acting, different from those of its individual "owners", then one has begun the real study of the modern business corporation. That study did, in fact, emerge out of the metaphysical nebula here being examined.

¹⁰ G. Sorel, *La Révolution dreyfusienne* (Paris, 1909).

¹¹ "The opponents of democracy could argue that it ignored the real man, with his real interests and his real groupings; the abstract citizen, counted and represented in parliament, was a figment of the theorists' imagination. This was the criticism the monarchists brought against the Republic: in place of the real man, participating in matters of immediate concern and within his competence through a variety of natural organizations (local, professional, religious or family), democracy had substituted the elector, whose only right was to pronounce at intervals on matters about which he knew nothing. The Revolution has been described as an expression of the *esprit géométrique*; with it the mechanistic rationalism of Descartes was transferred to the state. In Bergsonian terms, democracy was based upon analysis—*ordre géométrique*—and thus failed to grasp the reality of the *ordre vital*. The point was made by Pirou in 1910 when he said of the syndicalist theoreticians that they saw democracy as the political expression of intellectualism and universal suffrage as a philosophy of discontinuity, a misunderstanding of the deep, internal unity of social reality. Proposals for a more real, more organic structure of society were advanced on all sides: social catholicism, guild socialism, solidarism and communism in the days when it still favored government by soviets. Such proposals formed part of the same movement as the fascists' call for a corporate state, the monarchists' for a nation of states and provinces, and the syndicalists' for a society based on trade unions."

F. F. Ridley, *Revolutionary Syndicalism in France: The Direct Action of its Time* (New York and Cambridge: Cambridge University Press, 1970), pp. 211–12.

¹² The most concise statement of his ideas on this subject is in *Les Préoccupations métaphysiques des physiciens modernes* (Paris, 1907). See also: Sir Isaiah Berlin's discussion, "Georges Sorel," in the *Times Literary Supplement* (31 December 1971), pp. 1617–22.

¹³ W. Gallie, *Peirce and Pragmatism* (London: Penguin, 1952), pp. 23–4. Gallie observes that the second law of thermodynamics, "the doctrine of the running down or heat death of the universe made up the so-called nineteenth-century nightmare, a curious complex of theoretical

beliefs and emotional reactions, without reference to which little of the philosophy of the late nineteenth and early twentieth centuries can be adequately understood."

Bergson complacently called that law "the most metaphysical of the laws of physics." On the metaphysical exploitation of it, see A. Rey, "Physique et philosophie de la nature à la fin du XIX siècle," in *Revue Philosophique* (vol. 51, 1926), pp. 321–70.

[14] G. Sorel, *De l'utilité du pragmatisme* (2nd edn, Paris, 1928), pp. 246–71, and "Le système des mathématiques" in *Revue de métaphysique et de morale* (1900), pp. 407–28. Sorel considered this argument to be the most exquisite demonstration both of Marx's economic interpretation of history and Bergson's *homo faber* account of intelligence.

[15] In so far as they took this to mean that technology determined culture, these "vulgar Marxists" had certainly misunderstood Marx. See Lukacs's attack on Bukharin for this error in a review of the latter's *Theory of Historical Materialism*, reproduced in *Schriften zur Ideologie*, pp. 188–200.

[16] G. Sorel, *Insegnamenti sociali della economia contemporanea: Degenerazione capitalistica e degenerazione socialista* (Milan, 1907).

[17] Notably in G. Sorel, *Saggi di critica del marxismo* (Palermo, 1903), and in Sorel's preface to Seligman, *L'Interprétation économique de l'histoire,* tr. Barrault (Paris, 1911).

[18] G. Sorel, *Matériaux d'une théorie du prolétariat*, pp. 383–4.

[19] Ibid., p. 18.

[20] Ibid., pp. 170–73.

[21] *Réflexions sur la violence*, (11th edn, Paris, 1950), p. 202. There are many editions of the English translation by T. E. Hulme, *Reflections on Violence,* first published in 1915.

[22] G. Sorel, *Matériaux*, p. 69.

[23] G. Sorel, *Réflexions*, p. 219.

[24] Ibid., pp. 371–87.

[25] G. Sorel, *Les Illusions du progrès* (5th edn, Paris, 1947), pp. 317–36. This has recently been translated by the University of California Press with a foreword by Robert Nisbet. *The Illusions of Progress* (Berkeley, 1969).

[26] Ibid., p. 354.

3. Gramsci: Marx and/or Mussolini

[1] In English there exists an anthology: Gramsci, *The Modern Prince and other writings* (London: Lawrence & Wishart, 1957). In French there are: Gramsci, *Lettres de la prison* (Paris, 1953), and *Le Materialisme historique et la philosophie de Benedetto Croce* (Paris, 1948).

[2] A. Caracciolo and G. Scalia (ed.), *La Città futura: Saggi sulla figura e il pensiero di Antonio Gramsci* (Milan, 1959), p. 9 and elsewhere.

[3] On Gramsci's life, see John M. Cammett, *Antonio Gramsci and the Origins of Italian Communism* (Stanford: Stanford University Press, 1967). For his theories, see C. Riechers, *Antonio Gramsci: Marxismus in Italien* (Frankfurt, 1970) and the works mentioned in V. Frosini, *Storia della critica al marxismo in Italia* (Catania, 1965).

[4] For this period see E. Avidgor, "Il movimento operaio torinese durante la prima guerra mondiale," in *La Città futura.*

⁵ Enzo Santarelli, *La Revisione del marxismo in Italia* (Milan, 1964), Chapter 5, and Gaetano Arfé, *Storia del socialismo italiano* (Turin, 1965), Chapter 25. The detailed history of the Leghorn split is in Helmut König, *Lenin und der italienische Sozialismus* (Tubingen, 1967).

⁶ Cf. A. Caracciolo, "Serrati, Bordiga e la polemica gramsciana contro il 'blanquismo' o settarismo di partito," in *La Città futura*.

⁷ The books thus compiled, and published by Einaudi (Turin), are *Il materialismo storico e la filosofia di Benedetto Croce* (1948), *Gli intellettuali e l'organizzazione della cultura* (1949), *Il Risorgimento* (1949), *Note sul Machiavelli, sulla politica e sullo stato moderno* (1949), and *Passato e presente* (1951). In addition, *Letteratura e vita nazionale* (1950) contains extracts from the Notebooks as well as drama reviews published in *Avanti!*

⁸ Gramsci, *Scritti giovanili* (Turin, 1958). Most, but not all, of his articles are published in *L'Ordine Nuovo* 1919–20 (Turin, 1954). There is a selection of the main ones in *Antologia popolare degli scritti e delle lettere di Antonio Gramsci* (Rome, 1957).

⁹ From an article published in August 1919, but not included in the *Opere* book, *L'Ordine Nuovo*; cited by Caracciolo in *La Città futura*, p. 96.

¹⁰ See Sorel's January 1920 essay published as "Ultime Meditazioni" in the Roman review *Nuova Antologia* in 1928 (vol. 262, pp. 289–307), and of which the present writer gave the original text (restoring the cuts made by the fascist editors of 1928) in "Georges Sorel: Aperçu sur les Utopies, les Soviets et le Droit Nouveau," in *Etudes de Marxologie*, January 1962. Gramsci read Sorel's essay in jail and discusses it in *Materialismo storico*, pp. 105–11.

¹¹ A. Gramsci, *Lettere dal carcere* (Turin, 1947).

¹² A. Gramsci, *Materialismo storico*, pp. 199–200.

¹³ Ibid., p. 76.

¹⁴ Ibid., pp. 75, 80–81. "Hegemony" is a key-word in Gramsci, implying opposition to "dictatorship" in the sense that cultural predominance can be distinguished from political power. When they coincide, that is revolution.

¹⁵ A. Gramsci, *Passato e presente*, pp. 55–7.

¹⁶ A. Gramsci, *Materialismo storico*, pp. 32, 41.

¹⁷ The interpretation of Machiavelli's *Prince* as a Sorelian myth symbolizing the Italian people is to be found in the *Note sul Machiavelli*. The principal passages have been translated in Gramsci, *The Modern Prince*, from which the following quotations are taken, pp. 137–9.

¹⁸ A. Gramsci, *Materialismo storico*, p. 32.

¹⁹ Cf. G. Cottier, *Du romantisme au marxisme* (Paris, 1961), of which the last section, pp. 207–26, deals with Gramsci.

²⁰ Croce, "Come nacque e come morì il marxismo teorico in Italia 1895–1900," published as an appendix to Antonio Labriola, *La concezione materialistica della storia* (4th edn, Bari, 1953). Cf. Neil McInnes, "Les débuts du marxisme théorique en France et en Italie 1880–97," in *Etudes de Marxologie* (June 1960).

²¹ A. Gramsci, *Materialismo storico*, pp. 50, 160.

4. Lukacs: the Restoration of Idealism

¹ "Zur Frage des Parlamentarismus," in *Kommunismus I* (1920), pp. 161–72. Reprinted in Georg Lukacs, *Schriften zur Ideologie und Politik*, hereafter

referred to as *Schriften*. The *Schriften* include extensive biographical and bibliographical information prepared by their editor, Peter Ludz.

[2] *Geschichte und Klassenbewusstsein*. An English translation by R. Livingstone appeared in London (Merlin Press, 1971).

[3] The so-called Blum Theses. Reprinted in *Schriften*, pp. 290–322.

[4] David Kettler, *Marxismus und Kultur: Mannheim und Lukacs in den ungarischen Revolutionen*, 1918–19 (Neuwied and Berlin, 1967), translated from an unidentified American original. Lukacs himself, speaking in 1967 of his 1923 views, called this attitude "abstract utopianism in the realm of cultural politics."

[5] G. Lukacs, *Lenin* (Berlin and Vienna, 1924).

[6] G. Lukacs, *Geschichte und Klassenbewusstsein*, p. 152.

[7] Alasdair MacIntyre, "Marxist Mask and Romantic Face: Lukacs on Thomas Mann," *Encounter*, April 1965, pp. 64–72.

[8] G. E. Rusconi, *La Teoria critica della società* (Bologna, 1968), covers all the "critical school," from Lukacs and Korsch to Adorno, Horkheimer, and Marcuse.

[9] A. Gramsci, *Passato e Presente*, p. 66.

[10] Franz Borkenau, *World Communism* (new edn, Ann Arbor, 1962), pp. 171–4.

[11] "Offener Brief des Exekutivkomitees der Kommunistischen Internationale an die Mitglieder der Kommunistischen Partei Ungarns" (1928), reproduced in *Schriften*, pp. 727–52.

[12] Morris Watnick, "Relativism and Class Consciousness: Georg Lukacs," *Revisionism*, ed. L. Labedz (London: Allen & Unwin, 1962).

[13] *Die Zerstörung der Vernunft* (Berlin, 1954). In French as *La Destruction de la Raison* (Paris, 1958).

[14] See the essays, lectures and interviews collected in Lukacs, *Marxismo e politica culturale* (Turin, 1968), and in *Schriften*, pp. 593–706.

[15] Lukacs assigns this task to socialist ideology, and to socialist realist art in particular, in the course of an essay on Solzhenitsyn (1970). Indeed, *The First Circle, Cancer Ward* and *Ivan Denisovich* are efforts to master the past—but they happen to be forbidden works. Lukacs's position once again was untenable: the literature he commended in the name of communist theory was banned by communist society. He consented to occupy the office of grand old man of communist letters although he was not free to say that communist letters are worthless nor that the valuable works written by such masters as Solzhenitsyn were censored.

[16] Francisco Fernandez-Santos, *Historia y Filosofia* (Barcelona, 1966), p. 226.

[17] Lukacs, *The Meaning of Contemporary Realism*, tr. Mander (London: Merlin Press, 1963), p. 81.

[18] T. Pinkus (ed.), *Gespräche mit Georg Lukacs* (Hamburg, 1967).

5. In the Shadow of Hegel: from Marx to Marcuse

[1] Marx also believed that once the symptom stood revealed as a symbol, it would disappear. He wrote to Feuerbach that Schelling's first philosophy was "a youthful and fantastic dream" of which Feuerbach had discovered the symbolic sense, adding, "Schelling is therefore your *anticipated caricature*,

and as soon as reality comes out against a caricature, the latter must vanish like a mist." Quoted by G. V. Plekhanov, *Fundamental Problems of Marxism*, p. 24.

² He called it *"ein sinnlich übersinnliches Ding,"* and "a most complex thing, full of metaphysical subtleties and theological caprices." The socialists of 1890 could make nothing of that but today all the restorers of *anticipated caricatures* can see in it Hegel's object, in which spirit lies estranged, and young Marx's goods, in which man's mutilated humanity lies alienated.

³ Including Lenin himself in 1894. Cf. Karl Korsch, "L'ancienne dialectique hégélienne et la nouvelle science matérialiste," *Etudes de Marxologie*, no. 7 (1963), p. 182.

⁴ V. Lenin, *Cahiers sur la dialectique de Hegel* (Paris, 1967), p. 241.

⁵ Ibid., p. 204.

⁶ L. Althusser, *Lenine et la Philosophie* (Paris, 1969), p. 18.

⁷ V. Lenin, *Cahiers*, p. 248.

⁸ Ibid., p. 160.

⁹ Ibid., p. 167.

¹⁰ L. Colletti, *Ideologia e società*, pp. 166–7.

¹¹ B. Jeu, *La Philosophie soviétique et l'Occident*, pp. 343–6.

¹² Max Eastman, *Marx, Lenin and the Science of Revolution* (London: Allen & Unwin, 1926.)

¹³ V. Lenin, *Cahiers*, p. 204.

¹⁴ Lenin later advised "militant materialists" to constitute "a sort of society of materialist friends of Hegel's dialectic" by publishing *"fragments* from Hegel's principal works to interpret them materialistically, commenting on them by examples of the application of dialectics in Marx, and also by those examples of dialectics in the field of economic and political relations which recent history, especially contemporary imperialist war and revolution, provides *in large numbers.*" (Italics added.) Quoted in G. Petrovic, *Marx in the Mid-Twentieth Century* (New York, 1967).

¹⁵ V. Lenin, *Cahiers*, pp. 257–8, 278–86.

¹⁶ Ibid., pp. 195, 205.

¹⁷ Ibid., p. 205.

¹⁸ G. Lukacs, "Mein Weg zu Marx," in *Schriften*, pp. 325–6.

¹⁹ D. Kettler, *Marxismus und Kultur: Mannheim und Lukacs in den ungarischen Revolutionen.*

²⁰ G. Lukacs, *Lenin: Studie über den Zusammenhang seiner Gedanken.*

²¹ Cf. L. Colletti, *Ideologia e società*, pp. 181–2.

²² G. Lukacs, *Geschichte und Klassenbewusstsein*, pp. 198–203.

²³ Ibid., pp. 61–3, 86–8, 190–91.

²⁴ M. Merleau-Ponty, *Les Aventures de la dialectique*, p. 71.

²⁵ For Lenin's role in the defeat of Italian socialism by fascism, see H. Konig, *Lenin und der italienische Sozialismus.*

²⁶ A. Gramsci, *Il Materialismo storico e la filosofia di Benedetto Croce*, pp. 69–70.

²⁷ Ibid., pp. 75–6, 223–7.

²⁸ Ibid., pp. 80–81.

²⁹ Ibid., p. 159.

³⁰ Ibid., p. 199.

³¹ Ibid., p. 91.
³² Ibid., pp. 79–87.
³³ Ibid., p. 159.
³⁴ Ibid., pp. 55–6, 142–3.
³⁵ Ibid., pp. 69, 199.
³⁶ A. Gramsci, *Note sul Machiavelli, sulla politica e sullo stato moderno.*
³⁷ A. Gramsci, *Passato e Presente*, pp. 65–7, 70.
³⁸ A. Gramsci, *Materialismo storico*, p. 39.
³⁹ C. Riechers, *Antonio Gramsci: Marxismus in Italien*, pp. 167–8.
⁴⁰ A. Gramsci, *Materialismo storico*, pp. 18–19.
⁴¹ H. Marcuse, *Kultur und Gesellschaft*, vol. I (Frankfurt, 1965), p. 55.
⁴² Ibid., p. 46.
⁴³ H. Marcuse, *Hegels Ontologie und die Theorie der Geschichtlichkeit* (new edition, Frankfurt, 1968).
⁴⁴ H. Marcuse, *Negations*, p. 55.
⁴⁵ Ibid., pp. 66–7.
⁴⁶ The dates are those of essays now collected in *Negations* or in *Kultur und Gesellschaft.*
⁴⁷ H. Marcuse, *Negations*, p. 168.
⁴⁸ Ibid., p. 189.
⁴⁹ Ibid., pp. 190–91.
⁵⁰ Ibid., p. 192.
⁵¹ H. Marcuse, *Reason and Revolution: Hegel and the Rise of Social Theory* (Boston: Beacon Press, 1960; London: Oxford University Press, 1941).
⁵² H. Marcuse, "Neue Quellen zur Grundlegung des historischen Materialismus," in *Die Gesellschaft* (1932).
⁵³ H. Marcuse, *An Essay on Liberation* (Boston: Beacon Press, 1969; London: Allen Lane, The Penguin Press, 1969), pp. 14–15: "The First International was the last attempt to realize the solidarity of the species by grounding it in that social class in which the subjective and objective interest, the particular and the universal, coincided (the International is the late concretization of the abstract philosophical concept of 'man as man,' human being, *Gattungswesen*, which plays such a decisive role in Marx and Engels's early writings) ... the distinction between the real and the immediate interests of the exploited ... far from being an abstract idea, was guiding the strategy of the Marxist movement."
⁵⁴ H. Marcuse, *Eros and Civilization* (Boston: Beacon Press, 1955; London: Allen Lane, The Penguin Press, 1969).
⁵⁵ M. Ambacher, *Marcuse et la civilisation américaine* (Paris, 1969). Cf. R. Tucker, *Philosophy and Myth in Karl Marx*, p. 50: "Hegel's world-self is a neurotic personality."
⁵⁶ G. Rohrmoser, *Das Elend des kritischen Theorie* (Freiburg im Breisgau, 1970), pp. 67–71.
⁵⁷ H. Marcuse, *Psychoanalyse und Politik.*
⁵⁸ Thus falling far below Lukacs who not only denies atomism but makes that denial the basis of his literary criticism. Novelists who set characters in a social milieu are "naturalists," like Emile Zola and Victor Hugo. In

contrast, novelists who fuse character and social milieu by portraying men as the vehicles of social movements and as the incarnations of conflicting moralities and institutions are "realists" like Balzac, Dickens, Tolstoy. See G. Lukacs, *Balzac et le réalisme français*, tr. Laveau (Paris, 1967).

⁵⁹ A. MacIntyre, *Marcuse* (London: Fontana, 1970), pp. 53–4. On the sexual proclivities of the Young Hegelians, including for a time Marx and Engels, see L. Feuer, *Marx and the Intellectuals* (New York: Anchor edn, 1969), pp. 70–83.

⁶⁰ J. Laplanche, "Notes sur Marcuse et la psychanalyse" in *La Nef*, no. 36 (Paris, 1969).

⁶¹ H. Marcuse, *Five Lectures* (Boston: Beacon Press, 1970; London: Allen Lane, The Penguin Press, 1970), p. 30.

⁶² Marcuse declared Freudianism "obsolescent" from 1963 (*Five Lectures*, pp. 44–61). The coming of Imagination, anticipated in *Eros and Civilization*, is revealed in *An Essay on Liberation*.

⁶³ F. Schiller, *On the Aesthetic Education of Man*. The letters relevant to Marcuse's reading of Schiller are the second, sixth, and seventh.

⁶⁴ H. Marcuse, *Liberation*, pp. 24–45. Politics as art is a favorite theme with fascists, which is no doubt why Joseph Goebbels in his novel *Michael* also plundered Schiller. On the Nazi veneration for Schiller see the Introduction to the *Aesthetic Education* by E. M. Wilkinson and L. A. Willoughby, pp. cxli–ii. On politics as art cf. Rohrmoser, *Das Elend des kritischen Theorie*, pp. 76–81.

⁶⁵ Colletti, *Ideologia e società*, pp. 174–8. Cf. J.-P. Sartre, *La Nausée* (Paris, 1963), p. 177; "Elles sont là, grotesques, têtues, géantes et . . . je suis au milieu des Choses, les innommables. Seul, sans mots, sans défenses, elles m'environnent, sous moi, derrière moi, audessus de moi . . . seul en face de cette masse noire et noueuse, entièrement brute et qui me faisait peur."

⁶⁶ H. Marcuse, *La Fin de l'Utopie* (Neuchatel, 1968), pp. 43–4; *Liberation*, pp. 49–71.

⁶⁷ Marcuse's quandary about elitism is plainest in R. P. Wolff *et al.*, *Critique of Pure Tolerance*, pp. 114–37.

⁶⁸ On the missing second dimension as a cultural aristocracy see L. W. Nauta, *Theorie en Praxis bij Marcuse* (Baarn, 1969).

⁶⁹ The theory of playful aristocratic logic that rejects the plebeian empiricism of non-contradiction is laid out with more consistent insolence than Marcuse can manage by Ortega in *La idea de principio en Leibniz y la evolución de la teoria deductiva* (Buenos Aires, 1958).

6. Ideologists of the New Left

¹ Most of the quotations are drawn from Carl Oglesby (ed.), *The New Left Reader* (New York: Grove Press, 1969). Additionally, I have drawn on E. Guevara, *Diario del Che en Bolivia*; Nikolaus Ryschkowsky, *Die linke Linke* (Munich, 1968); Régis Debray, *Révolution dans la révolution?* (Maspero edn, Paris, 1969); Leo Huberman and Paul Sweezy (eds.), *Régis Debray and the Latin American Revolution* (New York and London: Monthly Review Press, 1968); Frantz Fanon, *Les Damnés de la Terre* (Paris, 1961) and *Pour la*

révolution africaine (Paris, 1964). There are paperback editions (Penguin, and others) of most of the writings of Debray and Fanon, not to mention Herbert Marcuse. The reader is also referred to the massive anthology by Massino Teodori, *New Left: A Documentary History* (New York: Bobbs-Merrill, 1970; London: Cape, 1970), and to the critical volume of essays edited by Maurice Cranston, *The New Left* (New York: The Library Press, 1971; London: Bodley Head, 1970).

² Lukacs saw the connection between the New Left and his work of the 1920s, for he said in 1967, in the preface to the new edition, "the conception of revolutionary praxis in this book takes on extravagant overtones that are more in keeping with the current messianic utopianism of the communist Left than with authentic Marxist doctrine." Irving Howe has put together a useful collection, *Beyond the New Left* (New York: McCall, 1970). The so-called Modern Masters Series, published by Fontana/Collins in London and Viking in New York, has a number of relevant volumes, with brief bibliographies for further reading: see Alasdair MacIntyre, *Marcuse*; David Caute, *Fanon*; John Lyons, *Chomsky*; George Lichtheim, *Lukacs*; Andrew Sinclair, *Guevara*.

³ Lewis Feuer, "Neo-Primitivism: the New Marxism of the Alienated Intellectuals", in *Marx and the Intellectuals*.

⁴ Paul Breines, "Marcuse and the New Left in America", in J. Habermas (ed.), *Antworten auf Herbert Marcuse* (Frankfurt, 1968).

⁵ Alasdair MacIntyre, *Marcuse* (New York: Viking, 1970; London: Fontana, 1970).

⁶ H. H. Holz, *Utopie und Anarchismus: Zur Kritik der kritischen Theorie Herbert Marcuses* (Cologne, 1968).

7. From the Associated Producers to the Flower People

¹ J.-F. Revel, *Ni Marx ni Jésus* (Paris, 1970), p. 35; and Raymond Aron, preface to new edition of *L'Opium des Intellectuels* (Paris, 1968), p. 10. The translations are: *Beyond Marx and Jesus* (New York: Doubleday, 1971; London: Paladin, 1972), and *The Opium of the Intellectuals* (New York: Norton, 1962).

² R. Tucker, *Philosophy and Myth in Karl Marx*, pp. 234–8; M. Nicolaus in C. Oglesby (ed.), *New Left Reader*, pp. 105–7.

³ Actually, Marcuse's assumptions in 1969 were more extensive than those of Plutarch's Lycurgus in the first century A.D. (ascribed by Plutarch to the ninth century B.C.). Lycurgus's utopia was possible provided there was frugality at the common table, no eating at home, no magnificence in building or furniture, sexual chastity, and laconic speech. Marcuse, despite the supposed miracles of automation, says his utopia still presupposes a totally new humanity, new values, new words, a new character and even a new human *biology*. See: *An Essay on Liberation*, pp. 5–9. Even then, Marcuse warns, we must expect a decline in productivity and an end to "luxury"—which he defines as most of the goods we now consume. This sort of communist prophetism is the ancient tautology that abundance is possible as soon as we all accept a low enough standard of living.

[4] F. Perroux, *François Perroux interroge Herbert Marcuse.*

[5] J. K. Galbraith, *The New Industrial State* (Boston: Houghton Mifflin, 1967; London: Hamish Hamilton, 1967), pp. 57–9, 370–99.

[6] G. Lukacs *et al, Gespräche mit Georg Lukacs,* pp. 46–9.

[7] J. Monnerot, *Sociologie de la révolution* (Paris, 1969), pp. 695–9.

[8] K. Marx, *Texte zu Methode und Praxis,* II, *Pariser Manuskripte.*

[9] K. Marx. *Grundrisse der Kritik der Politischen Oekonomie (Rohentwurf).*

[10] K. Marx, *Capital,* pp. 45–6 and 53–4.

[11] Ibid., p. 874. As to stifling limitations on production, Marx's next sentence is a reference to the cyclical depressions of capitalism, soon to be swept away in a "universal crisis."

[12] For a history of this movement, see: G. E. Rusconi, *La Teoria critica della società;* G. Lichtheim, "From Marx to Hegel: Reflections on Georg Lukacs, T. W. Adorno and Herbert Marcuse," in *Triquarterly,* July 1968, pp. 5–42; and G. Rohrmoser, *Das Elend der kritischen Theorie: Adorno, Marcuse, Habermas.*

[13] "The categorical judgement is typical of pre-bourgeois society: matters stand thus and man can change nothing. The hypothetical and disjunctive forms of judgement are peculiar to the bourgeois world: under certain circumstances this effect can occur; either matters stand thus or otherwise. Critical Theory declares: matters need not stand thus; men can change being; the appropriate circumstances are now at hand." M. Horkheimer, *Traditionelle und kritische Theorie,* p. 44. The passage quoted dates from 1937.

[14] W. F. Haug, "Das Ganze und das ganz Andere," in J. Habermas (ed.), *Antworten auf Herbert Marcuse.*

[15] H. Marcuse, *Negations,* pp. 214–15.

[16] For those theories see *Venceremos! The Speeches and writings of Che Guevara,* ed. John Gerassi (New York: Simon & Schuster, 1969; London: Weidenfeld & Nicolson, 1968), pp. 250–56, 280–85, 292–316, and 387–409.

[17] The quotations are from Horkheimer, op. cit., pp. 12–64; T. W. Adorno, *Zur Metakritik der Erkenntnistheorie* (Stuttgart, 1956), pp. 33 ff.; Herbert Marcuse, *Reason and Revolution* and *One-Dimensional Man* (Boston: Beacon Press, 1964; London: Routledge, 1964).

[18] K. Marx, *Grundrisse,* p. 89.

[19] Revel, *Ni Marx ni Jésus,* p. 71: "These Left-wing intellectuals, those with by far the most prestige and influence, are ruled by old-fashioned ideas and hostility to science. They are mainly engaged in devising, with tireless ingenuity, modernized and often clever reproductions of doctrinal models from a pre-scientific universe; moreover, they are marked by an extreme cultural aristocratism. For them as for the medieval clerk, culture is a way of marking themselves off from the rest of humanity, of feeling superior to the mass. . . . Since this culture is also impregnated with currents of revolutionary origin (Marxism, psycho-analysis, surrealism), it ends up creating an inextricable amalgam of the Leftist mood and the anti-scientific and anti-technological mood. Science *is* capitalism, that is the slogan it ends with."

[20] Adorno, *Negative Dialektik* (Frankfurt, 1965), p. 275.

[21] Marcuse, *An Essay on Liberation,* Chapter 2.

Surrealism's combination of Marx and Fourier had been anticipated by the poet of Critical Theory, Walter Benjamin. "Sometimes [Benjamin] used to talk to us about his [theory of a phalansterist revival] as an esoteric doctrine, at once erotic and artisanal, that underlay his explicit Marxist conceptions. Communism of the means of production would enable us to substitute for the old social classes a division of society into *emotional classes.* Liberated industrial production, instead of repressing the emotions, would let their forms blossom out and it would organize emotional exchanges, in the sense that work would become the accomplice of lust instead of being a primitive compensation for it." Pierre Klossowski, "Entre Fourier et Marx," in *Le Monde*, 31 May 1969.

André Breton discovered Fourier in 1940, the year of Benjamin's suicide, and his ode to Fourier dates from 1947. The surrealist international exhibition, *Ecart Absolu*, dedicated to Fourier, was held in Paris in 1965. The surrealist protest against capitalist alienation and the consumer society, in the name of the total realization of human potentiality in a new and man-made world, was thus popularized in time for the events of May 1968 in France. The crop of books on Fourier since then has, indeed, another cause: the women's "liberation" movement as conceived by those he called *les saphiennes* and their male helpers, of whom he was one. In this variety of Marxism, the place of the proletariat is taken by lesbians, as Simone Debout proclaims. "L'Illusion réelle," in *Topique: Revue freudienne* (Paris, October 1970), p. 23.

[22] C. Oglesby, *New Left Reader*, p. 9.

[23] "Appeal from the Sorbonne," 13–14 June 1968, Thesis 23.

[24] R. Berthelot, *Un romantisme utilitaire: étude sur le mouvement pragmatiste* (Paris, 1911); J. Sageret, *La Vague mystique* (Paris, 1920); V. Lee, *Les Mensonges vitaux* (Paris, 1921); and R. B. Perry, *Present Philosophical Tendencies* (New York, 1912).

[25] H. Bergson, *Creative Evolution*, tr. A. Mitchell (New York, 1944; London: Macmillan, 1965), pp. 99, 179–81, and 141–2.

[26] L. Colletti, *Il marxismo e Hegel* (Bari, 1969), pp. 317–56.

[27] Ibid., pp. 329–30.

[28] See Lukacs's 1967 preface to his 1923 book: "Since the object, the thing, exists in Hegel only as an alienation of self-consciousness, its recuperation by the subject would mean the end of objective reality, hence the end of reality in general. Now, *History and Class Consciousness* follows Hegel in this, that in that book alienation is put on the same level as objectification (to use the terminology of Marx's Paris Manuscripts). This gross and fundamental error surely contributed in notable measure to the success of *History and Class Consciousness*."

[29] G. Lukacs, *Geschichte und Klassenbewusstsein*, pp. 20–21.

[30] Ibid., p. 23.

[31] Ibid., p. 136.

[32] Ibid., p. 178.

[33] Ibid., pp. 198–203.

[34] However, for the intellectual climate see G. Lichtheim, *Lukacs* (New York: Viking, 1970; London: Fontana, 1970).

[35] Lukacs, *Marxismo e politica culturale* (Turin, 1968), p. 70.

³⁶ Adorno, *Negative Dialektik*, pp. 240 ff. When New Left agitators over-looked these objections, Adorno uttered the famous protest, "I set out a theoretical model. How was I to dream that people would try to make it come true by using Molotov cocktails?"

³⁷ In the 1968 preface to his collected essays of the 1930s and 1940s, *Kritische Theorie* (Frankfurt, 1968). When Horkheimer's objections were overlooked in turn, he protested that he could not be held responsible because the world student uprising happened everywhere, "even where no one has read my books." On this issue of "responsibility" see S. Encel, "Sociology and Student Unrest," *Australian and New Zealand Journal of Sociology*, April 1970. Against the direct, immediate causality that Hork-heimer and Encel have in mind, my own analysis presupposes a slow and anonymous permeation, over several decades, of the desperate revolutionism of the Critical Theory of the 1930s, notably in the teachings of its academic exponents.

On that process, see the dialogue in D. Desanti, "San Francisco: Des Hippies pour Fourier," in *Topique*, no. 4–5, p. 205. " 'We're Fourierists,' declares the leader with the hair and beard of a ginger Christ, dressed in a very long unbleached smock, looking like the Christs they used once to sell in the Place Saint Sulpice. 'Have your read Fourier?' Hesitation. Tell a lie and fall in under the star-spangled banner of universal culture? Or confess you prefer myth to knowledge, dreams to books? A flutter of the eye betrays the torment of a choice quickly made. 'We've been told.' " It is not suggested that many members of the New Left have read the books discussed in this chapter. They have "been told."

³⁸ T. W. Adorno and W. Dirks (eds.), *Soziologische Exkurse*, vol. 4 of the *Frankfurter Beiträge zur Soziologie* (Frankfurt, 1956).

³⁹ K. Marx, *Capital*, p. 50.

⁴⁰ *Pariser Manuskripte*, 1844, pp. 166–71, 173–4, 179–80.

⁴¹ It follows that de-alienation is a speculative notion, corresponding to something the world has never yet seen. This does not bother the neo-Marxists. "Consequently, if it is the *inadequacy* of some forms of objectification that may properly be called alienation, it is not true that objectivity equals 'estranged human relations,' although it may be true that the objectivity of civilized society as we have known it *so far* carried with it estranged human relations. By contrast, an adequate form of human objectification would produce social objectivity as *objectified* but *non-alienated* human relations . . ." Istvan Meszaros, *Marx's Theory of Alienation*, pp. 172–3.

8. The Irrational Totality, or the Life and Death of Reason

¹ Max Horkheimer, *Verwaltete Welt?* (Zurich, 1970), pp. 18–20 and 30.

² This could lead to some strange anxieties. Marx (or Engels) once said that before the rise of technique, the only division of labor was in the sexual act. They had no doubt forgotten that harmless joke when on other occasions they insisted that the revolution would suppress the division of labor. If one takes both these absurdities literally, the problem arises whether after the revolution one will make love.

"What will happen not only to *love* but also to the *sexual act*—the original form of the division of labor—after that radical suppression of all division of labor by which must pass the enterprise of human de-alienation? With a new mode of economic and technological *production* will there come a new mode of *reproduction*?" This contribution to the science fiction of obstetrics is from Kostas Axelos, *Marx, penseur de la technique* (Paris, 1961), pp. 114–15.

[3] Maurice Godelier, *Rationalité et irrationalité en économie* (Paris, 1971), vol. I, pp. 14–22, 29–31. Godelier quotes an American theorist who is willing to go to the *reductio ad absurdum* of the equivalence of economics and rationality rather than limit the former to a given domain. He maintains that since economics is about the application of resources, a mother's relation with her baby is as much economics as an employer's with his worker.

[4] Max Weber, *The Protestant Ethic and the Spirit of Capitalism*, tr. Talcott Parsons (London: Allen & Unwin, 1930).

[5] Franz Borkenau, *Der Übergang vom feudalen zum bürgerlichen Weltbild* (Paris, 1934), p. 161.

[6] Easton and Guddat, *Writings of the Young Marx*, pp. 243–8; most of Marx's italics have been omitted.

[7] For example, by suggesting that for Marx *Judentum* meant "commerce". David McLellan, *Marx Before Marxism* (New York: Harper & Row, 1970; London: Macmillan, 1970), p. 142. In that case Marx would be proffering the tautology that Western society became commercialized when it was commercialized. He is saying, in fact, that it became "Judaized" when it became commercialized.

[8] "It is one of the most important insights that emerge from all the researches of Max Weber that the original stock from which issued the manufacturing entrepreneurs who first systematically introduced capitalistic methods into the production process arose not from the money and trade bourgeoisie but from the budding handicrafts. Between these two classes, adventurous money capital and solid manufacturing capital, there was bitter opposition." Borkenau, *Übergang*, p. 155.

[9] The literature, to that point in time, is summarized by Henryk Grossmann, "Die gesellschaftlichen Grundlagen der mechanistischen Philosophie und die Manufaktur," in *Zeitschrift für Sozialforschung*, IV, 2 (Paris, 1935), pp. 176–82. Grossmann's article was reproduced along with Borkenau's book in an undated photostat edition in West Germany about 1970.

[10] When ordering the retreat, Lenin disingenuously called the previous policy "temporary war-time communism." Actually, it had been introduced neither as something temporary nor as conditioned by war, but as plain communism. See: G. F. Hudson, *Fifty Years of Communism* (Baltimore and London: Pelican edn, 1971), p. 89.

[11] Annie Kriegel, *Les communistes français* (2nd edn, Paris, 1970), pp. 110–11.

[12] Widespread resistance to economic modes of thought can persist long after the rise of an active class of entrepreneurs in such a society. For example: "But the Italian Catholic party, even when it implemented a policy that gave full satisfaction to the industrial class (in the time of De Gasperi) has always held itself aloof from the industrial world, has never understood it and has almost always had an unfavorable prejudice against it, a prejudice that consisted in seeing less the function of capitalism (in the meaning that even Marx gave that concept) than the problem of the riches

of the capitalists . . ." Giorgio Galli, *Il bipartismo imperfetto: comunisti e democristiani in Italia* (Bologna, 1966), p. 76.

[13] Cf. Borkenau, *Übergang*, pp. 170–71.

[14] Wolf Lepenies, "Il Mercenario: Ästhetik und Gewalt im posthistoire," in Martin Jürgens *et al.*, *Ästhetik und Gewalt* (Gütersloh, 1970), p. 65.

[15] H. Marcuse, *An Essay on Liberation*, p. 45.

[16] As Lukacs had already shown, *à propos* Rousseau and Schiller: *Geschichte und Klassenbewusstsein*, pp. 150–54.

[17] *François Perroux interroge Herbert Marcuse*, p. 41.

[18] H. Marcuse, "On Changing the World," in *Monthly Review*, October 1967, pp. 42–8.

[19] *Eros et Civilization*, tr. J.-G. Nény and B. Fraenkel (Paris, 1963), p. 87.

[20] H. Marcuse, *Five Lectures*, p. 54.

[21] H. Marcuse, *Psychoanalyse und Politik*, p. 8.

[22] T. W. Adorno, "Marx est-il dépassé?", in UNESCO, *Marx and Contemporary Scientific Thought* (Paris and The Hague, 1969), pp. 288–9: "The domination of men continues to operate through the economic process. For a long while now, this process has had for its victims not only the masses but also the owners of capital. . . . [This is] a structure that the anti-socialist Nietzsche described in advance as 'No shepherd and a flock.' But hidden in it is what he did not wish to see: the ancient social oppression which has simply become anonymous."

[23] Daniel Callahan, "Resistance and Technology," in *Commonweal*, 22 December 1967: "Unlike C. Wright Mills, Marcuse does not have to posit a power elite: the impersonal force of technology supplies the repressive domination."

[24] L. Colletti, *Ideologia e società*, p. 57. Cf. Merleau-Ponty, *Les Aventures de la Dialectique*, pp. 15–42.

Index

Absolute idealism, 32–40, 137–8
Abstract labor, 50–63
Adorno, T. W., 87, 170, 176, 182–3, 187–9, 200
Bergson, 69–75, 179–80
Borkenau, 192–3, 195–6
Calvinism, 192, 195
Castro, Fidel, 151–68
Cohn-Bendit, D., 128, 151–68
Colletti, L., 180, 183
Communist party, 101, 119–21, 138–46, 167, 189
Critical Theory, 176–85
Croce, 27, 101–3, 140–1
Debray, Regis, 128, 151–68
Division of labor, 51–63, 148, 179
Engels, 9, 15, 17, 21–4, 42–3, 57, 64, 70, 78, 118
Fanon, F., 38–9, 156–66
Freudianism, 13, 41, 146–8
Gramsci, 27–8, 88–104, 119, 130–1, 139–42, 150–1
Guevara, E., 151–68, 178
Hegel, 9–25, 29–33, 39–41, 54–5, 59–60, 66, 117, 130–50
Hook, S., 45–8
Horkheimer, M., 31, 50, 170, 176, 182, 189
IWW, 8, 165
Joule, 58–9
Judaism, 192–3, 195–6
Korsch, K., 25–9, 111
Labriola, Antonio, 23
Labriola, Arturo, 44–5
Lenin, 40–3, 70, 97–9, 111–2, 130, 133–7, 194–5
Lukacs, 29–30, 33–7, 48–50, 103, 105–30, 137–9, 157, 159–60, 165, 181–2

Marcuse, H., 26–7, 31, 33–7, 50, 65, 87, 131, 142–50, 151–68, 170, 176, 197, 199–200
Merleau-Ponty, 22, 139
Monnerot, J., 171–2
Perroux, F., 186, 198
Planning, 49–50, 60–1, 63, 186, 188, 195
Pragmatism, 43–8, 179
Schiller, F., 20, 52–6, 148–9, 197
Sorel, G., 7–8, 22–3, 65, 68–87, 93–4, 98, 207
Weber, M., 36, 118, 193, 203, 205–6
Young Hegelians, 15, 20–2, 26–7, 39, 147, 164, 167